THE BIRTH OF COLORADO

The Birth of Colorado

A Civil War Perspective

By Duane A. Smith

UNIVERSITY OF OKLAHOMA PRESS : NORMAN AND LONDON

By Duane A. Smith

Silver Saga: The Story of Caribou Colorado (Boulder, Colo., 1974)

Colorado Mining: A Photographic History (Albuquerque, 1977)

Fortunes Are for the Few: Letters of a Forty-niner (San Diego, 1977) (ed. with David J. Weber)

Rocky Mountain Boom Town: A History of Durango (Albuquerque, 1980; Boulder, Colo., 1986)

Secure the Shadow: Lachlan McLean Colorado Mining Photographer (Golden, Colo., 1980)

A Land Alone: Colorado's Western Slope (Boulder, Colo., 1981) (with Duane Vandenbusche)

A Colorado Reader (Boulder, Colo., 1982) (with Maxine Benson and Carl Ubbelohde)

Song of the Hammer and Drill: The Colorado San Juans, 1860–1914 (Golden, Colo., 1982)

Natural Resources in Colorado and Wyoming (ed.) (Manhattan, Kans., 1982)

A Taste of the West: Essays in Honor of Robert G. Athearn (ed.) (Boulder, Colo., 1983)

When Coal was King: A History of Crested Butte, Colorado 1880–1952 (Golden, Colo., 1984)

Colorado: Heritage of the Highest State (Boulder, Colo., 1984) (with Fay Metcalf and Thomas Noel)

Pioneers and Politicians: Ten Colorado Governors in Profile (Boulder, Colo., 1984) (with Richard D. Lamm)

Mining America: The Industry and the Environment, 1800–1980 (Lawrence, Kans., 1987)

Mesa Verde National Park: Shadows of the Centuries (Lawrence, Kans., 1988)

The Birth of Colorado: A Civil War Perspective (Norman, 1989)

Library of Congress Cataloging-in-Publication Data

Smith, Duane A.
The birth of Colorado

Bibliography: p. 255.
Includes index.
1. Colorado—History—Civil War, 1861–1865. I. Title.
E498.9.S65   1989   978.8'02   88-40548
ISBN 0-8061-2180-7 (alk. paper)

The paper in this book meets the guidelines for permanence and durability of the Committee on Production Guidelines for Book Longevity of the Council on Library Resources, Inc.

For

Rodman W. Paul

and

Clark C. Spence

Contents

Illustrations

Civil War Coloradans

People and Places

Map

Preface

IN 1861 THE NORTH and the South went to war, destroying one America and laying the groundwork for another. This same year, the land that the Pike's Peak gold rush had opened two years earlier received its name, Colorado. Far from the battlefield, this frontier territory forged ahead, its development overshadowed by the distant thunder of guns and drums.

Exuberant Denver newspaper editor William Byers marked the end of his paper's second volume by writing, "Spring is dawning with far brighter prospects than any that have gone before." With unwavering faith, he concluded: "That there is great wealth is no longer questioned, and the absolute certainty of every person of industry and perseverance, sooner or later reaping a rich reward, is greater than in any other mining country in the world."

Meanwhile, a young Denver merchant, David Moffat, was receiving some encouragement from his worried Aunt Jannette. She was relieved that he was "well off at the Peak place . . . not troubled with the war spirit."

Both were correct in their assessment of Colorado's situation: Its future loomed bright that spring, and Moffat and the others were fortunate to be in Pike's Peak country. The story about to unfold is theirs and that of their territory during the four turbulent war years. The Colorado that emerged in the spring of 1865 would no longer be the frontier that had found itself in a war. That frontier, that time, and that way of life would pass, to be replaced by something new and yet hauntingly familiar.

The saga of what went on remained alive in the memories of the people who had been there. The purpose of this study can be simply stated: to let them, the famous and the forgotten, tell their stories. In no way does this pretend to be a military history; much of what happened in Colorado, though influenced by the war, was not directly connected to it. Hopes and dreams, disappointment and heartbreak mingled with might-have-beens and rousing successes in a land that offered the centuries-old promise of the American West, in peacetime or in war.

The war, however, did shape and influence Colorado and Coloradans; they could not escape it. They probably did not fully understand the conflict or why it had happened. Bruce Catton was later moved to point out that "it ended as it had begun, in a mystery of darkness and passion. If no one could say exactly why it had come about in the first place, no one could quite say what it meant now that it was finished." Coloradans had their own memories and questions, some of which would persist through the years.

Long ago I toured the battlefield of First Manassas with Wade Hampton Morgan, whose fascinating stories told of his namesake and relative, who had fought there. Somewhere that day I glimpsed a time and place brought back to life, and I was captivated by the Civil War era. A few years later, Colorado won my heart, and this study is a marriage of those two loves.

I owe a great debt of thanks to the staffs of libraries and archives throughout the country for their untiring work on my behalf. For twenty years, with occasional time-outs for other projects, I have researched my Colorado Civil War project at the Huntington Library, Bancroft Library, National Archives, Denver Federal Records Center, Western Americana Collection at Yale University, Colorado Archives, Library of Congress, and, much more frequently, at the Colorado Historical Society, Western History Department of the Denver Public Library, and the Western Historical Collections at the University of Colorado.

Over the years, the staff of the Fort Lewis College Library has been cheerfully helpful in finding and borrowing materials on my behalf. My thanks also to the Amon Carter Museum for its assistance in securing photographs. To the staff of the University of Oklahoma Press, who shepherded the manuscript into a book, goes my sincere appreciation for their encouragement and profes-sionalism.

As she has done so faithfully for my other books, my wife Gay helped edit and polish what you are about to read. Words simply cannot convey my indebtedness. To my parents, who spent hours taking me through one Civil War battlefield and museum after another in Virginia, and along the way sparked my excite-ment about the era into a lifelong passion, my deepest gratitude.

This book is dedicated to two long-time friends and mentors, whose friendship, encouragement, scholarship, and love for mining history have inspired me to strive to match their stan-dards of excellence.

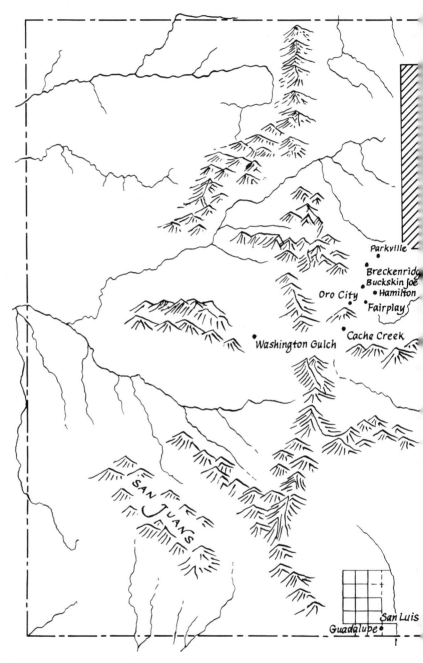

Colorado Territory, 1861

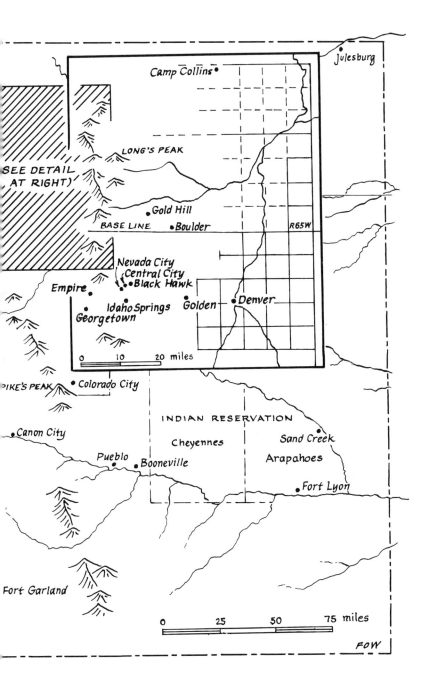

Julesburg

Camp Collins •

(SEE DETAIL AT RIGHT)

LONG'S PEAK

Gold Hill

BASE LINE   • Boulder   R65W

Nevada City
Central City
• Black Hawk
Empire •
• Idaho Springs   Golden   • Denver
Georgetown

0   10   20 miles

PIKE'S PEAK   • Colorado City

INDIAN RESERVATION

• Canon City
                    Cheyennes   Sand Creek
        Pueblo   Arapahoes
        • • Booneville
                                    • Fort Lyon

Fort Garland

0   25   50   75 miles

FOW

THE BIRTH OF COLORADO

Prologue

THE MORNING OF APRIL 12, 1861, dawned "bright and clear" over the plains, a welcome relief from the snow and disagreeable weather of recent days for Boulder County farmer Sylvanus Wellman. The day kept its early promise. Wellman worked his "boys," otherwise known as hired hands, breaking ground with five oxen and cutting willows. As the hours wore on, he chewed some of the tobacco plug he had purchased the previous day in Boulder for 20 cents.

This settlement, a still rough-hewn little village not yet three years old, nestled along Boulder Creek at the mouth of its canyon. The gateway to the mountains and the mines beyond, Boulder owed its existence to those mines, but already it exhibited greater aspirations than being simply another mining town. It was, as a later visitor observed, "the most Yankee of any settlement I have seen in Colorado."

In the mountains southwest of Boulder, young miner Frank Hall waited for his partner to return from a prospecting tour across the "snowy range," known eventually as the Continental Divide. Hall lived near Spanish Bar on the south fork of Clear Creek, a mining district once considered the promised land. But that was back in the exciting days of 1859; now the Western Slope beckoned the footloose with tempting stories of wealth. Frank Hall had come west in 1860 with every intention of making his fortune and returning home within a year or two. Wealth did not come as quickly as expected, however, and Hall's plans

3

changed accordingly. As he wrote to his brother, "I expect to make this country my home for the next five years unless I should be so fortunate as to make a 'big strike' before that time." And he did expect to strike it rich, as did the others of his generation who had hastened to Colorado in the Pike's Peak gold rush. "I feel confident that time Faith and Energy will give me all I want of this world's goods & I'm bound to stick to it like grim death to a nigger."

And still they came. Edward Seymour and a party were on their way to Denver that very day. For them, too, it was pleasant, and before camping they would drive some thirty-one miles, finally reaching Pat Mullally's ranch on Plumb Creek. Traveling along the familiar Oregon Trail, Seymour followed in the wagon tracks of a generation of pioneers. Sharing a common experience, the party saw a few buffalo that afternoon, a sight that was worthy of note in one's diary.

Leaving his friends, his wife, and his family back in Ohio had not been easy for Seymour, and it seemed he had been away much longer than the four weeks that had passed. He vividly expressed his worries and fears: " . . . am I to come back, Heaven only knows. But necessity compels me to do something and I cannot do it at home and Pike's Peak, I believe is the place for me to go." Others had worried similarly, a fact of little consolation to Seymour. He pushed on, "not knowing when I shall come back, if ever."

Seymour's goal, Denver, was the largest settlement in the Colorado Territory. The census taker the previous year had counted 4,749 people living there. The previous month, on March 20, editor William Byers of the territory's leading newspaper, the *Rocky Mountain News,* had taken stock of the "metropolis" of the Rocky Mountain region. Byers boldly proclaimed that Denver was destined to become the largest inland city on the American continent, noting that it had shown wonderful development in the past year. Well-defined streets replaced paths; churches, schools, and municipal government graced the community. Frame and brick construction was replacing log, and society, Byers rhapsodized, had shown great improvement. In his eyes, Denver was showing the "footprints of respectability, of personal worth, of the blessings of civilization and progress."

At the moment, though, Byers complained about the muddy streets, the result of the storm and snow of the past thirty-six hours. Denver, too, was awakening to a nice spring day on April 12, but underfoot the streets thawed, turning "really muddy."

Fifteen-hundred miles away as the crow flies, the citizens of Charleston, South Carolina, did not have the luxury of such a leisurely April morning. For them, a tension-filled night reached an anticipated, and for many a long-desired, climax. At 4:30 A.M. the sharp crack of a single cannon announced that the artillery bombardment on Fort Sumter had begun. Caught in a cross fire, the outgunned federals gamely fired back, trying to silence the first cannonade of the army of the new Confederate States of America. The Civil War thus began with a forty-hour bloodless battle, a silent comment on either the fortifications or the aim of the artillerymen. On April 13 the garrison surrendered.

Blissfully unaware of these events, Coloradans went about their usual business. Territorial newspapers had kept them well informed, in a delayed manner, of what had been occurring in the States. They knew of South Carolina's secession in December, of the other states that had followed, and of the formation of the Confederacy. Byers had even prophesied back on December 27, 1860, that "We cannot conceive a dismemberment or dissolution of this Union . . . without war, and the worst of all wars, a strife between those who but yesterday were brothers." Now news of the conflict raced across the country. St. Louis newspapers reported the events within hours. Denver folks read about it on April 19, as did Canon Citians via a *Canon City Times* extra on April 26. The editor was more than pleased to have received the news in so few days from St. Louis. Those Coloradans scattered in remote mountain mining camps and cabins heard the news later. (Most of them, except the extremely isolated ones, probably knew by May that the Civil War had begun.)

In Washington, amid the rumors, confusion, and mounting pressures of a capital gripped by the start of a war, newly appointed Colorado governor William Gilpin prepared to head west. In the prime of life, this forty-five-year-old bachelor, sometime army officer, explorer, flowery writer, and western promoter had lived in Missouri for years. Gilpin had even crossed the future site of Denver in 1843 on one of his western treks.

Bearded and lanky, the six-foot Gilpin seemed an excellent choice for governor, known to Coloradans as one of their own. Somewhat of a dreamer and visionary (traits that abound in his 1860 book *The Central Gold Region*), he had endeared himself to the settlers by predicting a glorious future for Denver as the center of the new civilization.

Gilpin's critics proved not so kind: They scorned his flights of rhetoric as being pompous and self-serving and stressed that he remained untried as a governor. Not one to fret about such things, however, Gilpin was eager to start the trip west. He scurried around Washington doing last-minute business and personal errands and received what few instructions the harassed Lincoln administration could offer amid the recurring crises that absorbed it and the city. Finally he left, journeying to his native Philadelphia and to New York before heading west.

Gilpin knew more than most easterners about Colorado. This land of promise and gold had temporarily directed national headlines away from the North/South dispute in the winter of 1858–59. Gold has been found—far more gold, it was said, than even that mother lode of golden riches, California, had yielded to the 1849ers. That meant bonanza!

The stampede had come in the late winter and spring of 1859. They called it the Pike's Peak gold rush, because that peak was the only well-known geographical feature in the region. The gold deposits were nowhere near there, however; they lay sixty miles to the north around a little settlement soon to be known as Denver, and miles beyond in the mountains to the west. One hundred thousand people, give or take a few, had answered the siren song of gold. Most panned out as "go-backers"; those who stayed provided the foundation for Colorado. Throughout the late spring and summer prospectors, recent farmers, storekeepers, teachers, and other nonminers poked and pried along the streams, canyons, and eventually in the hills, ever searching for their fortunes.

While few planned to make the territory their permanent home, many stayed longer than expected when their fortunes did not come easily. They lingered a season, then two, searching for the elusive ore. Some gave up prospecting to become farmers;

others had come west to pursue a trade or business. Out of all this excitement and energy came Colorado.

In 1860 a second rush of fortune hunters came from the States to the Rocky Mountains. The Western Slope, across the Continental Divide, had been reached the previous year, and now the more venturesome were probing into the rugged, snowy, isolated San Juans of southwestern Colorado. By this time, as the census takers discovered, over 34,000 people lived in the region, most of them in the mountains near the mines. Whereas they had originally searched for free gold in placer mining, Coloradans now turned to underground or deep mining, following the quartz veins down into solid rock. This mining technique required more investment, more mining experience, and more machinery, and Coloradans had to look beyond themselves to get it.

The national crisis over slavery and sectionalism soon reached even here. A new territory could not be organized while Northerners and Southerners argued in Congress. Not until after the South seceded did the new Colorado Territory become a reality, in February 1861. Even then, a fight over the name and boundaries delayed what should have occurred a year earlier. All this Gilpin understood as he came west.

The new governor also realized that both Southerners and Northerners lived in the territory, and the war "back in the States" would never be far away. Plans were already underway for the transcontinental telegraph, assuring that in a fraction of a second news would reach lonely Julesburg, a settlement on the prairie in the territory's northeast corner. Gone was thinking in terms of days and weeks. The rest of Colorado, however, continued to rely on the stagecoach and travelers for telegraphed and any other news.

The Civil War seemed far away to people in Denver, Boulder, Canon City, and those places in between. But their attitudes were nonetheless strong, and feelings hardened in the days following Fort Sumter. Colorado and the United States had plunged into a war, and the outcome was uncertain, at best. It would be, some predicted, a single-battle conflict, after which everyone could return to more peaceful pursuits. But others, less hopeful, prepared for the worst.

Part I

A TIME FOR WAR: 1861–62

1

"Stand ON THE SIDE OF THE UNION!"

ON THE FRONT PAGE of the April 19, 1861 issue of the *Rocky Mountain News*, Denverites read the long-dreaded news—the fighting had begun at "Fort Sumpter" (Editor Byers insisted on the incorrect spelling of the fort's name). "The blow has come at last, and civil war is upon our once happy land." In subsequent issues more details followed, Sumter was spelled correctly, and the editor made his position clear:

We are at a loss for the language sufficiently strong and condemnatory to characterize as it deserves this greatest outrage ever committed against the Republic.

For ourselves, we take our stand ON THE SIDE OF THE UNION! . . . to this cause we pledge the best of our ability, the last dollar of our property, and if necessary our last expiring breath! (April 22, 1861).

Fortunately, William Byers did not have to expend his "last expiring breath," although in his own mind he questioned neither the need nor his own willingness to make the supreme sacrifice.

For the next few weeks, readers in the Colorado Territory, like readers back in the States, were deluged with information about military affairs, current political developments in the South, and any other items that struck an editor's fancy. The war was still a novelty, and Americans relished every tidbit of news.

Nothing escaped the attention of thirty-year-old William Byers, whether it was in or out of the territory. Community gadfly and promoter, Byers had ambitiously established his paper as the territory's foremost. He aspired to higher goals, and his readers, at least those who agreed with his Republican and Denver chauvinism and his full-steam-ahead editorials, assumed he was destined for greater things.

He had brought his wife, the prim and proper Elizabeth, and his children to Colorado, something others with less faith in the future hesitated to do. Beginning with the paper's first issue in 1859, Byers had vigorously advocated agriculture, mining, and anything else that would enhance his adopted home. William Byers was a man to be reckoned with in Denver and throughout the mining districts.

At the moment, Byers was in a stew. Territorial government organized in Washington was one thing; territorial government functioning in Colorado was quite another. He relayed to his readers as much as he knew about their future governor and encouraged plans for a grand reception, a rousing Colorado welcome to get William Gilpin started on the right foot.

Of more immediate concern to Byers, however, were the Southerners who seemed to be lurking behind every door or prowling around the mountains up to no good. A Confederate flag had already been flown smack in the middle of downtown Denver on Larimer Street, a "rattlesnake" flag, Byers snarled. In these tumultuous times almost any rumor invited some credence, and as late as October Byers was reporting a balloon over Denver that trailed its own "secesh" rag. The sobriety of the informant was in question, and even Byers suspected the whole thing was a hoax, but no one could be absolutely sure.

Byers did everything in his power to whip up pro-Union enthusiasm. He reported on Union rallies, provided information about where to purchase Union badges and rosettes, and noted that a wagon passed by his office with the twin mottoes, Our Union Forever and Death to Traitors. He promised to speed copies of the News to his "mountain friends" via the Pony Express—forty-eight minutes to Golden City and less than three hours to Central City. War news would arrive in record time.

Fellow Union stalwart Matthew Dale, living in Nevada City, a steep mile beyond Central, was relieved that he had heard of only one "rattlesnake" flag being flown. Yet there were too many Southerners around for his liking. Be that as it may, he believed his neighbors stood ten to one for the Union. Meanwhile, C. S. Hinman wrote home from Trail Creek (above Idaho Springs) that although they were probably having an exciting time in the States, "I am glad that I am not there for I expect I should be foolish enough to enlist." He was not alone in his gratitude for Colorado's isolation.

Many and varied were the concerns in those first weeks of what most predicted would be a short war. Gilpin, meanwhile, had left the east behind him in a Central Overland California and Pike's Peak Express Company stage with eight other passengers, including two women. Bumping and swaying over dusty prairie roads, the passengers enjoyed, as much as they could, the splendid summerlike days of May. At half past four on Monday, May 27, Gilpin alighted from the stage in Denver. The new governor and the new territory welcomed each other with alacrity; now it was time to get down to business.

That evening at the brightly lighted Tremont House, Denver's finest hostelry, William Gilpin was formally greeted with cheers and cannon salvo. A "large number of Denver's fairest ladies" graced the reception for the unmarried Gilpin, and a band serenaded the crowd with patriotic music. Famous for his verbosity, Gilpin responded with a "somewhat lengthy" speech to a nonetheless enthusiastic audience. The festivities concluded with three cheers for Colorado and the Union, followed by a cannon salute for each of the thirty-four states, as well as one for the "young embryo state of Colorado."

Presbyterian missionary Amos Billingsley thought it a splendid reception, with a crowd of fifteen hundred. "May God direct & bless the Governor," he implored later that evening in his diary.

Gilpin would need God's help as he tackled the territory's problems. Never lacking enthusiasm, the new governor gamely set off on a tour of the mountain mining districts to meet their inhabitants and take a census. With eye-pleasing June days as background, the tour proved to be a rousing success. From Boulder on the north to Pueblo and Canon City on the south, the governor was greeted eagerly with toasts, speeches, receptions, and balls. Gilpin enjoyed a splendid, if tiring, time.

The census documented 25,329 people in the territory. Denver's population of 2,603 (down considerably from the 1860 census) led the list, followed by Central City (2,465) and the mining districts—the Nevada and Russell Gulch districts, for example, reported 2,705. One demographic feature came into sharp focus—Colorado was highly urbanized, with the centers of population in the mining districts and camps. The ink on the paper had scarcely dried when doubts were cast on the accuracy of the canvass; John Irwin in Mountain House district (north of Black Hawk) bemoaned that the report gave his district only 25 inhabitants when the actual population was 91! Byers doubted the results, too; he felt sure the total population would not fall short of 30,000.

The warm greetings Byers had showered on Gilpin cooled as rapidly as a mountain evening. The governor had made a grievous error by including newspaperman Thomas Gibson on his June tour. The two subsequently became close friends, a fact that did not endear the governor to Byers. Locked in a bitter newspaper war, Gibson and Byers minced no words. The often "cranky" Gibson and the occasionally bullheaded Byers had once been partners on the News, which only embittered the current feud. Gilpin should have known better than to show favoritism; he had seen similar fights in other frontier towns.

When Gibson loyally defended his friend, Byers would sulk, criticize, and ultimately stab his editorial pen at the governor. Gilpin had compounded his error in Byers's eyes by granting the territorial printing contract to Gibson's Colorado Republican and Rocky Mountain Herald.

Undaunted, Gilpin proceeded with his work, calling for a territorial legislative election, creating electoral districts, and setting up election procedures. The August voting results gave an easy victory to the Republicans, sending ex-Nebraskan Hiram Bennet to the House of Representatives as Colorado's first delegate to Congress. The News hailed Bennet's victory and looked forward to his able representation of local interests in Washington.

Bennet quickly discovered exactly what the job entailed when he found himself embroiled, much to his annoyance, in a squabble over printing. When the Territorial Legislature gave its printing to Byers, Gilpin protested and the matter landed in Washington, where the Lincoln administration was struggling to maintain the Union after its humiliating defeat at Bull Run in July. The dispute ended in the lap of Secretary of State William Seward, who ordered that public printing be divided equally between the two loyal papers published in Denver, the *News* and the *Herald*.

The matter refused to die. Byers blasted Territorial Secretary Lewis Weld in an affidavit for refusing to follow Seward's order, and Weld rejoined in kind, calling the *News* "not a sheet reputable in this community either for honesty of purpose or loyalty to the government." Weld further stated that he had "very strong reason to believe that it [the *News*] is the open apologist for the worst and most dangerous class of people in our midst."

The tempest continued into March 1862. Bennet defended the legislature's right to contract its own printing and called for the removal of Weld. Washington, though puzzled by the commotion Gilpin had stirred up out west, paid as little attention to the brouhaha as possible. The more pressing matters of the eastern front, where the Union army was preparing for its spring campaign, demanded the government's full attention. Maybe, if ignored, Colorado's problem would settle itself.

The Territorial Legislature had, in the meantime, convened on September 10, opened by an invigorating speech from Gilpin. Even the *News* was moved to praise: "In its beauty of style, smoothness and elegance of composition, it can hardly be excelled by any writer of the age." A snowstorm the previous night had mantled the peaks west of Denver with a fresh silvery crest, and Gilpin rose to the occasion with his address. The future, he promised, glistened for mining, farming, and Colorado's prosperity and power. He predicted that the railroad would soon arrive. If Gilpin's words proved true, all of these accomplishments would be achieved within the first three years of settlement. He warned, however, that Coloradans must remain ever alert, ever valiant:

Our great country demands a period of stern virtue of holy zeal, of regenerating patriotism of devoted citizens. It is to you representatives, and to the people of the young Territory of Colorado, that I speak. To exalt your intrepid enthusiasm is my aim—with us are the continental eagles and the continental cause, immortalized by the purity of Washington, illuminated by the wisdom of Jefferson, vindicated and restored by the illustrious Jackson. Let us condense around those eagles and advance, devoted to maintain their purity and exalt their glory.

This was Gilpin at his promotional best—Gilpin the visionary, Gilpin the dreamer. The governor raced from past through present to future, leaving his listeners eager for action.

The legislature, which was comfortably situated on Larimer Street, seemed energized by Gilpin's flights of oratory. Before completing their session in November, the two branches (House and Council) created seventeen counties, including one named for Gilpin and another for Weld; enacted a legal code; authorized a school system; and adopted measures to survey the territory for the first official map. They borrowed some of their ideas from older states, especially Illinois, but they had been nonetheless busy. They incorporated roads, mining companies, tunnels, and town companies; organized the militia; prescribed the rate of interest; protected the rights of married women; passed an act concerning divorce and alimony and one for the protection of trout; and looked ahead to a greater future by establishing the University of Colorado, at least on paper. They also petitioned Congress for the establishment of a branch mint and mail routes. In one session these pioneer politicians made the Territory of Colorado a political reality and provided a governing base. They could go home satisfied.

Some disagreement had naturally arisen about where the capital should be located. Several sites had been proposed by enthusiastic legislators, including the obvious Denver, as well as the not-so-obvious towns of Hamilton, Canon City, and Julesburg. The lawmakers ultimately chose Colorado City, near Pike's Peak, despite the heated protests of the Denver delegation. Byers steamed and blustered when the representative from Central City commented that he voted for the winner because he "found only two persons in Denver who were friendly to the Executive Department of Colorado . . . [and] desired to remove those officers away from such a disagreeable locality."

Gilpin got along famously with the legislators initially, and he and Weld even found time to sketch the territory's official seal. The Governor's Ball in October at Broadwell House proved to be the crowning social event of the season, the "grandest and most extensive affair" ever known in the region, according to Byers. Altogether, it was an auspicious legislative start.

Byers, however, learned a lesson about candidates. He was forced to remind both winners and losers early in December, in all "goodness and justice," to square up their bills. Between crossing swords with the governor and attempting to settle overdue accounts, Byers had had a difficult time the past six months.

Gilpin had not enjoyed an easy time, either. One ominous cloud hung over his relations with Coloradans—his summer tour of the mountains had convinced him that the Confederate faction was growing large and threatening. The governor therefore set out to save Colorado for the Union with all the vigor his nervous temperament could sustain.

Reactions to Gilpin's assessment varied. S. Newton Pettis, who served briefly as a territorial judge, desperately wished that the issue would just go away: "There can be no excuse for pandering to passion here now. The consequences of political lunacy are not desired for a moment." Newspaperman and writer Ovando Hollister, on the other hand, agreed with Gilpin, believing it was "patent to everyone" that some force would be necessary to preserve Colorado for the Union.

Coloradans watched and wondered, like Americans north and south, as two governments tried to turn volunteer mobs and unbridled enthusiasm into trained professional killers and military order. "On to Richmond," cried the Northern press; when the Union army tried that strategy in July, the consequences were disastrous. The Battle of Bull Run proved aptly named when the Union troops hightailed it back to Washington. The *News* headlines (July 29, 1861) captured the moment:

GREAT BATTLE NEAR MANASSAS JUNCTION
TERRIBLE LOSS OF LIFE
RETREAT OF THE FEDERAL ARMY

According to the accompanying text, "a general feeling of gloom

and depression was experienced yesterday amongst the Union
men, on receipt of the news of the disaster." Byers did not waver
in his support and called for the defeat to be "most promptly
avenged. There will be no more temporizing with the traitors and
assassins. . . . Northern people will not listen to any further prop-
ositions for a peaceful solution." The North and South could not
even agree on nomenclature; hence, Bull Run was also Manassas.
Talk among Unionists of a one-battle war quickly came to an end.

Fortunately for the Northern cause, the victorious Confederates found themselves almost as exhausted as their victims and
could not follow up their victory. A season of regrouping ensued
on the eastern front. To provincial eastern newspapers, no other
front of any significance existed. Colorado lay in the disdained
and ignored far western theater.

Hollister believed that Bull Run invigorated the Confederate
sympathizers in Colorado. Daniel Conner, a loyal Southerner,
agreed. This fifty-niner miner was visiting a Fairplay saloon (or
"deadfall," as the proper folk called these groggeries) when someone in the crowd saluted the Confederate victory. Instantly, cries
arose to find the traitor, but no one pursued him and the gambling
and drinking soon resumed. William Byers, almost as nervous as
Gilpin, puzzled over a young Denver woman's decision to wear
secession rings and show partiality for that cause.

Obviously, many Southerners had rushed to Colorado, and
many had stayed to prospect and mine. How many remained and
how disloyal they might be was debatable. Justice Benjamin Hall,
a strong Union man, informed Lincoln in September that at least
six thousand men leaned in the Confederate direction; were fully
posted as to the situation in the border states of Texas, Arkansas,
and Missouri; and had begun to form secret enclaves, variously
termed "Blue lodges, Golden circles and Rangers."

For his part, Gilpin had warned Secretary of War Simon
Cameron the previous month that Colorado was encircled by
hostile elements. The customary Indian problems and fears, plus
the fact that Colorado was "utterly destitute" of arms, ammunition, and weapons for self-preservation, drove the governor nearly frantic. In his opinion, beleaguered and helpless Coloradans had

no place to turn for support. Mormons to the west, New Mexicans of questionable loyalty to the south, and Indians
everywhere else forced Gilpin to beg Washington for help.
Cameron, sinking in his own inefficiency, could not grant Gilpin's
request for two field batteries, muskets, equipment, ammunition,
and other supplies.

If given the necessary provisions, Gilpin believed that Coloradans could preserve themselves and assist their country's
cause: "Energy, loyalty, and bravery preeminently belong to the
mountain people. To conquer their enemies appears to them more
glorious than to perish." Afraid that guns would fall into
Southern hands, he secretly began to buy up those offered on the
market. This practice encouraged an increase in prices, and soon a
small arms race enriched those who had guns to sell. After Gilpin
obtained the firearms, he turned to the task of finding men to
shoulder them. The governor had hoped to secure federal troops
from Utah or New Mexico, but none could be spared. Thus he
set to raising volunteers.

Recruiting Coloradans proved easy. Lawyer Henry Teller had
told Cameron back in May that "Here in these mountains we
have hundreds anxious to contribute to the support of the
Government and to assist in maintaining the integrity of the flag
of our country." Would the government accept volunteers? No,
the secretary replied, the distance from the scene of conflict was
too great. So Mountain City did not send men "inured to toil and
hardships" to save the Union. But when the action came to Colorado, Gilpin welcomed Mountain Citians and anyone else willing to rally 'round the flag.

Recruiting for the First Regiment of Colorado Volunteers went
forward vigorously in July, August, and September. Central City
miner George Aux enlisted under Capt. Samuel Tappan, whose
persuasive tactics managed to gather 103 men within twenty-
four hours.

Capt. Richard Sopris opened a recruiting office in Hamilton,
calling for one hundred able-bodied men, ages eighteen to forty-
five, to serve three years or for the duration of the war. Enlistment provided an excellent opportunity for young men tired of

prospecting to "engage themselves at sure, fair wages [fifteen dollars a month]" and to receive plenty of grub, as promised by the captains.

Patriotic young men heeded the call. Within a fortnight, forty-three volunteers marched off to Denver's Camp Weld. From Hamilton, Buckskin Joe, Delaware Flats, and other once-promising mining districts they came, a "noble looking set of men." The recruits were "good sized, stout, hardy, sober, intelligent," according to the proud editor of the Tarryall Miners' Record (September 14, 1861).

Even though the recruitment campaign had been successful, Gilpin wrote to Gen. Edward Canby, commander of the Department of New Mexico, that the "malignant element" in the territory numbered seventy-five hundred and would require extraordinary measures to control. The fact that Southerners were leaving Colorado to return to their home states did not calm the governor's fears. He expected them to return with overwhelming strength and to encourage neighboring Indians to attack. Canby attempted to reassure Gilpin, but the governor refused to listen. Gilpin's friend Hall interjected another concern when he wrote Seward that same month, describing the "destroying angels" of Brigham Young and the Mormons' long-standing distrust of gentiles. The cup of worries overflowed.

Denver rippled with rumors, and Southerners made their presence known. Denver's first mayor, John C. Moore, left to join the Confederate army, and in September A. B. Miller openly recruited followers to join him in going south. Before leaving, he and a few friends flaunted their cause in street demonstrations. Byers became so agitated that when several other Reb supporters were arrested, he exclaimed, "In times like the present even 'Free Speech' is sometimes a dangerous privilege." Union readers of that October 2 issue probably agreed that Southerners were going too far.

The popular Criterion Saloon on Larimer Street drew the most adverse attention. Here its proprietor, Charley Harrison, held court. This soft-spoken Southerner, a suave and dapper gambler, had been a Denver feature for several years and the Criterion a source of annoyance to Unionists for months. No one fooled needlessly with the dangerous Harrison, who was a reputed killer and ranked as one of the "fast guns."

Denver had never before seen the likes of New York–born Charles Harrison in all its three-year history. Coming out of Utah, trailing the rumor of having loved one of the plural wives of a Mormon leader neither wisely nor well, Harrison quickly established himself in his new home. Visiting easterners could find in Harrison the dime-novel image of the western gambler and gunfighter they were looking for.

Harrison made no unusual effort to maintain his image—it came naturally. He hobnobbed with acceptable people and promoted Denver, its theater, and other refinements, while still consorting with the saloon crowd. Once the war broke out, he attracted a sympathetic following of Southerners. The *News* pointed out on August 2 that the company performing at the Criterion was getting "better and better" every show; however, "the secession song last night expressed bad taste & bad patriotism." The gracious Harrison took all the criticism in stride and one time even rescued editor Byers—a fellow Mason—from Harrison's irate friends after a blistering anti-Harrison editorial.

Trouble developed in and around the Criterion, and Harrison overplayed his hand when he confronted Gilpin and the First Colorado. Disturbances at his Rebel rendezvous had increasingly incensed Unionists, and ultimately several soldiers were wounded by gunfire coming from the saloon. Arrested for this last transgression, brought to trial in September, found guilty and fined, Harrison was ordered to leave the city.

The banished proprietor sold the Criterion and left for the States on the September 19, 7:00 A.M. stage. Being a Denver legend no longer sufficed if one openly supported the South.

Six weeks later, the elusive A. B. Miller's wagon train was captured in southern Kansas. Miller and his family escaped in the Concord coach that they had been using to travel to Cherokee country in Indian Territory, which seemed to prove the rumor that Miller and the men with him had intended to join forces with the Texans. Arrested but eventually paroled, the rest of Miller's party left behind equipment and animals, which led to a curiously named case, *The United States v. Twelve Mules.* The unfortunate defendants (standing in for forty ponies, one jackass, and various accoutrements) were finally freed from federal custody the following May.

Gilpin had won another round: Southern sympathizers were unquestionably departing Colorado. The appearance of volunteer companies should have further put to rest Denverites' fears of Confederate invasion and potential Indian attacks. Unfortunately, however, the community was faced with the greater headache of deciding what to do with the would-be soldiers when they came to town.

Not all the "stout patriotic boys" of the First Colorado fit that description. Abijah Babbit of Company B absconded to Denver from nearby Camp Weld and never came back. A standing thirty-dollar reward awaited anyone who returned this light-complexioned, twenty-nine-year-old "with a wild look, dark brown hair—cut short." Others created chaos in their own ways.

The First Colorado did not cover itself with glory in its opening engagements. One of its first reported outings was a visit to a "house of questionable repute," where outnumbered "gallant pimps" managed to drive off the soldiers. Battles with the bottle frequently made the newspaper, in humorous and not so humorous stories. The First Colorado, far from displaying the disciplined military ideal, had evolved as something of a nuisance.

Drilling, training, guard duty, and the other mundane tasks of military life did not sit well with the boys who had volunteered to be heroes. Inactivity and boredom gave birth to a variety of schemes, particularly ones designed to supplement the soldiers' diets. Farmers and gardeners fell victim as trophies of pigs, chickens, tomatoes, and corn improved many a meal. By October Byers was complaining loudly about the petty depredations and outrages of drunken soldiers who insulted citizens, took merchandise from stores, and behaved in every manner except that expected of gallant heroes. He and others advocated the prohibition of liquor sales to boys of the First, in hopes of quelling their pranks. Malicious activity reached a high point the following January when the editor reported that drunken soldiers and officers had ridden recklessly into town on their horses, careening madly through the streets, tearing down awnings, breaking up sidewalks, and "whooping and yelling like savages." Their mission, to rescue a comrade locked in Denver's jail, was successful.

Ovando Hollister, a member of the regiment, defended his fellows, blaming most of their pranks on inactivity, the "Devil's opportunity." But even he was forced to admit, with more than a hint of truth, that they were accused of being "chicken thieves, jayhawkers, turbulent and seditious, a disgrace to themselves and the country." In his 1863 history of the regiment, *Boldly They Rode*, Hollister candidly recounted some of the scraps he knew about, including a Christmas Eve foray through darkened Denver that netted chickens, oysters, cheese, and champagne—all the makings of a great dinner. He spent another three pages telling how some of the boys avoided capture after raiding the store of a Jewish Denver merchant. Colorado City was also subjected to company raids. A patrol swept up unsuspecting chickens and pigs, for which the captain paid "at least ten fold" after confronting the irate owners.

Despite such shenanigans, Hollister stoutly defended his fellows, maintaining that there was not "a manlier, better disposed thousand men in the United States service than the First Colorados." He placed a good share of the blame on the soldiers' four months without pay. A worried Gilpin did not have money to raise and pay his troops.

The governor, never one to hesitate in such a crisis, began issuing drafts to local and a few out-of-territory merchants to purchase supplies, clothing, and other essentials for his troops. Before long, $375,000 in promissory notes had been distributed. Unfortunately, the governor acted without federal authorization, which was not realized at first. His failure to seek permission soon became apparent; by mid-September merchants were getting edgy. These individuals warranted concern, but more to the point was the fact that much of the capital of the territory was locked into those notes.

Gilpin assumed that he had authority to issue drafts based on a vague, late-evening conversation with Cameron and Lincoln. When the secretary of the treasury, not privy to such midnight capers, refused to honor the drafts, their value plummeted and with it the fortunes of quite a few Denver merchants. Public support for Gilpin dropped at about the same rate.

By late fall Gilpin faced a crisis of confidence. Byers believed that the drafts would eventually be paid, but he lashed out at the blundering governor anyway. Gibson defended him as expected, and the newspaper war rattled on, with the governor as the featured attraction. Nothing he could do seemed to help; finally, in late December, he hurried to Washington to defend his actions. No other governor, Byers judged, had ever entered upon his labors with more encouraging prospects or more heartily endorsed, only to find himself, in six short months, occupying a position less than enviable.

Gilpin made matters worse by equating his enemies with traitors or, at the least, Southern sympathizers. This mistake did not endear him to those Coloradans opposed only to their governor's precipitous actions.

While defending himself, Gilpin apparently found time to write—or be interviewed for—an article for the *New York Times* (January 27, 1862). The unsigned article recounted recent events and praised the governor for saving the day. Byers jumped on it immediately, particularly the accusation that Coloradans were infected with secession and that only the "excellent Governor" had pulled them through in the "life and death struggle . . . in that hand-to-hand struggle for political existence."

Gilpin became even less popular when he insulted the women by saying there were so few that they were not worth mentioning. An irate Coloradan from Nevada City answered, "We ladies have many friends in the East and we don't like to have it circulated abroad that we are not recognized, whatever, in our flourishing new Territory, where the society of ladies, above all things, should be most appreciated." Byers gleefully printed the letter, signed simply "A Female," and for weeks the *News* battered Gilpin.

By March it was painfully obvious that Gilpin had become a liability to the territory and an embarrassment to the Lincoln administration. Byers's junior editor, Edward Bliss, bluntly stated that one more year of Gilpin's administration would effectually prostrate every department of business, retard immigration, and ruin the territory. Though the case was overstated, many people in Colorado agreed with Bliss. Gibson's assertion that "the courageous bold front of Gov. Gilpin awed the leaders of the Rebel gang," in the February 27 issue of the *Herald* did not stem the tide of dissatisfaction.

Complaints about the governor poured into Washington. Gib-son's continued stout defense failed to save his friend; Lincoln removed Gilpin in March. The decision had been made while Gilpin was returning to the territory. John Evans from Illinois would take his place.

Ironically, Gilpin's actions were soon vindicated when, as Byers described it, a "Texan Horde" began to advance up the Rio Grande from El Paso. Confederate Gen. Henry H. Sibley suc-cessfully brushed aside Union forces, leaving Canby little choice but to withdraw and concentrate his forces at Fort Union, north and east of Santa Fe. There with his outnumbered, battered, and worried New Mexico volunteers and regular troops, he awaited the oncoming Texans and, he hoped, reinforcements. The vic-torious Confederates meanwhile occupied Albuquerque and San-ta Fe and seemingly held within their grasp the gate to Colorado. They had accomplished all this in only eight weeks.

Colorado's gold and potential Southern volunteers had been factors in the decision to march north. Nor had the Confederacy overlooked the fact that the conquest of so much territory was bound to look impressive to European diplomats inexperienced in western matters. Militarily the campaign would pin down troops and perhaps force Washington to turn some of its attention away from the eastern front.

The only defensive barrier in the open country between Fort Union and Denver was a will-o'-the-wisp picket line of lonely patrols anchored by two tiny, nondescript forts—Garland and Wise (disgustingly named, from ardent Unionists' viewpoint, for an ex-governor of Virginia who had joined the Confederacy). No wonder Byers, Gilpin, and others panicked.

Once part of the Western Department headquartered in St. Louis and commanded by the hero of young America, John C. Fremont (a better explorer than Civil War officer), Colorado, in a

November reorganization, became part of the Department of
Kansas. Despite this logical change, the territory still did not gain
much attention from the hard-pressed Lincoln administration.

Some of Gilpin's troops went to Fort Wise, soon to be renamed
Fort Lyon in honor of Gen. Nathaniel Lyon, who was killed that
August in southwest Missouri during the battle of Wilson's
Creek. Denverites cheered them off and Byers concluded that the
"boys" were gratified at the "prospect of any kind of active
duty." He further revealed that they would prefer to be called to
Missouri rather than garrison "an Indian post." The army looked
upon the fort with much more favor, however, because it "is so
important (both as regards our Indian relations and our communications with the East)."

Among those who went to the post was Mollie Sanford, wife
of Byron Sanford, the captain of Company H. She described why
duty at Fort Lyon was not the most desirable, even with her
beloved By there. "This is a lonely place, on a level plain, no
timber in sight," Mollie wrote, and "there is no place to go, and
few to see outside our company." Regulation rations meant little
variety for meals, especially since "we are destitute of any kind of
vegetables." Beef and whiskey seemed to be the "staple articles."
One redeeming quality was the pleasant quarters, built of stone
with white pine floors, which poor Mollie had to use as a bed
when she became sick; they had no bedstead. After six weeks the
two Colorado companies were ordered to rejoin their regiment,
and the wives were sent back to Denver. "Farewell, old Fort.
May I never see you again as the wife of a soldier or until peace
again reigns in our land."

The untested, maligned First Colorado proved its worth.
Ordered south in February by Canby, in one stretch they
marched ninety-two miles in thirty-six hours. They reached Fort
Union, four hundred miles from Denver, in thirteen days. The
regiment's officers, including a Methodist minister become ardent
military man, John Chivington, were as glad to leave Denver and
find active service as Denverites were happy to see them depart.

Everything turned out well; Hollister and Chivington could not
have been prouder of their boys. In a battle later dubbed the
"Gettysburg of the West," they defeated Sibley's forces at

Glorieta Pass on March 26–27. The "fighting parson" played a conspicuous role when he led a bold encircling maneuver that took his men over sheer cliffs to the rear of Sibley's line. There they destroyed the Confederate's supply train, forcing the Tex-ans to retreat. "Gilpin's Pet Lambs" were heroes; the "Texan Horde" had been routed.

In May the Treasury Department announced it would pay Gilpin's unauthorized drafts, which elicited some invectives from the unforgiving Byers. The thousands who had suffered from uncertainty could rejoice, he intoned, over the rectification of "Gilpin's stupid blunders," tardy though it be.

Gone, too, were the Southerners who might have been inclined to cause trouble. James Pierce, a member of the original 1858 Russell party, which had found the gold that started the Pike's Peak excitement, expressed his feelings after leaving. He and his friends had intended to stay in Colorado but could not stand the insults heaped on them. "I do not believe there would have ever been any trouble here at the time war came on, if it had not been for forced conditions." If Gilpin had "only shown more conser-vatism," there would have been no need for troops and trauma. In the case of William Gilpin, that "if" was a big one.

So ended the turbulent first year of Colorado's political history, with one governor axed and another eagerly anticipated. The ac-companying rhetoric sounded familiar; Byers hailed the appoint-ment of the well-known, sound, clear-headed John Evans. Gilpin would stay as acting governor until his successor arrived. One more social triumph awaited him, the Governor's Ball and supper. According to Thomas Gibson, "It was the grandest, largest, most brilliant 'biggest thing' of the age and of the country."

Over the protests of his friends, Gilpin was forced to go. He had lost the support of a substantial number of Coloradans, who looked upon him as impractical and erratic, at best. If Lincoln wanted a smoother second year in Colorado, Gilpin's removal was imperative. Bitter feelings lingered, however, causing a movement to rename Gilpin County. Not until a year later did an August petition, signed by some of that county's prominent citizens, including Henry Teller and Eben Smith, put this ill-deserved vindictiveness in the grave. Gilpin deserved cheers for

his accomplishments in getting government started and in promoting Colorado. Now, hail the new governor, who promised to
bring a period of stability and quiet.

Perhaps his friend Benjamin Hall best summarized what Gilpin
had run up against—malcontented office seekers, open rebels, and
others ready to fight him over contracts and related matters. "I
presume that they are the worst people on the face of the earth to
govern." The outgoing governor could take solace in knowing
that Colorado remained loyal to the Union and that the Southern
cause had ceased to be a factor in the territory.

2

"Like a lottery, the prizes attract"

BORN OF THE GOLD-RUSH FEVER of fifty-nine, Colorado lived and died by mining when the Civil War broke out. Chasing rumor and prospecting fact, mining had ebbed and flowed throughout the territory for two years. Men still came, lured by the bewitching call of gold, just as they had in 1858, 1859, and 1860; the war made no difference.

Edward Seymour, who arrived in Denver on April 23, left the city within four days in his rush to reach the diggings at California Gulch. Before the summer was over, he had sampled nearly all the red-hot districts. His success, or lack of it, typified the experiences of most prospectors. Not until May 20 did he "rock out" his first gold, $4.30 worth. When California Gulch failed to meet his expectations, he tried nearby Bird's Eye Gulch and later Gilpin Gulch, which he "did not think it any account, don't like looks of the Gulch at all." Two futile months of searching went by before he started for Buckskin Joe and beyond to the Independent district in late July.

Seymour filed on a claim and surveyed his surroundings: the "scenery here is the wildest and grandest that I ever saw." Prospects proved unpromising, however, and he returned to California Gulch, where he soon tried his luck at Cache Creek, south down the Arkansas River, but found no claims worth taking. Finally, on October 13, he left at 10:00 in the morning for the long trip back to the States and his family in Ohio.

Despite his great expectations and effort, thirty-three-year-old
Seymour had drawn a blank. He lacked the necessary skills and
had been forced to learn them as he went along, but that deficiency did not hurt him as much as his late arrival in every district he
prospected. The best claims were already taken, and the search
for more yielded little success.

Scotsman James Fergus sadly confessed to his wife Pamelia,
who stayed in Little Falls, Minnesota, that "the longer I stay
here the poorer I get. I believe there are more broken men in
these mountains than in Minnesota." Breckenridge, Black Hawk,
and Mountain City had bestowed no golden nuggets on this
forty-eight-year-old, would-be miner.

Like other lonely wives, Pamelia worried about her husband
and the impact the gold fields might have on him. "Now father
don't work so hard . . . you say you still hope to make your pile if
you should happen to find a streak of luck don't be too gready
[sic] and never get home." The weary woman had to raise their
children, manage James's business affairs, and handle the day-to-
day problems without her husband:

Now Fergus I do not know what to say about your business here in
your town. Our county taxes are not payed yet nor won't be if I do not
watch it. You had better come home and do something with this property it is good for nothing.

Pamelia's fortitude pulled her through, and James gave up and
returned to Little Falls, sans pile, in September. Left-at-home
wives, like Pamelia, deserved as much recognition as the husbands who ventured to Colorado; without the women's support,
the men would not have felt so free to travel west.

With the family reunited, James set about trying to resolve his
Minnesota problems. Summarizing his adventures, he wrote his
brother that "in every respect except making money it has been
beneficial to me." His health, thanks to Colorado's climate and
his hard outdoor work, was excellent, and he could "stand almost
any amount of fatigue."

Colorado had come a long way since the days of fifty-nine. The
easy diggings for "free" gold along the branches of Clear Creek,
the Arkansas River, and South Park disappeared into history.

The days of the pan and rocker, the latter a device that resembled a baby's rocker and allowed for more gravel to be washed, had nearly passed, as well. Prospectors used the pan to follow the float to the golden ore, where mining then began in earnest. Many of the old placer districts had declined, their former residents having drifted on to more promising areas.

Gilpin County, the site of John Gregory's great discovery, had already turned to quartz mining and the required skills, money, and technical knowledge. Working with a pan had been all right for the short haul, but Americans wanted to make money as fast as possible. That obsession quickly led to hydraulic mining in the placer districts, with its high-pressure nozzles, hoses, flumes, reservoirs, sluices, and companies to pay for all the equipment. Seymour had undoubtedly heard of one or two of these operations cutting away a hillside or a stream bank. Miners combined their resources and claims to start this kind of operation, or outside capital was used to finance miners. The risks ran high (a Lake Creek company spent two thousand dollars completing its work), yet so could profits (a Tarryall group earned eighteen hundred dollars in one week).

Seymour understood that it now required some investment to make money in mining, unless a person was very, very lucky. He looked around him and could still see vestiges of the early days (the pan, rocker, and sluice), which traced their heritage back to California in the days of forty-nine and beyond. He also saw, perhaps, the mining wave of the future with its companies, hired hands, and large expenditures. Just as he and most of his contemporaries had come from the East and Midwest, so now came the machinery and money. California's ties to Colorado, strong in the early placer days because of the experienced miners who came from there, now loosened as that state's attention and resources turned to Nevada and Comstock silver.

As Seymour prospected over the mountains, bucking large snow drifts that surprised this Ohioan, he migrated from the old to the new and back again. Colorado mining, though not dead, seemed not so lively as last year, and new discoveries were made less frequently. He also found, legend notwithstanding, that mining was not the easy road to wealth.

Seymour never saw Central City and its mining districts, the heart of Colorado mining from the beginning. Here in fifty-nine had lain the rich placer claims; now rich quartz mines augmented them. Here the evolution from pan to rocker to sluice box to hard-rock mining had occurred with breathtaking speed. And here both forms of mining existed side by side, depending more on wealth and ambition than on evolutionary progress.

Like Seymour, these miners found mining to be a combination of tribulation and disappointment. Placer miners continually found themselves facing shortages of water, even though they built ditches to bring in more. Winter closed down their opera-tions instantaneously, freezing their water sources. Water was also the key to running the mills, which the quartz miners needed to crush their ore and save the gold. Ironically, the deeper the mines went, the more water the miners encountered, necessita-ting the expense of pumps.

The Consolidated Ditch was dug to ease Central City's placer problems. It served its purpose well, and its backers hoped to pro-fit from their venture. Unfortunately, complaints about fees, ser-vice, stolen water, unpaid bills, and damage from leaking ditches generated frustration and led to litigation, threats, and much ill will.

Hard-rock miners were not exempt from problems, though theirs differed from those of their placer neighbors. They found as they burrowed into the mountains that mining required skill and capital that they too often did not possess. As they dug deeper, some of them hit refractory ore which stymied mill men. Then a few hit what they called cap (barren rock), and the ore values crashed. The mill men were no better off. The simple process of crushing the ore with stamps, then mixing in mercury (to form an amalgam with gold) no longer seemed to work so well. Various experiments aimed at overcoming the problem were attempted, but results were discouraging. Other mills lay idle in the summer of sixty-one for want of ore.

Then there were always the unexpected problems that cropped up to bedevil mining. The downpour in Central City's neighbor-ing community, Russell Gulch, in July was an example: "Men could be seen in every direction endeavoring to capture stray sluice boxes and I have heard [wrote a correspondent to the *News,* July 15] that one man rode in safety from Pullman's mill down to Pleasant Valley." Though the truth of that assertion is doubtful, there is no question that a great deal of damage had been done to ditches, pits, and sluices, and that mercury (used to separate gold from its oft companion, black sand) had been lost. Hard-rock mining fell victim to cave-ins and a host of other mining accidents that did not often plague surface operations. Dampness and foul air also bothered miners; pumping out water and providing fresh air for the lower workings were not easy operations.

A shortage of powder nearly brought Gilpin County's mining to a standstill in the early months of 1862. Speculators and hoarders were blamed, a most detestable twosome in the eyes of those who did not have powder, or the money to pay for it, when prices soared. Not until mid-March, when wagon trains finally reached the mountains, did the price break (from $40 to $14 a barrel) and powder become abundant.

If Central City was to maintain its position as the premier mining district, these problems and others had to be solved. Cries were already being heard for more reliance on scientific mining; for experienced miners; for new and better equipment; for more efficient mills, which saved a higher percentage of gold; and for a major influx of money to pay for everything.

The Seymours of the world, though, still did not see the reality of Central City, blinded as they were by their dreams. With luck, those dreams might be realized, and Buckskin Joe seemed to offer the best opportunity in sixty-one, as had Gregory diggings in fifty-nine.

Buckskin Joe lured Seymour and hundreds of others from less exciting mining districts. Those staunch New Englanders Horace and Augusta Tabor and their son Maxey had come. Fifty-niners who had panned at Payne's Bar on south Clear Creek and then gone to California Gulch in its palmy days of 1860, they followed the flow of mining once more.

Stamp mills and arrastras, the old Spanish method of crushing ore using horse power and rocks, were found side by side in this new district. Placer claims coexisted with quartz mines. The rush

to Buskskin Joe spawned other discoveries, among them the Independent district, which Seymour visited near the head waters
of the Platte River.

The old and the new, the dying and the developing, the bust
and the boom—Colorado offered some of each. For a while Iowa
Gulch, near California Gulch, bid fair to surpass its neighbor.
Tabor mined there but moved on when the gulch did not pan out.
The familiar gulches in the Breckenridge area, the first district to
open beyond the Continental Divide, still attracted attention:
Delaware Flats was all the rage, Gold Run was not being worked, Gibson's Gulch was said to be rich, Humbug Gulch was pur-
portedly paying the best of any in the territory, French Gulch
was not being mined extensively. Each prospect acquired its own
tag line. These little mining districts, struggling for existence, exemplified the saga of the mining frontier in one river valley. As
the year ended, too late in the season for extensive prospecting,
news of yet another discovery reached the foothills. The Silver
Lake district at the head of the Blue River had been found.
Rumor made it "in extent and richness the most remarkable on
record."

Indeed, in so well-established a region as Gilpin County,
districts rose and fell. Spring Gulch's deserted appearance
showed it to be very nearly washed out. A few miles away, the
new Vermillion district was just being prospected that summer
with pan and sluice. To the north, Boulder County held out great
hope, as it had since the beginning. Hurt by smaller and poorer
gold deposits and a lack of publicity, that county trailed its much
smaller southern neighbor. Only now did a good road make acces-
sible Gold Hill, one of the three original discoveries of 1859. Prospectors had never given up on the county and opened the Grand
Island district in April 1861, reporting both gold and silver. The
nearby Ward district held even more potential; it only needed
capitalists, better roads, and, according to a correspondent in
January, almanacs so they could stop "marking days of the week
on shingles."

All things considered, most of the excitement was generated by
anticipation of unknown discoveries in as yet unprospected regions. A miner could rush in on the ground floor, stake a claim,

make a fortune, and retire back East, just as in the days of 1859. That year, 1861, held out two such hopes.

Washington Gulch, in what later became Gunnison County, was discovered in 1860, survived through 1861, and then declin-ed. Handicapped by the Ute Indians' aversion to harboring min-ers so deep in their territory, shallow deposits, extremely expen-sive provisions, and mountain isolation, Washington Gulch was doomed. Optimism and "astonishing yields" could not overcome the fact that California Gulch, the nearest settlement, lay one hundred roundabout, mountainous miles to the northeast.

Fifty-niner John X. Beidler could testify to Washington Gulch's problems. He ran a pack train there and just barely struggled out in December, battling cold, snow, elevation, fatigue, and hunger all the way. Too slim rewards would not tempt this thirty-two-year-old to continue freighting into such a region.

Even more isolated and inhospitable were the San Juans, which for a fleeting moment in 1861 promised bonanza. Late the previous year, rumors had begun to circulate describing $.50 to the pan, $2.50 to the pan, another California, and Colorado's mother lode. Winter quickly thwarted Coloradans' enterprise, however; it was no time to venture into the area's highest and most spectacularly rugged mountains. Suddenly, news and letters from the new mother-lode country ground to a halt. Byers de-nounced the "San Juan humbug," a rush that threatened Denver with a rival in either Canon City or some town in New Mexico, if rumor proved out. Canon City, in fact, based much of its future on the San Juans.

Byers's epithet was validated. By early summer San Juaners, recognized by their "toil-worn and weary appearance," were re-turning. Wolfe Londoner remembered the "sad and weary crowd" that reappeared in California Gulch. Ben Eaton nearly starved to death before making his way back to civilization and turning to farming. Others boiled their moccasins for a "tasty" soup before they struggled out.

Reliance on false information had created the fiasco: a few pen-nies to the pan hardly constituted a bonanza. A mountainous, rugged environment, three months of "mighty late fall and nine months of winter," unbelievable isolation, and unwelcoming Ute

Indians doomed the venture. Byers gloated as the San Juan excitement collapsed, while others counted themselves lucky to
have returned from the mountains alive.

"Like a lottery, the prizes attract," concluded eastern mining
investor John Wetherbee. A few miners found wealth in Colorado; many more made only a passable living, and others were
completely disillusioned. As Nevada Citian Samuel Mallory
wrote, "some getting rich and many getting poor, and wishing
themselves back to the States."

That was Colorado in 1861–62. The "feverish, nervous"
temperament that characterized earlier days still permeated the
region and incited prospecting and mining. So mining lived and
with it the territory.

What kept these people going? Excitement, stubbornness, embarrassment over not striking a fortune, adventure, lack of funds
to pursue alternatives—the reasons were as varied as the individuals involved. They all hoped to be like the miner who
thought he had discovered the original source of all gold deposits
(*Miners' Record*, August 24, 1861). This was the dreamed-of fortune. He had not found it, but the possibility did create excitement in the Silver Lake district. Undaunted, others tried various
ways to strike it rich.

Matthew Dale gave up unremunerative prospecting for a salary
of one hundred dollars a month as a mill superintendent. Pleased
with his "very large salary," he wrote his parents, "you know
brains will always command more than mere automatons in any
business." Dale learned all the new gold saving techniques and
set off confidently, exemplifying the motto that "Everything is
done in the west with a rush." That practice explained in part
why so many mills were failing. Inexperienced hands operated
too many mills without the proper mix of mechanics, chemistry,
and metallurgy.

Sniktau (nom de plume of E. H. Patterson) wrote from Gold
Hill on June 29 to the *News* that

In a mining country, men must "live and learn," and the sooner men
divest themselves of the idea that they "know it all," the quicker they
will be in a position to profit by the experience of others and commence
mining understandingly.

He proffered good advice that went too little heeded.

Living at Hamilton, teenager Irving Howbert probably never read Sniktau, but he practiced the advice. Miners learned that yellow pine, not spruce, proved best for durable sluice boxes. Since the miners had no nearby sources of the needed lumber, Howbert used his family's team to haul logs to the sawmill at five dollars a load, thereby earning himself a fine summer income. Overcoming some unexpected problems, the fifteen-year-old used his wits to handle emergencies during his first trips, thereby learning to think for himself and maturing beyond his years. Lumbering and jobs such as young Irving's exemplified mining's ability to stimulate other industries needed to support it, some of which took permanent hold.

C. S. Hinman believed he had learned from experience; tired of prospecting on his own for little return, he and two partners hired out for two dollars a day to prospect for others. Mining had indeed become a business. He informed his parents that if he did not make something in six months, he planned to return home and be content. Always optimistic, he reported that some of the claims they found near Trail Creek promised to be "better than the famous Bobtail." He proved a poor prophet.

To comfort his worried mother, who feared for him in the hostile environment at Mountain City and Trail Creek, Hinman wrote:

> Mother spoke something about that she was afraid that some of the boys were inclined to be reckless and that I might bee influenced by them. All I hav to say is that they have no made it manifest since we hav been hear. I do not believe there is a stiddier set of men in the mountains. We have all worked hard and tried to make something as yet we hav no made much money but I think we hav got a pretty good foundation laid for making som.

The spelling would have appalled his teachers, but, even with all the mistakes, he well summarized the conditions of most of his contemporaries that summer.

At least one former teacher would have understood—twenty-five-year-old William Dutt, a restless soul who came west to seek his fortune. To Hinman's insights Dutt added a few ideas of his own about how Colorado had changed him. From sad experience,

William learned to sew without a thimble, wash without a board, make biscuits without shortening, and drink coffee without cream. An ardent reader, Dutt believed he "should die of horrors here in the wilds of Colorado if I could get nothing to read." With books of any description costing double the price back in the States, and a "common weekly paper" costing ten to fifteen cents, this new Coloradan tightened his belt and bought them. He read the cold winter away and looked for an opportunity to strike his bonanza.

Anticipating a golden fortune, Chicagoan George Pullman and a partner purchased a stamp mill. Because George was the younger of the two and unmarried, he volunteered to come to Colorado in 1860 to check it out. Before he went back to Chicago in June 1861, Pullman had also purchased mines, run a freighting business, and kept a store, in addition to operating the mill. All these enterprises left him little time for anything but work. He did not return to Colorado until March 1862. James Lyon, his new partner, took charge in his absence. Pullman demonstrated one way to make money—by diversifying his investments in hopes that one or more would pay off.

The Tabors had migrated west in 1859, planning to make enough money to clear the mortgage from their Kansas farm. Not until they reached California Gulch, however, did they come close to the success they hoped to achieve. Here they ac-cumulated a small fortune, seven thousand dollars according to Augusta, before moving on to Buckskin Joe. They also came to understand that the road to wealth followed paths other than mining. They opened a store, served as postmasters, and boarded miners, always working as a team. Horace continued to prospect for his own bonanza and grubstaked others with a few supplies for a share of their discoveries. The Tabors worked hard and long hours and emerged as solid middle-class residents of Buckskin Joe.

Many, of course, stayed with mining exclusively. Those "old pioneer miners and prospectors," the Russells (William Green and Levi J.), had been here first in 1858. Having found the gold that started it all, they subsequently missed out on the Gregory diggings but bounced back to open neighboring Russell Gulch.

Southerners, they had not rallied to the Union flag and continued
to earn a steady income throughout 1861 by working their
claims. For the moment at least, Colorado held more attraction
for them than the South. Neighbor Pat Casey, an illiterate Irish
immigrant, had also followed his dream of wealth to Colorado.
He staked a claim above Central City on Quartz Hill, near the little camp of Nevada. Hard work failed to produce a bonanza, but
he never gave up and his situation looked promising. His
generosity and love of the good life gained him more prestige than
most of his fellow Irishmen achieved back east, soothing
somewhat his mining disappointments.

For some, the reward of their toil had been death. Mining has
always been a treacherous occupation. Twenty-nine-year-old
Alfred Payne died of mercury poisoning after inhaling fumes
while retorting gold amalgam. (This common procedure was used
to separate gold from mercury.) Another man, identified only as
Brown, was killed in a cave-in while working in the Bobtail lode
near Black Hawk. He left a wife and two children. Others were
injured in mines, placers, and while prospecting. Many simply
disappeared, never to be heard from again.

One heritage of the 1859 rush slowly disappeared in 1861—the
need for extralegal miners' meetings, courts, and mining district
laws beyond those related to mining. A product of the time when
no official legal system existed, these practical remedies had
saved the day then. Now Colorado Territory had organized and
brought into being courts, laws, officials, and a legislature.

As miners opened up new discoveries, though, they continued
to form mining districts. The Mosquito district and the Independent district, for example, came out of the rush to Buckskin Joe.
The latter was four miles square each way from "Skin's house on
the Platte River." Its laws, typical of the times, defined the size of
a claim and the method to record and hold a claim (the recording
fee, fifty cents), and established two officers, a president and a
recorder. In the months that followed, meetings were called to
discuss water claims and tunneling (they had neglected to pass
laws on that subject), to elect new officers, to settle a claim
dispute, and to set a time by which claims had to be worked or

forfeited. Claim disputes created most of the trouble because of vague or overlapping boundaries. A multitude of claims could be filed—gulch, water, mill, spring, timber, tunnel, bar, lode, and even ranch claims to cover stock grazing. Miners wanted any dispute settled as quickly, easily, and cheaply as possible, and the mining districts provided that expedient. Occasionally a tax was levied to improve the roads, or a law passed to "prevent the sale of licquer" or to handle civil matters. Legislative action by mining districts was becoming more unusual, however, and residents of the mountain districts successfully pressured the legislature to model territorial mining law on local district laws.

Another problem common to miners and merchants was the establishment of a standard price for gold. Because gold cir-culated as currency, a standard needed to be set. Gold might be valued at twenty dollars per ounce back east, but not in Col-orado. The discrepancy resulted from the retorting; some gold was clean, some dirty. The problem was further complicated by a scoundrel who occasionally shaved a little brass into his gold pouch to see if he could pass it off as pure.

In May 1861, Denver and Central merchants tried to find a solution to pricing gold by establishing twelve dollars for badly retorted dust and going up to twenty dollars per ounce for Platte River gold, which was considered the finest. Gold from most districts was valued between seventeen and eighteen dollars. The plan collapsed amid accusations that Denver was trying to rob honest miners of their just reward. Miners in Georgia and California gulches considered their gold every bit as valuable as that from the higher-priced Clear Creek and Platte River dig-gings.

Distrust of Denver, already a fact of life in Colorado, only inten-sified after this incident. Denver, with its transportation and business dominance, its head start and publicity, and its continual aggressiveness in all areas, was not beloved by the mountain communities.

The logical method for solving this currency problem was to coin the gold. Denver's Clark and Gruber Mint managed to do so with some success; coins minted in Tarryall and Georgia Gulch proved less successful. The ultimate answer, a federal mint in Denver, became the goal that Coloradans worked to achieve.

As the winter of 1861–62 descended on the mountain districts, the miners drifted out to Colorado City, Denver, and other more temperate climes. The winter months rekindled enthusiasm dampened by problems of the past season. Absence rejuvenated imagination. Why, it was only a matter of time before silver, already reported in several places, would rival gold; other valuable minerals only awaited discovery. Perhaps some basis of fact underlay the report that opals could be found in high mountains above the Clear Creek Valley!

So spring returned, and with it a promise that every claim would be rich and every mill successful. A January 2 editorial in the *Republican* cheerfully proclaimed that "the inexhaustible wealth of the country is proven, the fact that Colorado is one of the richest mineral countries in the world is fully established."

But there was something wrong in Eden; why else would miners be tempted to go to the new and enticing Salmon River mines in Idaho? Byers felt moved to issue a warning on April 12: "We again repeat our old caution. Stick to what you have got. Let monster gold stories, new discoveries and 'the richest mines in the world' go. Colorado is good enough." But was it?

3

The "Star of Empire" Rolling Westward

POPULAR YOUNG DENVER MERCHANT David Moffat did not appreciate the scolding he received from his Omaha friend and business associate, Joseph H. Millard:

Now Dave I am going to talk to you about *overdraft*. Your act. is overdrawn $24.41 and has been for a long time. . . . This little overdraft of yours is very small and was I doing business alone would not say a word but you know such is not the case and you being my very particular friend. I of course hear of this quite often and I know it's as unpleasant for you to hear of it from me as for me to hear of it from others.

Angered by this reminder, Moffat fired off a heated reply. Taken aback by his friend's response, Millard replied, "I am a good deal surprised you should write me so." No insult had been intended, and he wanted to continue their friendship.

Not finished chastising his young friend, however, Millard turned to another business problem in a May 18 letter:

We have been bored to death here just by the foolish way your men have traded at Denver. Allowing 16$ for dust that is not worth 14$. I trust experience has been a good teacher to all of you. Your bankers know full well that the dust is worth no such money . . . If people at the mountains will let the Bankers buy *all* the Dust then it will be all right and people can make something at it.

Hundreds of prairie miles separated Omaha and Denver; Millard and Moffat could not fully understand each other's current problems. They were united, however, in their desire to make a profit, although Millard seemed more concerned about the second great problem confronting western merchants—the war. "These are war times and no one in this latitude can expect to make much money. We think now days more of hanging traitors and keeping the country together than any thing else."

The two remained friends, despite their sometimes irate exchanges. In fact, Moffat nearly managed to get Millard into hot water with his wife:

Dave I don't want you fellows to send me any more pictures of your *female* friends. The time to send me such things is past and I hope you won't do it again. When away from home I always tell my wife to open any letters that may come for me and you know such a thing as that to get opened when away would not be pleasant. I have no recollection of having ever seen the individual but suppose she *was an intimate friend* of my old Omaha companions.

Bachelor Moffat did not yet understand the problems that could confront the newly married.

Down on Larimer Street, Moffat ran Denver's most popular book and stationery store. The enterprising twenty-two-year-old had come to Colorado back in 1860. His store offered a splendid assortment of goods to tempt the customer, and the proprietors were not averse to profiting from partisans of both sides in the war. Millard's concern about hanging traitors notwithstanding, Moffat and Woolworth advertised both Union and Secession envelopes in May. During the Christmas season, they tempted customers with more traditional children's books, "elegantly" bound poems, Bibles, and holiday books.

Always on the lookout for further opportunities, Moffat secured an appointment as telegraph agent in September, an important political position. He controlled the delivery of telegraphic reports when they arrived on the stage from Julesburg, the telegraph line not yet having reached Denver. Supplying one newspaper with a late-breaking story could tip the readership in its favor for a time. The *Herald* did not fear that Moffat would give undue preference to his friend Byers and forecast that he would make an efficient agent. Moffat seems to have been a friend of almost everybody.

When Moffat departed on a trip east in October, Byers wished him a pleasant and prosperous visit. That wish proved fortuitous: two months later the *News* saluted his marriage to Miss Fannie Buckhout of Mechanicsville, New York, wishing them a "happy and prosperous" journey through life. The young bride and groom returned to Denver in January, following a cold stage ride across frozen plains.

Dave Moffat was having a good year. His Aunt Jannette need not have worried when she wrote him in April from war-fevered Adel, Iowa: "You are well off at the Peak place and are not troubled with the war spirit but I hope and trust that your heart is in the right place." Moffat's heart was in the right place, even though his aunt remembered him as a Democrat. She conceded, however, that he could "be that and be a union man too." Her nephew was a Union man, but he also understood the fact that war days were good for profits.

Moffat and his Main Street contemporaries were as much pioneers as the miners in the mountains. They rushed to the urban world of Colorado to make money and settle permanently. With more invested, they stood to gain more from that permanence than some of their fellow Coloradans. Like businessmen everywhere, they faced competition and the rise and fall of the marketplace. A misjudgment in stock purchases or poor site selection could jeopardize a business here just as it did in the Midwest or East. Unlike their more established colleagues, businessmen in Colorado were frustrated by long, costly transportation lines, irritating delays in receiving shipments, and the transitory world of mining. No one knew if a mining district would pan out for more than a season, or which of a multitude of little rival camps would dominate and survive.

To make matters worse, outside competition—St. Joseph, St. Louis, and Chicago merchants, as well as a few professionals— advertised in Colorado papers. Even *Harper's Weekly* carried its share of advertisements, many of which gradually came to reflect the war times. In the December 21 and 28 issues, field manuals, cavalry tactics, and miscellaneous military books were promoted, along with a circular on artificial legs and arms and a Tiffany and Company advertisement for swords ("warranted to cut wrought iron"), caps, and gold epaulettes. One company parlayed the name of the military hero of that winter, George McClellan, by marketing the "McClellan Gift Writing Desk" for only 25 cents. Each desk included a jewelry gift, "eclipsing all and every gift [of] jewelry articles offered to the public."

The long odds against achieving success did not diminish the optimism and expectation that businessmen and other Coloradans brought with them. By the time of the Civil War, Denver had become the territory's dominant business center, thanks to a fortunate location, aggressive business leadership, and a thriving head start over its neighbors. All rival communities, willingly or not, fell into Denver's economic orbit.

This did not mean that outlying merchants were any less aggressive or had fewer aspirations than Moffat in Denver. Wolfe Londoner, isolated in Oro City, was every bit as "wide awake." The two men, in fact, had similar backgrounds. Both native New Yorkers, each had ventured out on his own while in his early teens, Moffat eventually ending up in Omaha as a banker and Wolfe, after traveling to California, settling in St. Louis as a merchant. Both were veteran businessmen by the time they reached Colorado, though they were only in their twenties. In his general store Londoner practiced the policy of quick sales and small profits. Hailed as one of the pioneering merchants of that region, the irrepressible Londoner was well liked, and his arrival in Canon City to purchase supplies always warranted reporting. Riding his yellow mule and sometimes trailed by his spotted "dorg" Bonito, the ebullient Londoner made friends wherever he traveled. So did Central City's popular hotelman, Glen Dickinson, who made a point of visiting newspaper offices while in Denver to garner some free publicity.

Alex Rey in Montgomery combined prospecting with merchandising and eked out his income by acting as agent for the *News*. Every merchant's perception of his community duplicated Rey's, who wrote that Montgomery was the best place for business. Although some opinions were justified, more proved to be wrong, but every camp and town needed whatever business it could attract.

Thanks to mining—its gold surplus and its urban ambience—Colorado's merchant community grew by leaps and bounds in the first three years, unlike the slow, steady evolution of an agrarian village. Here existed boom and bust, speculation, impatience, and optimism. Swift population increases and business turnovers were facts of life.

Specialization might be expected in a city of Denver's size. Travel south to Canon City revealed the same phenomenon on a smaller scale. In April, this year-and-a-half-old community, which fancied itself Denver's only southern rival, boasted of wholesale and retail merchants and professional practitioners, including a butcher, pharmacist, jeweler, baker, hotelman, blacksmith, real estate agent, attorneys, an architect and builder, and the ever-prestigious newspaper staff. These were only the businessmen who advertised; undoubtedly, others existed.

The farther one ventured into the mountains, the smaller the business districts became. In Wolfe Londoner's Oro City, his general store, actually a branch of Canon City's Dold and Company, monopolized the declining market. Several hotels and saloons constituted the rest of the businesses strung out along a nearly played-out gulch. But a miss in Oro City did not mean demise. Another new district, somewhere in the mountains, was always being born with the promise of a future metropolis.

Like Moffat in Denver, these mountain merchants were on the lookout for various ways to make a living, sometimes out of sheer necessity, other times out of ambition. Mat Riddlebarger in Canon City proved to be a virtuoso in the world of entrepreneurs. He owned a store, dealt in real estate (farming and mining), was part owner and "junior" editor of the Times, and served as district recorder. He wagered that his town of some four hundred people would become the kingpin of southern Colorado.

Everywhere Riddlebarger turned, however, he saw rivals, actual and potential. Every merchant in every community had to fight for survival in a no-holds-barred contest. In this competition, a town's very existence depended upon the presence of a newspaper. Without one, promotion and defense of one's territorial pride were virtually a lost cause. Fight or die, grow or die—the brutal struggle did not reward second place.

Canon City challenged Denver, praising its own natural advantages for mountain travel and its easier and faster connections with the East. The *Times* delighted in publishing letters praising Canon City as the "commercial metropolis" and describing how more immigration came up the Arkansas Valley than the Platte. Residents envisioned the day when Canon City would be the territorial capital, except for realistic A. C. Thomas, who wrote a friend: "I doubt very much myself, the influence of Denver being too great." Denver took all the bombast in stride, replying only when a barb stung particularly hard, or when the editor's humorous mood prompted a parody of a rival's aspirations. For Denverites, the arrows of aspersion came with being number one. Envy of this city surfaced early in Colorado.

Rivalries were not limited to competition with Denver; some involved competing mining camps struggling desperately to dominate or die. Hamilton and Tarryall stood as "ambitious rival cities" in South Park. So heated became the contest that the local *Miners' Record* took the unusual step of threatening to move to another part of the valley if the issue were not resolved. The site of the newspaper's office had become a bone of contention that jeopardized the paper's existence.

The *Miners' Record*, despite its warning, was beyond saving. Receipts failed to pay current expenses, lamented the owners (who happened to be William Byers and the *News*), and neither job work nor advertising, the two staples of newspaper life, could support the publication. With flags flying and promises to return in another season, the readers were bid "adieu for a time." That time never came.

Denver was well newspapered, another advantage for the "City of the Plains." Tarryall, Colorado City, and Canon City were the only other cities with papers in 1861, and all had folded by year's end. Hence, Colorado was viewed through Denver's eyes, an unpleasant fact of life for residents of every other community. Location in Denver, however, provided no guarantee of journalistic success; several newspapers had already come and gone, and the rivalry that had trapped Gilpin continued unabated.

Every paper faced similar problems: a lack of community sup- port and advertising, failure of subscribers to pay or renew, short- ages of district news, and the threat of competitors seeking a share of the rather meager revenue pie. They attempted to over- come these problems by pledging to maintain high standards, to be the best friend of their town, to provide a "spicy" paper, and to devote themselves to local matters, commerce, and politics. The *Times* even went so far as to include "choice literary selec- tion" for the edification of its readers.

Of course, ambition was not confined solely to pursuits for journalistic excellence. The publishers of the *Times*, Mat Riddle- barger and H. S. Millett, were also closely involved with the Canon City town company as secretary, recorder, and treasurer. Their newspaper failure heralded the failure of the town com- pany and its dreams. They admitted that from the pecuniary point of view the paper had been a "most signal failure"; their "long self-sacrificing generosity" did not last past October.

In Denver, meanwhile, Gibson and Byers battled on; Gilpin had been merely a side issue in a long-standing fight. The *Herald* blasted the *News*, that "slimy reptile," on October 12, then add- ed a week later: "The few readers of the '*News*' are delighted with the blackguardism and buffoonery used by its editors in refutation of facts." Byers replied in kind, referring to the "smut machine," and twitted Gibson when George Pullman subscribed for five copies to send to eastern friends. "He states that from Il- linois to New York, wherever he visited, people and friends wanted to have him send them back the *News*. . . . We confess we are proud of this, and we don't care who knows it."

Pullman was an innocent bystander who just happened to get dragged into the fight when he stopped by Byers's office on his way back to Central City in April 1862. Readers relished seeing their names or the names of their mining claims or businesses in print, and editors obliged in the local column, the heart of any paper. Subscribers also wanted their community and mines defended and promoted down to the last drop of ink. Woe unto the newspaper that failed in this mission.

News from other places also provided a popular diversion; the shorthanded editors were forced to rely on correspondents to supply it. Some of the best correspondents, like Sniktau, managed to create a following and carried on minifeuds with their rivals.

The newspapers depended on prosperous times, and even they were forced to admit (a real concession) that prospects were not very good in 1861–62. Byers reported seeing large cards in some saloons in June: "Gents—If you have not got the MONEY, DUST or collateral, Do not play a . . . game, or call for a . . . drink!" Those bellwethers of a community's prosperity, the saloons and sporting halls, were doing a "very light business." A month later, in late July, Byers complained that everybody seemed determined to feel blue and complain about hard times. Byers objected to these attitudes and encouraged people to look on the bright side, blaming most of the problems on the "crisis in the States." The merchants, he admonished, should stop grumbling and realize whose fault it was that the country was overstocked with goods. He pointed out that competition had reduced prices and, consequently, profits.

Farther south, the same refrain was being sung. The *Canon City Times* put up a bold front for a time but finally admitted in July and August that the town was suffering a dull season. This admission helped hasten the paper's own demise, and the situation failed to improve the coming winter. The mountain districts fared no better. C. T. Campbell fumed to Moffat in June that times were "God awful dull. No money in circulation [in old California Gulch]." Matthew Dale had difficulty collecting money due him for labor during the summer months in the Central City district. The whole country was "nearer bankrupt than ever," he wrote his parents on October 21. He had hoped to make money on claims he sold on time payments, but the claims all came back to him because the parties had been unable to meet their obligations. After nearly three years, Dale was worse off than when he arrived in 1859. Colorado was not evolving into the promised land envisioned in more heady days.

These circumstances, combined with the Gilpin flap (particularly that damaging article in the *New York Times*, which implied
that Colorado faced anarchy, bloodshed, and strife as well as
prostrate business conditions) nearly caused Byers to panic. It
was imperative to reverse this image to keep the tide of 1862 immigration from going elsewhere. In dead earnest he wrote in a
March 1 editorial, "Wake Up," that the time had come for people
in Colorado to work earnestly to remove the "erroneous impressions respecting our territory so prevalent in the States. Do not
stand idly by." To make matters worse, the Salmon River mines
in the future state of Idaho were now beckoning.

Colorado needed to lure immigrants vigorously. In the nomadic
life of nineteenth-century mining, gold's will-o'-the-wisp attraction caused stampedes of people from one place to another.
Miners were likely to pack up and rush to a new discovery on a
moment's notice, and, at this particular time, Colorado had
nothing new to offer. Somehow the "Star of Empire," as the
Times and others described it, must be kept rolling westward to
Colorado.

Immigrants did continue to come, but not in the numbers of
1859 and 1860. William Dutt thought he knew why: "Young
America has gone to the war instead of seeking her fortune
elsewhere as she had probably designed." Making the best of an
embarrassing situation, Byers found encouragement even in decline. The 1861 arrivals were far less transient and a "better
class—when industry and stability are considered." Yet the influx
barely equaled the outgo and Colorado, caught up in the grow-or-
die philosphy of the nineteenth century, faced a gloomy future.

Ore seekers trekked to the Salmon River mines and elsewhere;
some stayed, some returned to the States. Byers's morale suffered for having to admit that travel back to the war-torn "Happy
Land of Canaan" ran exceedingly heavy that fall. The same pattern had been in evidence earlier, as many people never thought
of the territory as their permanent home. They made their pile
and went back east. Ever on the alert to turn a discouraging
trend into something positive, Byers reminded those who must
go east not to forget to call at the *News* office to subscribe to the
"only paper" from this interesting region.

The territory needed more than mining to create a permanent

economic base. Coloradans—those who had not succumbed com-
pletely to mining fever—readily admitted that. No one was more
determined to promote agriculture and broaden that base than
Byers. He had relentlessly pushed his pet agricultural theme since
1859 and practiced what he preached by farming on the Platte
near Denver. Joined by other newspapers, he chronicled the
successes and occasionally the setbacks of local farmers and
ranchers.

The appearance of the season's first crops on the local markets
provided fodder for favorable publicity. In 1862 homegrown
radishes and lettuce from near Golden garnished Denverites'
meals as early as March. Experiments with virgin soil and an
untested growing season sometimes yielded failures, along with
the more abundant successes. In the fall of 1861 sweet corn,
tomatoes, melons, squash (including one weighing 163 pounds),
and even sugarcane showed up in Denver stores. "Who says this
is not agricultural country," crowed Gibson. Specialized occupations arrived soon after, as evidenced by M. C. Fisher, the
pioneer thrasher, who worked his way up the Platte Valley
thrashing and cleaning wheat, rye, oats, and barley. His thrashing
machine was the best, of the most-improved pattern, claimed
Byers.

Cattle and dairy cows had thrived in Colorado since the Pike's
Peak rush; for other animals, Colorado still relied on the outside
world. Two hundred fifty-two hogs driven from Missouri across
the prairie to Denver must have been a wonder to behold. The
arrival of a large flock of sheep, also driven from Missouri, was
news at Tarryall in August, as was the jumping of hay claims on
Trout Creek. The intruders were driven off posthaste by a group
from town who forcibly righted the wrong.

While Byers encouraged and rejoiced in development along the
Platte, the editors of the *Times* were boosting the Arkansas
Valley as second to none in Colorado for its ranching and farming
potential. They forecast that within a few years the local harvest would prove sufficient for "our great home consumption."
The promising crops of summer were reaped in the fall. Farmers
streamed into Canon City and the mountains beyond with their
"eatables." "God speed the plow!" cheered Millett and Riddlebarger.

Somewhat ignored in all the furor was the fact that crops and sheep had been raised for a decade in the southern end of the San Luis Valley. Settlers from New Mexico had established a toehold in little villages, where they farmed with irrigated fields, the first such effort since that by the Anasazi culture centuries earlier. Fifty-niners paid scant attention to these isolated, agricultural settlements. No gold lured them there.

Agricultural self-sufficiency—the end of reliance on uncertain outside sources—became the goal. The vicissitudes of weather, which left farmers cussing and discussing, and the problem of how to insure a steady water supply beyond the river bottoms, prevented attainment of the goal at this time. Unpredictable setbacks, such as the grasshopper invasion of the late spring of 1861, also hurt. The lonely farmer's vulnerability to Indian attacks once he moved away from populated areas proved a further deterrent to rapid development, even with high market prices for produce. Living in an urban and rural frontier at the same time, Coloradans sometimes misunderstood one another's concerns and needs.

Colorado remained dependent on overland shipments, a risky gamble. Thus the *News* advised its readers in April 1862 not to pay ruinous prices for flour: hundreds of sacks were being freighted toward Denver, and the shortage would soon end. Shortages in the mountains were common, and the price of beef rose to fifteen cents a pound. Equally scarce vegetables commanded high prices.

Somewhat less resolutely, Coloradans attempted to capitalize on a phenomenon they did not fully comprehend—what later would be called tourism. When correspondents touted such advantages as the salubrious climate and environment, they were encouraging readers to come for reasons other than profit. When Ovando Hollister, in *Boldly They Rode*, described such non-military matters as the romantic aspects of Garden of the Gods and the valuable medicinal properties of the soda springs above Colorado City, he was promoting. Others joined the still faint chorus.

The most forbidding deterrent to the promoters' success was transportation. As long as it took a week or more by stage and at least a month by wagon to reach the territory, Colorado tourism would suffer. Stage travel, the fastest and costliest mode of transportation often sacrificed comfort for speed. Samuel Clemens bounced west in '61, leaving behind his career as a Mississippi River pilot and the "damnable war." He later recalled:

Our coach was a great swinging and swaying stage. . . . As the sun went down and the evening chill came on, we made preparation for bed. We stirred up the hard leather letter-sacks, and the knotty canvas bags of printed matter . . . and redisposed them in such a way as to make our bed as level as possible.

We began to get into country, now, threaded here and there with little streams. These had high, steep banks on each side, and every time we flew down one bank and scrambled up the other, our party inside got mixed somewhat. First we would all be down in a pile at the forward end of the stage, nearly in a sitting posture, and in a second we would shoot to the other end, and stand on our heads. And we would sprawl and kick, too.

Welcome breaks in the journey came at the stage stations where, at mealtime, unique treats awaited Clemens and his friends.

The station-keeper upended a disk of last week's bread of the shape and size of an old-time cheese, and carved some slabs from it which were as good as Nicholson pavement, and tenderer.

He sliced off a piece of bacon for each man, but only the experienced old hands made out to eat it, for it was condemned bacon . . . the stage company had bought it cheap for the sustenance of their passengers and employees.

Finally, at noon on the fifth day out, "we arrived at the 'Crossing of the South Platte,' *alias* 'Julesburg,' *alias* 'Overland City,' four hundred and seventy miles from St. Joseph—the strangest, quaintest, funniest frontier town that our untraveled eyes had ever stared at and been astonished with."

Here travelers for Denver departed the overland stage and boarded the one for Denver. Samuel Clemens went on to Nevada and reemerged as Mark Twain. For the time being, staging exemplified the state of the art in Colorado transportation. The expense (Twain paid $150 for a ticket to Carson City, Nevada; the cost from the Missouri River to Denver was $100, with meals extra), however, forced most people to come by the slower, more common wagon trains.

On reaching Denver, passengers could make connections with stages heading into the mountains, sometimes at bargain rates, as in January 1862, when it cost one dollar to Golden and two to Central. Denver's role as a transportation hub did not hurt its aspirations. Only Canon City rivaled it for a while; in May 1861 the smaller city secured direct connections with Kansas City. The first stage, drawn by "four splendid white mules," rolled in-to town on Monday the thirteenth. Canon City could not main-tain its direct connections, however, and soon fell into Denver's orbit.

Freight wagons, Colorado's umbilical cord to the eastern states, lumbered over the same trail that Twain and others traveled. Unable to produce enough food, equipment, and other supplies, the territory depended on these overland shipments for sustenance. The wagon trains, vulnerable to weather, Con-federates, and Indians, created a constant state of anxiety for the citizens who relied so heavily on them. To the consumers' disgust, food often arrived with a distinctly strange taste.

Something faster, more reliable, was already in the works. First came Thomas L. Fortune of Mt. Pleasant, Kansas, with his steam wagon. Boasting a speed of seven miles per hour and the capabili-ty of hauling ten tons, the inventor promised that his machine could make a round trip from the Missouri River to Denver in ten days, three trips per month. Fortune introduced his invention that summer, once failing to navigate a street corner in Atchison and overrunning a store. The second trial ended in a mudhole. So did Coloradans' hopes for more efficient transportation in 1861.

Dreams of a railroad, part of the transcontinental route now before Congress in bill form, remained alive. With the South hav-ing seceded, little debate remained as to what route the railroad would follow—the central one, just north of the territory. That possibility held promise for a practical transportation solution, if financing and other prerequisites could be worked out during a war.

An improvement in communication came with the completion of the telegraph to Julesburg. When the transcontinental hookup was made in October, news flashed to that suddenly important hamlet in minutes from both coasts. The new technology doomed the more romantic Pony Express rider, whom Twain so eagerly waited to see. Now remained only the question of when the wires would be stretched to Denver and the mountain communities beyond. When that happened, Colorado would become part of the communications revolution that so astounded Americans.

By the end of the war's first year, Moffat and his fellow businessmen had made significant strides toward bringing Colorado into the mainstream of American progress and economy. How far had they really come in this land only three years removed from the wilderness? In May the Denver Foundry had cast the region's first iron, from local iron ore. Byers, as usual, enthusiastically predicted that within three years this country should be able to produce everything it needed. By the next January the Langford and Company Foundry was manufacturing shot and shell and casting pieces as heavy as thirteen hundred pounds. Unfortunately, failure to find coking coal left the company at the mercy of charcoal, which was less satisfactory in the firing process.

Denver's candle factory produced candles superior to those previously manufactured "in this country" and at a cheaper price. Soap, perhaps not so essential in some people's way of thinking, also evolved into a "home-grown" product. Another step forward came in the form of ice making; in the warmer months ice could be purchased to cool drinks, to preserve food, and to provide a treat for children on a hot afternoon.

Barney Ford, well-known professor of the "tonsorial art," fitted up a first-class restaurant next to his barbershop and was living proof that a black could succeed if given half a chance. That chance at success epitomized the lure of Colorado for many Americans of this generation.

Merchants in the mountains also wanted to succeed. Frank Sprague superintended a store at Cache Creek, which served customers in Lost Canon, Kale Creek, Kelley's Bar, and other nearby mining districts. Sprague, given the opportunity, nearly monopolized local business; his continued success during the upcoming winter was predicted by the News. Sprague gambled on more variables than his Denver counterparts but with luck and hard work would make it.

In Denver and elsewhere, the same could be said. Industrialists and businessmen were gaining ground. Denver played for the biggest stakes, striving to become the commercial emporium of the "Great Western Gold Fields." All this would happen, Byers piously intoned, if only Coloradans would patronize home manufacturers. He failed to mention that dealing with local businessmen would keep money at home, where it was needed for further development.

Customers searched for the best bargain, and Colorado businesses would have to provide it. Sometimes, in their enthusiasm for profits, they got carried away. Denver bakers were scolded in May when they tried to organize and raise the price of a loaf of bread to twenty cents. "Gentlemen, when you can't live at your trade without establishing these protective associations, quit it and go at something else."

In the end, these heralds of urbanization formed the hearts of their communities. They risked much to make much if they succeeded. They worked to build permanence against a swiftly changing mining life; for them, that strategy would be the long-range answer to profit. With a touch of pride they could have their photographs taken either by William Chamberlain or George Wakely in Denver, or by Central City's Rankin and Company or Henry Faul. If one were "desirous of getting fine ambrotypes" of house, store, street, or human "face divine," Chamberlain proclaimed, he need look no further.

A bit of immortality lay in those photographs, as well as a chance to exhibit one's success to folks back east. Four photographers in such a young territory gave hearty evidence to America that Colorado would take a backseat to none.

4

"I think this 'the place' "

FROM BUSTLING BUCKSKIN JOE in September 1861, John Ming wrote his friend David Moffat in Denver that "The town is small yet and *Rough* But there is more life and activity here than any place I have seen and I think there will be quite a village here by & by. In fact I think this 'the place.' "

Buckskin Joe *was* the place that season, lusty proof that the Colorado mining frontier still lived, despite reports to the contrary. Ming, along with his neighbors, the Tabors and others, had migrated to the district in the past year for the same reason people had rushed out in 1859—golden opportunity. Anything seemed possible while villages and camps were aborning, booming, and declining in a season or two. Even a docked life seemed better than one that existed only in a promoter's mind and often died there. Coloradans flocked to these primitive communities, huddling against the loneliness of the frontier and searching for profit.

From the foothills to deep into the mountains, settlements took root. The gateway towns stood staunchly as a picket line between plains and mountains. Of these, Denver predominated, but its rivals conceded nothing. Nearby Golden, nestled at the mouth of Clear Creek Canyon, provided easier access to the mining districts and aspired to everything Denver had, especially its designation as the capital city. Though a much smaller community, Golden did not suffer lack of ambition.

Massachusetts-born William Loveland was the key figure in

guiding Golden's destiny. William Byers took a shine to him, even though he voted Democratic and promoted an urban rival. A "good man and true," in Byers's opinion, Loveland rallied to the Union cause when war broke out. The experienced thirty-five-year-old miner-merchant had been both a California forty-niner and Colorado fifty-niner. A keen businessman, willing to spend money to develop his home and its resources, Loveland opened a thriving general merchandise store in Golden and owned a quartz mill in Nevada Gulch. He incurred Byers's displeasure, however, when he turned his efforts to making Golden the territorial capital. A large man physically, Loveland also loomed large politically, a worthy adversary for Denver.

Boulder, to the north, did not enjoy such a benefactor, but it did have a correspondent to the News, who signed himself "Dry Bones." He described Boulder's spring weather in these terms: "At times 'old boreas' favors us with a lusty howl, and for the time being, holds supreme control of outside affairs; in wild and fitful gusts down the rock canons he sweeps in fearful fury."

That windy April 1862 slowed down planting. Not only did Boulder provide passage to the mines, but it had also evolved into one of the territory's prosperous farming regions. Dry Bones expressed indignation with his neighbors, whom he saw as locked in a "Rip Van Winkle slumber" because they neglected to promote their community as the natural trading point for the mines and farming country. They should put their shoulders to the wheel, he advised, and make this "an A No. 1 locality." Their failure to build a bridge over Boulder Creek particularly disgusted him.

Boulder faced a long road and many wheels to push before it could hope to catch up with Denver. Even though the two settlements were launched about the same time, Boulder's founding fathers had not proven as aggressive, as Dry Bones pointed out, and the site they selected was not as geographically central. No itinerant newspaper, an essential appurtenance, had stopped to set up shop. Boulder languished.

Most of the other villages scattered along the foothills struggled, too. Colorado City never amounted to much, and Hollister dismissed it as a "mere assemblage of log cabins." Promoters' dreams failed here because of the remote location and poor mining prospects. The Civil War was another factor, first disrupting, then nearly closing the southern trails to Colorado, the natural trade and immigration routes from the States. Many disgruntled Colorado City denizens blamed Denver, as well, for down-playing land to the south as not worth seeking.

Farther south, Canon City was an 1859 settlement whose time had come and passed. An even smaller Pueblo, not considered worthy of mention by most correspondents and travelers, main-tained a store and a dozen houses as a reminder of its earlier status as a settlement established at the tag end of the fur trade.

Though one of the earliest settlements along the mountains, Pueblo could not claim to be the oldest in the territory. That honor belonged to the tiny villages in the far southern end of the San Luis Valley; Garcia, San Pedro, Guadalupe, San Acacio, and San Luis had all been settled by New Mexicans in the early 1850s. Steeped in Spanish and Catholic tradition and living in communities built in the familiar plaza style, these Coloradans had little in common with their distant Anglo neighbors.

It was in the mountains that a person could make a quick for-tune by landing on the ground floor of a community's rise to pros-perity. Camps seemed to grow like Topsy in these regions. Here was the action, the wave of the future.

In each district, camps scrapped for dominance. If the district provided at least a season's worth of gold, one camp would even-tually rise to the top of the heap. The rest fell into its economic orbit. They fought endlessly with more distant rivals and were not above taking on Denver to prove who was best.

Without question, Central City reigned as king of them all. Its early start, its rich placers followed by gold quartz mines, and its active, promotive merchants and city fathers, as well as a pinch of luck, kept it in the forefront. Denver's only real rival in size, in-fluence, and wealth, Central City, by the spring of 1862, had nearly everything Denver had in the way of businesses, though not in such large numbers. The primary exceptions were newspapers and good transportation connections. Denverites did not think Central City could match their status or select society, a contention with which Central Citians wholeheartedly disagreed. Tenuously perched along three gulches, cuddled amid the mountains with mines all around, Central, as it was called, looked every bit the part it had played for three years, a log-and-frame mining community.

So did Black Hawk Point, soon to be known generally as Black Hawk, a mile east down a winding road in north Clear Creek's canyon. Later in time than Central, slower to develop and smaller, it nevertheless that spring "bid fair to take the palm from her sister cities of the mountains." Similar optimism reached epidemic proportions in these communities. Black Hawk was building, which showed confidence that it would "be the great mountain city of the Territory." Central City would have to check that hope and watch its laurels to retain its crown.

Black Hawk was growing, Nevada City rebuilding. The highest of Gilpin County's towns, at an altitude of over ninety-one hundred feet, Nevada lay situated among the mines overlooking its rivals, Central and Black Hawk. A city of "enterprise and energy," as someone named Gunnybags had written from there in April 1861, Nevada met with a devastating calamity on Monday, November 4—fire, a fate that awaited many other Colorado communities.

For several days, residents of Nevada City had watched a fire burning on mile-distant Bald Mountain; mistakenly, they perceived no danger. Pushed by a strong west wind, the fire raced over the countryside and leaped into Nevada. Not selective in its destruction, it quickly consumed businesses, hotels, boarding houses, saloons, private homes, mine buildings—everything in its path. The next day's dawn revealed a bleak sight. Many people saved only what they could carry, and from the Methodist Church only the stove and Bible remained. The stove's survival was an unresolved mystery. Some merchants raced through the smoke and fire to move their goods into prospect holes and tunnels, which appeared to be the only safe places. But even these precautions provided no defense against thieves, who in the chaos and confusion made off with about seven hundred dollars' worth of supplies.

Like a phoenix, Nevada rose from its ashes in a race against cold and snow. By February 1862, Gunnybags could write that it presented a "very prosperous and thriving atmosphere." For-

tunately, Nevada had the mining base to rebuild more substan-
tially than before; thus the fire proved an indirect blessing, albeit
a well-disguised one on the day it occurred.

W. R. Campbell was amazed at Nevada's change in two
years—from pine and fir forest to the rattle and roar of quartz
mills, the "innocent prattle" of little children, and the booming
thunder of blasting. "What astonishing progress had been made."
Nevada was a stranger to its own past. Coloradans loved such
progress, equating it with civilization's march.

Clear Creek's other urban concentration lay along its south
branch from Idaho Springs to Georgetown. Development had
been slower here, reflecting less profitable mines and resulting in
less publicity. Georgetown held the most promise, but one would
have been hard pressed to recognize it at the moment. The
youngest and most isolated settlement, it remained unproved, in
spite of a visitor's prediction in May that Georgetown would be
the richest of all districts except Nevada. Empire, with its splendid water power, abundance of "enterprising citizens," appealing
location, and promising placer and quartz mines garnered much
more attention.

"Success to Empire City," wrote a correspondent to the
Republican in September. That success seemed to be on its way.
Empire residents were already talking about capturing the county
seat. Every village and hamlet hoped that its "enterprising"
residents (Colorado apparently was well stocked with "enterprise" in 1861) would create the permanence they all sought. A
good location, ease of transportation, and large ore reserves were
even more important in attaining that end.

To the southwest, over in South Park, another cluster of camps
had sprung up, in momentary anticipation of bonanza discoveries.
Buckskin Joe, the "liveliest little burg" in the group, was just getting established. It had all the trappings of a young quartz mining
camp going into boom and even enjoyed a second name, Lauret
(combining the names of Laura and Jeannette Dodge, wives of
early settlers), which confused the post office more than locals,
who supported the first designation. Culture soon arrived in the
form of a large tent and Mlle Rose Haydee's popular company,
which played to "tolerable good houses" until cold weather

closed them down. Culture had its attractions, but sitting in a cold tent was not one of them. Other Coloradans besides Ming and the Tabors had their eyes on Buckskin Joe as a coming camp.

Directly across the snowy range sat the last group of small min- ing camps, which included Parkville, Buckskin Joe's mortal rival for investors and publicity. Parkville, a placer camp reveling in its moment on center stage, also boasted a big tent theater, along with a large hall for dances and concerts. An admiring visitor called it a "snug little collection of stores, hotels, houses and shops." "The free and easy" dances rather shocked that writer, and, alas, no further elaboration of the dancing style was given.

The largest of these hamlets, Breckenridge, had patriotically changed the spelling of its name. Breckinridge (with an i) had originally honored Vice President John Breckinridge, who was now a Confederate general. That kind of disloyalty would not be tolerated in Colorado!

All of these communities, despite natural rivalries, had much in common. Their fate lay with mining—if it prospered, so did they. They constituted the heart of an urban territory, with an estimated seventy-five percent of the people living in or within a short walk of one of them. They amused and amazed visitors, whose reactions sometimes antagonized locals, who viewed themselves much more tolerantly. Each community, in its own opinion, stood just a step away from greatness and prosperity. Anyone who could not grasp that fact was to be pitied.

These towns served as centers of business and culture, as well as centers of politics and government (to the extent that several fought over which would be the capital). Most communities re- mained unorganized, miners believing the less government, the better. The cost of government and a lack of demonstrated need trounced the hopes of would-be politicians. Denver, of course, already provided city government and ordinances, an organized police force, and local elections. No eastern city could claim much more. The rest of Colorado trailed far behind.

Generally, governmental organization depended upon demonstrable need. The great fire in Nevada aroused Central Ci- tians to the danger of that frontier plague. They soon organized a hook and ladder company and appointed a committee to examine chimneys and stovepipes to ascertain their safety. Small fires in Denver alerted its citizenry to the need for action. The lack of money to carry out plans, however, created new problems and often sabotaged the best intentions.

Professionals were also found in the small communities, lawyers being by far the most common. Mining generates lawsuits nearly as fast as new discoveries. Coloradans exhibited a certain distrust of the legal profession; several districts banned lawyers from practicing, and the Union district in Clear Creek County threatened no fewer than twenty lashes if anyone defied the edict. Lawyers were viewed as agents bent on depriving an honest man of his just property through "book learning" or legal maneuvers.

Denver ranked first in the territory in the medical field, having at least six physicians and surgeons and a dentist by the fall of 1861; Central ranked a distant second. Some of the other communities had a doctor, or at the least a visiting physician, but the rest did without. For those Coloradans who looked upon a visit to the doctor as a last resort, home remedies provided all the care they needed or wanted. Isolation complicated many emergencies, when time sometimes meant life. Such was the case when a rattlesnake bit young Stephen Conray. An Indian doctor was hurriedly called, and with the aid of a plentiful supply of whiskey, he effected a cure.

Primarily general practitioners, doctors labored under the stigma of causing pain. Anesthetics languished in their infancy. Medical students learned procedures and remedies only slightly more advanced than folk medicine. One critic claimed that military medicine barely equaled that which was given to soldiers in the days of the Roman Empire.

Doctors were aware of their shortcomings. W. B. Mead, who opened a medical and dental practice in Missouri City, promised to perform painful operations in the most thorough manner, yet "causing the very least possible amount of suffering." Dr. Mead came highly recommended as both a physician and a dentist. In this day before toothbrushes and dental hygiene, Coloradans' mouths were in terrible condition, and those who didn't have problems in the present were certain to have them in the future.

A visit to the dentist could cause more pain than anything in a person's previous experience, oftentimes more pain than the actual disease. Thus, too frequently dental work was postponed until extraction was the only alternative, with no better general anesthesia available than a strong slug of whiskey.

The challenge of overcoming pain and offering something new provided abundant incentive for quacks. Dr. J. B. Young and his "medical and business clairvoyant," Miss Jackson, arrived in Denver in February 1862, promising to prescribe at leisure for all the diseases human flesh could fall heir to, "independent of asking any questions" of patients!

Up-to-date medically, Denver also aspired to that status socially and culturally, as did every other community with any faith in its future. Entertainment, like business, attracted customers to a camp.

The theater came early to Colorado and, as long as the good times prevailed, stayed to contribute to its culture. From permanent sites in Denver and Central to tours of the mountain camps, theatrical entertainment was available to almost all Coloradans. The performance might vary from Shakespeare to the era's hit play, *Uncle Tom's Cabin,* or from the Colorado Minstrels to Professor Barton, the "great Magician and Wizard of the Mountains." There was something to tempt all tastes and pocketbooks. Town boosters could crow about respectability, culture, and progressiveness. Only a rare farming community could boast of similar achievements in so short a time.

Veteran actor Jack Langrishe led the best-known theatrical troupe, which already had a season in Colorado to its credit. Both the thirty-two-year-old Irishman and his charming actress-wife, Jeannette, became Colorado favorites, accepted in polite society from Denver to Central City and beyond, an unusual accolade for theater folks. The Langrishes followed their patrons wherever they went, sometimes leasing a theater, such as Denver's Apollo, but generally renting whatever was available. At Parkville and neighboring Delaware Flats, Langrishe ran two theaters, giving plays on alternate nights, except on Friday. He produced plays that "few places in the States" saw performed "with better effect." Nevertheless, when winter descended, the Langrishes retreated to Denver and Central.

A typical stage bill offered a serious play, followed by a farce and perhaps olio acts—a full evening's entertainment. Each member of this versatile (by demand) company specialized in certain roles; that amiable comedian, Mike Dougherty, was the only one who rivaled Jack in popularity. A native Pennsylvanian and actor turned prospector, Dougherty returned to his first love and became an instant hit. He and Langrishe toured as long as the money and interest held out, giving Coloradans a taste of fun and culture.

During the winter season of 1861–62, the two entertainers operated the People's Theater on Larimer Street, "the perfect gem of a house." Theater-lover Byers could not contain himself in December: "Langrishe and Dougherty had their new People's Theatre crowded from pit to dome with the beauty, fashion, and gallantry of Denver."

Only the "celebrated" Colorado Troupe, featuring the remarkable and intriguing danseuse, Mlle Haydee, provided serious competition. Charming Rose, of the "interesting manner," won the esteem of Coloradans, and her marriage in November 1860 had broken the hearts of many who sought her affection. She took her last bow on the Colorado stage in February 1862 and retired to the east. Amateur groups, with varying success, provided occasional wintertime amusement.

An evening with friends at the theater could divert one's thoughts momentarily from a poor mining claim or failing prospects. An afternoon at the horse races or watching a baseball game, with the added attraction of gambling, might serve the same purpose. Denver even had a jockey club, the only one in the territory. If one did not relish betting on horses, he could turn to footraces that pitted his camp's fastest man against a challenger.

Denver also leaped ahead of its rivals with a "Base Ball Club," organized in March 1862. Byers quickly called for the organization of another club to facilitate some match games. Following a 28–18 game, Byers admitted that a few more practices would make the players more proficient:

Who will be the first, then, to inaugurate a move for forming a base ball club? It is a beautiful game as played according to modern rules, and many hold that it is infinitely superior to cricket. In fact, it is rapidly

becoming the National game of America, as cricket is to the mother
country. . . .

There is no reason why we here out in this "neck of woods," . . .
should be behind our eastern brethren in anything; much less in athletic
sports and games, considering the healthful and invigorating climate.

Denverites, he went on to say, had plenty of opportunities to enjoy outdoor sports, much more so than the miners, whose lives
during the summer season did not admit much pleasure other
than acquiring wealth. Urban and rural Coloradans already
marched to different beats.

Nothing pleased Denver boosters more than having their com-
munity seen as up-to-date, as were its eastern counterparts.
Baseball, in its infancy, had only recently begun to migrate from
New York City and Brooklyn, and Denver was in the vanguard.
Without gloves, on rough fields, with at best only a couple of
bats (probably homemade) and balls, and the rules debated,
Denver players latched onto the game. They also played cricket
(emulating the mother country), billiards, chess, and checkers;
and they fished—some wonderfully large catches were reported.
They even went boating on the Platte. All of these activities constituted "manly exercises," fit for the metropolis.

Boxing ranked as the most popular manly exercise in certain
circles and was, undeniably, the most controversial sport. Byers
reported just before war broke out that Denver had witnessed its
first prize fight. "We hope we shall have very few such exhibitions to chronicle."

He was wrong. Twenty-six-year-old Con Orem, erstwhile
Denver blacksmith, swept away all in his path to become Colorado's champion. A stocky 145 pounds fitted onto a 5'6½"
frame, Orem had never put on the gloves until the previous
winter; he fought in the April 6 match that upset the *News*
editor. Even Byers, however, came to like Orem, praising his
abstinence from tobacco and spirits.

The big match came on Saturday, August 24, when Orem
entered the ring against Englishman Enoch Davies, known
throughout western sporting circles as "Rough Enoch." Lasting
109 rounds (as soon as a fighter was knocked or fell down, the

round ended), Orem, in his red, white, and blue colors, carried the day, amid the most vociferous cheers. The *News* conceded that order prevailed on the grounds during the fight. The Reverend Amos Billingsley commented in his diary: "How brutal, low, demoralizing, yea humiliating. May God have mercy on us."

When Orem declared he would decline "henceforth" to enter the ring, Byers was relieved, if not repentant. "We must enter our protest against such amusements and hope never again to have to chronicle a fight of this kind in Colorado." He went on to say that, at best, "prize fighting is barbarous." Hailed as the champion of Colorado, Orem reopened his blacksmith shop. He did, however, leave the door open to future matches, saying he held himself ready to maintain and retain the championship.

Forty-two-year-old Davies, who had fought originally in 1835, had had enough of Orem. He went to Central, where in November he opened a sparring school, giving ten lessons for fifteen dollars, plus public exhibitions every Sunday evening. Miners there did not share Byers's aversion to professional fighting.

Con Orem continued to hammer away at his blacksmithing and talked about the honor of the championship. Those who wanted to succeed him as champion, he believed, must conquer him first. By April Colorado and Orem were ready for another bout.

The Reverend Amos Billingsley was also prepared for another round of opposition to boxing. Ohio-born, like Orem, he had come west to save souls, not to make money. Some easterners, wondering if God had stayed back at the Missouri River, raised money to send missionaries out west to establish and maintain a Christian toehold in what they perceived to be a pagan land. This forty-two-year-old Presbyterian entertained doubts about the same matter: "May God help and bless me," he entreated, following much prayer and meditation about his decision to go west. More than six days of stage riding landed him in a room at Cherokee House on Blake Street, amid the "business and stirring music" of a gambling saloon.

In the next months his congregations steadily grew and included a large percentage of women. On June 2, 1861, Billingsley was pleased to note tears in several eyes as he preached on "heaven as a place." Yet he could not be satisfied and confided in his diary five days later: "*Strange!* Strange that I can live in the midst of so many sinners whose 'pulses are beating the march to hell' promenading the road to ruin—piling the faggots for their own eternal burning." He had, nonetheless, attained the position necessary for success; those clerics willing to meet people halfway had loyal and dedicated followers. No doctrinaire sermons were called for, merely an attempt to understand the needs of the flock.

The master of this call to ministry, Methodist John Dyer— a semi-invalid—traveled to Colorado in search of health and a new mission. Not one to sit in Denver and worry about obstacles, he took his preaching to the camps, following in the footsteps of the miners. In his first four months of preaching, Dyer estimated that he walked nearly five hundred miles, delivering about three sermons a week. For these efforts he received forty-three dollars in offerings and wore out his clothes. He found it necessary to work at various jobs in his free time to maintain himself.

Dyer went everywhere, including into the heart of the isolated Gunnison country in September 1861, a classic missionary journey. Following obscure Indian trails through the high mountains, wading cold streams, and sleeping in the open air, this pioneer minister pressed onward, proudly claiming that "for once I got ahead of whisky" when he passed a pack train with a burro carrying several barrels of the liquor. At Kent's Gulch he preached on the subject "Repentance and Conversion" to a more attentive crowd than usual. One woman said "she had not time to hear; must do up her work, and so washed dishes until text read. She turned her back to her work hiding her dish-cloth in her hand, and never moved until the discourse was closed."

Invited to preach there again, Dyer pressed on to Washington Gulch, holding camp meetings in front of tents and services near camp fires. One man said it was the first sermon he had heard preached in eight years; for others, it was the first in several. Dyer recrossed the range to his regular circuit in the South Park districts. Nothing daunted this remarkable forty-nine-year-old.

The frontier was not for the young alone.

Back in Denver, Billingsley complained that the choir's singing did not do much good—he liked to hear the whole congregation sing with spirit. He eventually toured the mountains of the Central City area before at last organizing a Presbyterian church in Denver in December. His own "sinful, treacherous heart" caused him no end of grief (for what reason he failed to explain), and he fretted about it.

Like Dyer, Billingsley endured discomforts. Having few personal belongings, he slept on a tick of hay with no sheet and a borrowed pillow and used a faded comforter as a blanket. A broken looking glass and a borrowed stove completed his apartment, which he shared with mice that kept him awake at night.

In the end Dyer, Billingsley, and their fellow laborers in the vineyard persevered and built upon the foundation already laid by others. They toiled away from the limelight. Only one minister held the public's attention very long, the military hero John Chivington. Now caught up in fighting a different enemy, he continued to function within the Methodist church, when time permitted.

Only large towns could afford full-time ministers; smaller communities remained on circuits or depended upon an occasional visit. Putting the best possible light on their deprived circumstances, the editors of the *Canon City Times* (April 20, 1861) claimed, "Canon City is among the vacancies yet to be supplied with a [Methodist] minister. We take the omission as a compliment to our morality." Sunday schools, more often than church services, testified to God's having arrived permanently in Colorado.

The saints, the sinners, the backsliders, and the faithful came to listen and some to heed. Sometimes attendance was up, more times down, to the dismay of those trying to prove that Colorado had been tamed and civilized. Although the territory did not totally achieve that goal, the church, like the theater and school, proved to doubters that Colorado had moved beyond its rough-edged frontier days.

Another pleasing sign of progress was the arrival of women in increasing numbers. The time of an overwhelmingly masculine world had passed. A correspondent from Gold Dirt to the *News* (August 21, 1861) described the changes:

To woman's influence we can look for the softening of the rough ex-terior of the miner; however great a sacrifice she may have undergone in leaving friends at home, I am sure that upon serious reflection she is more than paid for the cares and troubles undergone, if one poor heart has been enlivened by the glad smiles and words of encouragement.

This truly Victorian attitude contained a large measure of truth amid its sentimentality.

Coloradans honored the Clara Blacks of their world and denigrated the Phebes. Young Clara had come from Newton, Iowa, with her husband to the Tarryall mines. "An affectionate wife and tender mother," she was dead at twenty-eight, a victim of one of the frontier's perils, childbirth. Her infant daughter and namesake soon followed her mother to the grave.

Phebe, on the other hand, a lady whose appearance exhibited "age before beauty," appeared somewhat regularly before the Denver police court. The charge, "domesticating in a house of doubtful character," exemplified the Victorian way of euphemiz-ing prostitution. Dubbed *nymphes du pavé*, the erring sisters were ubiquitous in the male-dominated world of mining, despite efforts of upright Coloradans to ignore them.

Though their numbers were increasing, women remained a decided minority. As such, they were in some ways treated bet-ter than their sisters in the East. In both regions, women were labeled second-class citizens and unequal before the law, had no vote, found jobs and professions closed to them because of their sex, and were segregated by lower salaries. In Colorado some of these barriers were being breached, if not broken. Women's status as a much-needed minority was a distinct advantage.

No longer did a wife find it so difficult to file and win a divorce action. Ellen Bateman found that out and became somewhat of a cause célèbre in the process. Deserted by her "tyrannical and cruel" husband, she petitioned the legislature to dissolve the mar-riage. This brought to a head the question of whether the courts or the legislature should handle such matters. At the moment, the latter did; Gilpin and many legislators believed it should be handled by the former. Because he did not want the legislature to spend an inordinate amount of time adjudicating such cases, the governor refused to sign the divorce bill. Eventually, the courts were recognized as the sole arbiter of divorce matters.

In the Buckskin Joe district in December 1861, Mary Stephenson took similar action. Having married James the previous September, she found, to her dismay, that he kept a mistress, "committing adultery with her." That went beyond the bounds of propriety; she asked for a meeting of the local miners' court, and the marriage was annulled on the spot. Whether such action was legal did not concern the parties involved.

Ellen and Mary willingly faced public censure by admitting that their marriages had failed. Even if a husband strayed, his wife would be blamed if the marriage collapsed, a classic example of the era's double standards. Sometimes marital disputes became so hot that neighbors intervened. One cold February night, a group of Golden boys dumped a wife-beating husband into icy Clear Creek to try to reform him. The results were not reported.

Women found more occupations open to them in Colorado than in the East; boarding house and restaurant operators, clerks, cooks, sheepherders, and seamstresses were among the positions they filled. They dominated the teaching profession and were occasionally pressed into service to run a business, farm, ranch, or mine. They were accepted as part of the community, judged usually by their success or failure at a job. Rarely were they ostracized for flouting the sexual stereotypes of their generation. Catherine Thurston discovered this truth when she contested a high carpenter's bill incurred in building her Empire Hall at Buckskin Joe. She won the case, and the male plaintiffs had to pay costs.

Once in a while a woman found Colorado's theatrical spotlight trained on her. Beautiful Mlle Carolista, well-known for her artistic and graceful dancing at the Criterion, became even more famous for her tightrope skills. Walking from "stage to the gallery blind-folded," the talented star made news, aside from her somewhat risque costume. Enthralled, some of Denver's young men raised a purse to entreat her, sans blindfold, to repeat the performance outside. She made several daring forays onto a rope strung between the Criterion and the New York Store across Larimer Street, pushing a wheelbarrow one time, dancing as she crossed on another July afternoon. Large crowds gathered to gape, including photographer George Wakely, a former actor, who caught the scene with his camera. Times change and interests wane; by the end of the year, "brave and noble little Carolista" was in St. Joseph, Missouri, delighting its citizens with her performances. The $170 that enthusiastic Denverites had collected for her accomplishments were, no doubt, long gone.

The Carolistas of the world are fleeting. Wives and mothers provided the foundation for making Colorado a better place to live and work. They made homes, supported churches, brought refinement, added gentility, and provided the missing ingredient at dances, dinners, parties, and Christmas celebrations. They put Cupid into Valentine's Day for Woolworth and Moffat, who offered elegant cards with lilting inscriptions to make "old maids renovated, old bachelors revamped."

Some poignant moments touched these Colorado pioneers' lives. Mollie Sanford, who moved west in 1860 and lived in Left Hand Canyon while her husband prospected, heard a strange noise one night. "I struck a match and lighted my candle, and there in the middle of the floor stood a little white kitten!" The lonely, pregnant Mollie took it as a "gift from fairyland, for there are no cats or kittens in these mountains." Sadly for her, it turned out to be the wandering pet of a neighbor, and she had to give up her newfound treasure.

Left Hand Canyon was no place to give birth, so in May Mollie went to Denver, where she lived until the baby came. She wrote in her journal on September 25:

On the 28th of August my little babe was born, a beautiful boy, but he did not stay with us. God took him to his fold, this one pet lamb. When I first looked on his little face, he was in his little coffin, dressed in one of the sweetest of the robes I had made, into whose stitches I had woven dreams of my angel baby.

Grieving was a painful process, but women carried on in spite of it. The activities of Oro City's ladies were chronicled by the *Miners' Record* on September 14, 1861. They entertained them-selves in their isolation with fishing, strawberry hunting, and touring the rural district of California Gulch. According to Augusta Tabor, "There were so many men who could not cook and did not like men's cooking and would insist upon boarding where there was a woman." That situation did not change when the Tabors moved to Buckskin Joe. Through hard work and fun, the women stayed, male Coloradans chauvinistically assuming their female counterparts enjoyed their pioneering status. An unidentified woman, writing from Nevada City to her father in Il-linois, aroused the *News*'s ire on April 24. After a "long and tiresome" journey, she concluded:

> If I had known what a journey it was to come out here, I would never have seen the Rocky Mountains. It is too hard for any woman to come here . . . My advice to all women is that they had better go to the Poor House than come here . . . It is an *awful* hard life here, and I have got enough of Pike's Peak.

A flabbergasted Byers despaired because the letter had been published in the *Galena Courier*, as it reflected so unfavorably on the fair name of Pike's Peak. Most women of his acquaintance felt very differently on the subject. Byers blamed the husband, who somehow must have failed in his responsibilities.

Among the most important things women accomplished were curbing lawlessness and smoothing society's ragged edges. They brought about these improvements by their mere presence and their desire to make Colorado a fit place for families. Two gigan-tic steps in this same direction came without much of a feminine impetus, however—the organization of the territorial government and the court system.

A number of annoyances continued to plague urban life, a superabundance of dogs being one of the most visible and noisy. Denver, with the most people, also gathered the most stray dogs. The city council's best efforts and ordinances notwithstanding, the dogs mastered the situation and roamed at will. The possi-bility of contracting incurable hydrophobia and rabies panicked adults and children alike. Fast driving was another nuisance that did not seem to be controlled by arrests or fines. Equally annoy, ing were debtors who fled from creditors, rowdies who disturbed the peace, and pranks that backfired, such as the one that caused Canon City laundress, Mrs. Sorel, to write a letter to the newspaper: "The parties that ruined my washing apparatus committed a base act upon a poor woman and deserve the contempt of all honest people."

More serious crimes, such as horse stealing (which troubled the whole territory in the summer of 1861), the passing of bogus gold dust, and murder, indicated that the lawless days had not disappeared entirely. Much to his shock, Central City butcher Joe Block found that even his partner could not be trusted—he fled with fourteen hundred dollars that belonged to the firm. Block had some anxious moments before the culprit was arrested in Denver and the funds recovered.

Colorado worked to overcome crime, but it had a long road to travel; law enforcement and the courts were only just getting organized. Denver's new (six months old), "convenient and efficient" jail did not prove to be impervious to escape. After the evening meal of February 27, 1862, nearly all of the thirty-six prisoners joined in a mass escape, fleeing through the city with satisfied spirits and appetites.

An even worse containment problem troubled the mountain communities. Frank Hall in Spanish Bar said their law enforcers shaved half the lawbreakers' heads, whipped them "like the devil," and gave them orders to leave the district within one half hour, never to be seen there again on penalty of instant death. "Sometimes they swear vengeance, but at such time permission is given to bystanders to shoot the prisoner on sight if ever found within the limits of the district." In some cases, the threats accomplished little. Hall recalled one young man who, caught with stolen cattle, was sentenced to a whipping and given fifty lashes on his bare back. A week later, he was apprehended stealing in Golden and again whipped; finally, after stabbing a man near the Cache la Poudre River, he was hanged. Hall laconically noted that the man had a "mighty rapid career of crime."

Justice without appeal could cause grief. Edward Seymour suffered through a trying time when his friend Roger, accused of stealing money from their partner, was turned over to a miners' meeting. Not convinced of Roger's guilt, in spite of strong circumstantial evidence believed by most others, Seymour stood loyally by him. "Not even to clear myself from suspicion will I believe any man really guilty till it is proved satisfactorily to my mind." Seymour further agonized, "I am in such a state of excitement that I cannot work at all, at the risk of being suspected of the theft myself." When the case was ultimately dismissed for lack of jurisdiction, Roger departed for the States. Seymour thought that was the best solution for all, still satisfied nothing could be proved against his friend. Guilty or innocent, poor Roger had apparently fallen victim to the frontier's more free and easy morality. On their way out, Seymour had noted that Roger had stopped going to church services and that his speech was "very bad."

Part of the problem in all legal matters lay with the failure of enforcement, which was blatantly displayed in the matter of gambling. The legislature passed an antigambling act, but it had little impact—gambling whirled right on. Because this activity constituted a vital part of the mining communities' business attraction, its profits overruled the law.

A similar consideration weighed heavily in Coloradans' response to their Indian neighbors. With Utes to the west, Cheyennes and Arapahoes to the east, and others roaming in and out, the Indians held the potential for threatening the stability, safety, and profitability of the territory. Both visitors and settlers were aware of them, and many harbored a built-in bias. Traveling across Nebraska in 1860, Mollie Sanford, even after seeing Plains Indians firsthand, wrote, "the Indians are peaceable, I suppose, but are too treacherous to trust out alone."

Newspapers incited fear by using loaded terms, such as *savages, inferiors, lazy, dirty,* and *half-naked* when referring to the longtime residents. The Ute Indians received less negative publicity, probably because they lived farther from the major settlement clusters and posed no threat to the vital overland trails. A prospecting party, which ventured out to the Eagle River area in the summer of 1861, complimented the Utes for their civility and orderliness, a fact the *Miners' Record* reported on July 20. Samuel Mallory, after traveling 150 miles southwest of Nevada City, said that he saw some Indians but had had no trouble. His attitude was rare. Most people feared them, wished they would go away, certainly did not understand their culture, and failed to see the Indians as anything but an obstacle to greater development of Colorado. A time bomb ticked.

Coloradans would long remember the good and bad times of the first year of the war. Granted, the war's outbreak made the year exceptional in many respects, yet much remained typical for these pioneers. They had fought the pesky mosquitoes to a draw, perhaps using the popular camphor remedy to drive them off. They had complained about the weather, worried about running out of wood (and were relieved to find that local coal was coming onto the market), and lamented that "mother earth" was being torn up by hydraulic mining. They praised those Coloradans who beautified the landscape by planting ornamental trees and flowers. The *News* proposed game laws to protect animals, birds, and fish. Others sought solutions to eliminating kitchen odors—pieces of charcoal supposedly worked, as did throwing a couple of red peppers into a boiling pot of ham and cabbage. The post office was accused of "careless neglect." These problems were forgotten, however, when one viewed the scenery: "There is no sight more beautiful than an April morning in Canon City."

For those concerned about a less-than-beautiful appearance, Dr. Tumblety's Pimple Banisher (only one dollar a bottle) promised that they could obtain a handsome complexion, exempt from pimples and blotches. Dr. Tumblety further claimed that he could make old faces "look young and beautiful." And for only twenty-five cents, "Matrimony Made Easy" pledged to tell how either sex might be suitably married.

When they weren't solving complexion and marital problems, Coloradans could sit back and enjoy some of the hit songs of the war, because, all else aside, Civil War America sang. Julia Ward Howe's "Glory, Hallelujah," as it was originally known, became a popular hit with Unionists, as did "The Girl I Left Behind Me" and "The Bold Soldier Boy." "Dixie" appealed to both sides, and when *Harper's Weekly* (November 23, 1861) illustrated some popular songs, the charismatic General George McClellan personified "Hail to the Chief."

Coloradans delighted in the humor of their newspapers and nodded in agreement with the popular Ben Franklin–type wisdom of almanac and paper:

Why is Jeff Davis like the Platte River? Because he has been up, and is now falling.

A handful of common sense is worth a bushel of learning.

"I will kiss you, Eve!" said the Father of us all, to our common mother. "I don't care, A-dam if you do," she said.

"My son, haven't I told you three times to go shut that gate," said a father to a four-year-old. "Yes," said Young America, "and haven't I told you three times I wouldn't do it? You must be stupid."

To prevent starvation—eat very frequently.

Beadle's dime books, which Woolworth and Moffat offered on sale by the "wagon load," were also popular, and readers may have wondered whether they were fulfilling the western image portrayed in some of them. The *Tribune Almanac* told Coloradans what might lie in their future; the *Prairie Farmer* reminded them of their midwestern heritage and provided agricultural tidbits. War maps allowed one to follow military developments, and *Harper's, Leslie's,* and the other New York weeklies kept one informed about current fashion trends and literary, social, and national developments. *Godey's Lady's Book* answered home and women's needs. The December 1861 issue presented "highly instructive and entertaining reading," fashion plates, and lifelike engravings that might have ended up on some cabin wall to add a touch of class to a drab room.

Whether the latest novel, *Maum Guinea,* would prove more popular than the famous *Uncle Tom's Cabin,* individual Coloradans would have to decide. Novels, Byers declared, had become a "necessary evil." For those who preferred novels in small doses, Charles Dickens's *Great Expectations* ran serially in *Harper's Weekly.* At least one Coloradan's main concern was the correct use of compound words, evidenced by a complaint to the *News* (April 5, 1862):

The rule is that compound words ending in full or ful, and generally those which have the important word last, form the plural regularly; as spoonful, spoonfuls; cupfull, cupfulls. . . . But compounds in which the principal word stands first pluralize the first word: as—commanders-in-chief . . .

Life went on as it always had, with its highs and its lows. Edward Wynkoop, who gained some fame as an amateur actor and who was now a soldier, married Louise Brown. Frank Hall complained to his brother, "I guess that you & I are bound to live & die old bachelors or in other words single blessedness. Well who cares, responsibility will sit so much more lightly upon our shoulders." Already famous for his *Washington Crossing the Delaware,* painter Emanuel Leutze, commissioned to do a "picture of emigration" for the Capitol, journeyed to Colorado to sketch, then went back to Washington. That winter the *News*'s junior editor, Edward Bliss, visited the hospitable Leutze, who had already started working on his "great painting."

A promising and talented lawyer, William Perry came to Denver to open a law practice and fared so well that he felt secure in bringing his family west from Leavenworth. A couple of weeks later in October, when his wife and two children arrived, they found he had died after a brief illness. And Thomas Korp-stein, twenty-five years old, vanished from sight, much to the distress of his brother in Mt. Sterling, Illinois, who advertised for information about Tom.

Colorado, now three years old, had progressed rapidly since 1859. The future looked promising, the present exciting, in the spring of 1862. The cause of the struggling Union, however, appeared less sanguine.

Civil War Coloradans

Most of the time these people hardly seemed
To realize they wanted to be remembered,
Because the mountains told them not to die.

I wasn't here, yet I remember them.

—Thomas Hornsby Ferril, "Two Rivers"

William and Elizabeth Byers and children (From author's collection)

Reportedly Augusta and Horace Tabor, second and third from right, back row (Courtesy Amon Carter Museum)

Mike Dougherty (Courtesy Denver Public Library, Western History Department)

John ("Con") Orem (Courtesy Denver Public Library, Western History
Department)

Frank Hall (Courtesy Denver Public Library, Western History Department)

Daniel and Clara Witter (From author's collection)

Hal Sayre (Courtesy Colorado Historical Society)

Maria and George Kassler (Courtesy Denver Public Library, Western History Department)

Romine Ostrander
(Courtesy *History of
Clear Creek Boulder
Valley, Colorado*)

William Cozens
(Courtesy Denver
Public Library,
Western History
Department)

Alice and Nathaniel Hill (Courtesy Colorado Historical Society)

Camp Weld Council, September 28, 1864. Black Kettle, center, sitting; Edward Wynkoop and Silas Soule, kneeling. (Courtesy Denver Public Library, Western History Department)

Part II

A TIME FOR WAITING: 1862–63

5

"Their rights . . . paramount to all others"

COLORADO MINING was starting to show its age in 1862–63, a somewhat disconcerting phenomenon for a region only a few years beyond discovery. Attractive new diggings tempted Coloradans elsewhere in their rush to fulfill promises of grassroots gold. The Salmon River mines in Idaho attracted the most attention in the spring of 1862, despite efforts by the *News* to discourage it. Then came reports of even better discoveries in the future state of Montana, made, interestingly, by a Colorado party on their way to Idaho.

Trying to stem the ebbing tide, Byers printed letters such as the one dated May 16 from "Observer" in California Gulch, who concluded that the excitement was fast dying away in his vicinity: " 'Salmon River' is considered entirely too fishy." "J" in Montgomery reiterated that theme a month later; praising recently discovered lodes in Colorado, all of which prospected well, he argued that they gave "the best evidence that Pike's Peak has not 'played out.' " Byers himself took pen in hand in a July 19 editorial to convince his readers that every day showed "more and more clearly" that Colorado was destined to become the greatest mining country yet discovered. Byers predicted that thousands of disappointed "Salmons" would return next year, tired of gold hunting, and settle down. Rounds, who identified himself only as being in the mountains, thought the emigration all to the good. This new fever had cleaned the Pike's Peak country of "rubbish," although Rounds also admitted of some good men.

Were they whistling in the dark? Was Colorado mining really on the decline, burdened as it was with mining and milling problems? Were Coloradans being drawn elsewhere? These and other nagging questions badgered the young territory.

Coloradans were undeniably being attracted elsewhere. Throughout the spring and early summer, numerous reports told of people leaving. Alexander Toponce made money in 1861, invested it in claims in Georgia Gulch in 1862, and then lost everything when the claims did not pan out. That calamity forced him to head for the gold diggings in Montana in February. Even in the dead of winter, Toponce and others were lured by what he admitted were "wild stories of how rich the diggings were." In April 1863, H. G. Otis, pioneer miner and merchant of the Gregory district, followed the same route to Bannack City. If that country met his expectations, he intended to go to the States for his family; otherwise, he would return to Central City with his family and a large stock of merchandise.

Colorado could ill afford to lose the likes of the Toponces and the Otises. The drifting crowd was of little concern, but solid citizens were desperately needed. This exodus did not mean that immigration to Colorado had ceased—the pilgrims kept coming, though not in the large numbers of previous years.

A quick glance at Colorado mining showed signs of both optimism and despair. That astute observer, Ovando Hollister, saw placer mining dying out but quartz mining doing well. Expectations stayed high, even in such a worked-out district as California Gulch, which offered every possible inducement (according to a local correspondent) for enterprising miners, with or without capital. Swan River miners, especially in Delaware Gulch, avowed the same; their only problem stemmed from scarce provisions and their prices, which were, "to use plain English, d——d high." Boulder County mines needed only capital and accompanying energy (all too familiar complaints) to develop them.

New discoveries to whet excitement failed to surface. The San Juans had played out and were abandoned, amid recriminations and disgust; the Gunnison country still harbored a few prospectors, one of whom returned in February, calling it "one grand humbug." Buckskin Joe, which had proven the best of last year's lot, settled into a more routine life.

Small discoveries—long on hope, short on results—seemed to be all Colorado could muster. A new gulch at Sugar Loaf in Boulder County yielded thirty cents to the pan; aspirants flocked there, "expecting to make a big strike." "Musquito" district, above Buckskin Joe, also advertised "big pay." These finds hardly matched the ones described in Idaho and Montana and were only pale imitations of Colorado's earlier discoveries.

As always, winter slowed or stopped mining, but the advent of spring did not produce its usual buds of optimism. For the first time in its history, Colorado found itself mired in the ordinary—mining was becoming drudgery. An article discussing Cache Creek described how miners had overcome lack of capital only through hard work and hoped finally to reap the rewards of their labor by 1863. The phenomenon of one dollar to the pan, two hundred dollars to the cord, and mother lode discoveries had all evaporated.

Ezra Stahl, former Hoosier and Coloradan since 1860, lived in Delaware City and mined in the gulch of the same name. His terse diary entries describe the frustrations and endless toil. From July 3–14 he worked every day, except two Sundays, running a sluice and occasionally "ground sluicing." His only relaxation consisted of several nights at the theater and one preaching service. Cleanup netted ninety dollars in dust for Stahl and his partners. In September, he gave up and went home.

The placer districts were mired in misfortune; their nearly exhausted deposits had proved neither so rich nor extensive as California's. The transition to hard-rock mining in those districts blessed with gold locked in mountain depths preserved the territory's future.

None of those sites seemed more promising than Central City and Gilpin County. The only drawback lay in their lack of opportunity for individuals, a vital element for promoting Colorado. Just as the Salmon River diggings held something for the poor man, his chance of a lifetime, so once had the famous Gregory diggings. Now came hard-rock mining, with paid miners, high expenses, more machinery that demanded different knowledge and experience, and the threat of corporate control. Mining had evolved through the full cycle in a mere four years.

Byers visited the district in June and reported all mills working, deep shafts mostly through cap rock, steam engines set up on a number of principal leads, and hardly an idle man anywhere with wages at $2.50 to $3.50 per day. Central City's brand new *Colorado Mining Life* illustrated the scene in its first issue (July 5); the editor explained that the experience of the past two years had worked a wonderful change in the methods of gold mining. He went on to comment insightfully that only a few of the several thousand lodes discovered in these mountains would pay. What had happened to the never-say-die spirit of 1859?

Unrealistic expectations crumbled, and improvements were demanded. Cries for better roads, more capital, and greater development sounded familiar, and complaints about cap rock and milling gave evidence of new problems with hard-rock mining. Fresh discoveries were dwindling and often came as a lucky accident, as when Squire Jones of Nevada hit a prospect while digging a posthole. Only Russell Gulch reported large amounts of placering, and even there reports of hitting "damnable cap" indicated that placer days were numbered. Despite such complaints, Gilpin County and its major town, Central, reigned as the somewhat tarnished crown jewel of Colorado mining.

Short of capital, running into unexpected mining and milling problems, and encountering complex ore as the shafts deepened, Gilpin miners nevertheless represented the future of Colorado. They must persevere or the territory would be doomed.

Mill man Nathaniel Keith, inventor of the Keith process, was one of those trying to solve the perplexing milling problems. Ore values near the surface failed to hold up as miners penetrated to the depths of refractory ore. The mills could not save the gold; one startling example involved a cord of ore that assayed at $6,000 but yielded less than $300 after being worked. Old-timers believed sulfuret ores caused the problem, and soon thereafter Keith developed a desulfurizer process. After pulverizing the ore, he roasted it, then mixed it with "pure quicksilver and acid." A successful January trial saved over $1,300 per cord on ore previously yielding $150.

Eager miners overran his Black Hawk mill, forcing Sheppy, as Keith signed his letters, to fasten the doors and put up No Admittance signs. Triumphantly, he wrote his wife that "folks ought to pay us something for a process which will save them that much each and every day." Unfortunately for everybody, equipment failures forced the operation to close, and the jury remained out on the Keith process.

Gilpin's only legitimate rival remained the neighboring south Clear Creek mines. Mining there juxtaposed past, present, and future prospects in placer and quartz mining.

Desertion afflicted Spanish Bar, which had created big news in 1860; only a few hardy souls still held the faith. Other districts, worked occasionally, gave only a fair yield, according to the *Colorado Mining Life*'s reporter in September, which sounded suspiciously as though it were an epitaph for mined-out sites. Mill City, Downieville, and "mythical Bloomington" slumped to near abandonment for, it was said, want of capital.

Yet Georgetown, hailed as having the most promising quartz leads in the mountains, bid "fair to be one of the most flourishing mining sections" in another year. Trail Creek, meanwhile, developed steadily and quietly. Miners there persistently dug into lodes, not realizing anything "very big," but as a general rule being "very well paid for their labor."

The bright prospects at Trail Creek and Georgetown boded well for Colorado, especially since the Union district, the "great summum bonum" of Clear Creek and Empire City, the "future Rocky Mountain metropolis," boomed in 1862. With two mills running, superior water power, a large supply of timber, no great amount of cap rock encountered, and its famous Tenth Legion lode, the Union district garnered the news. Miners were further cheered upon discovering that Lion Gulch and other nearby streams held out placer opportunities, with hydraulics already eating away at the golden dirt.

"Bully for Empire," rang the headlines, as people flocked there in the summer and early fall. The Tenth Legion lode generated the bulk of the excitement; the rest were caught up in its wake. Reported averages of $150, $230, and $300 to the cord and $15 a day per hand in the placer workings whetted enthusiasm even more. In a somewhat dull year, this turn of events warranted all the attention it received. Colorado mining was not finished yet; 1863 might be a good year after all.

If Clear Creek exemplified mining contrasts and varied developmental stages, it typified all of Colorado. Reports of arrastras and sluices appeared alongside those of hydraulic operations, pumps and engines to dewater mines, and tunnels to open an entire mountain. An article on mine ventilation stressed the importance of good health to miners, something of no concern earlier. And in Central City, businessman Charles Hendrie and John Butler, a practical mechanic, opened a foundry to provide the machines, engines, and mills needed in the new world of hard-rock mining. The firm faced formidable obstacles, including freighting iron from the States, at six cents per pound; along with the iron came eastern coke and coal.

Iowan Charles Hendrie, the senior member of the firm, had the experience to make the business a success. Owning foundries in Burlington and Council Bluffs, this most energetic, thoroughgoing, enterprising businessman came west in 1859 to ascertain the needs of Colorado. Realizing his lack of knowledge about mining, he journeyed to California the next year to study methods and machines, then returned to Colorado. "Just such a man as needed in a new country," hailed the local press.

Hendrie and Butler promised any "description of quartz mill or engine" manufactured and delivered within sixty days. Particular attention, an ad said, was given to building steam engines to hoist ore or water from shafts, and machinery of all kinds could be repaired on short notice, "in a workman like manner and on reasonable terms." Nothing else in the mining field showed more faith in the future of quartz mining, nor indicated more clearly the steady transition from placer mining.

If Charles Hendrie represented the changing times, Pat Casey embodied the promise of the past and the possibilities of the present. "The celebrated king miner of Colorado" had spent the winter in the East, enjoying the rewards of his previous efforts. No doubt, he enjoyed describing how he arrived with no capital other than a "pair of brawny hands and an iron will"; in a few short years, he had progressed far along the road to wealth. It was even forecast that in a few more years he would be one of Colorado's millionaires.

Gossip already circulated that Casey's mining claims could not be purchased for $100,000, and his other property had attained worth in the neighborhood of $50,000. Fortune smiled on Casey; his dreams of 1859 could become reality. On his return trip to Nevada City he purchased additional stamps for his mill and bought more mining property; his faith stood fast.

No man in the mountains stood as tall, or acquired so much notoriety, as Casey; everything he did appeared to be worth a comment or two. Casey, however, was coming to enjoy the good life, so he traveled back to the States in September. From there, rumor had it, he intended to go on to Europe and, on his return, build a handsome residence in Golden. In Gilpin County, however, his wealth and fame had already embroiled him in legal disputes, which reportedly resulted from taking ore from claims he did not own.

Casey did not make it to Europe. He returned to Central by late December, and in February was involved in a riot at Black Hawk. It seemed that the owners of the ditch supplying water to his mill and others shut off the supply because one mill owner (not Casey) refused to pay required fees. Casey and some of his hands promptly hit town to remonstrate against this injustice and barely avoided a fight. The editor of the *Tri-Weekly Miners' Register* chastised Casey, a man held in esteem, for encouraging mob violence and setting a bad example for his employees.

Casey did not resent the reprimand. His "night hands" loved him, especially when he refused to pay them in inflationary green-backs. Some owners followed that practice to cut expenses, but not Casey: "No, by the powers, every mother's soul of 'em shall be paid in the same 'circulating medium' which they work hard to dig out." Later on, he reversed his position, causing no small amount of grumbling.

Casey took special pride in feeding his boys the best food available. His miners (one "cannot find anywhere else in the Territory as many exiles of Erin") were famous in their own right, and eventually all were immortalized, at least from their Gilpin County home to Denver.

The question of greenbacks versus gold generated some heat in Colorado, when the federal government began printing paper money to help finance the war. Soon dubbed "greenbacks," their value in relation to gold began to decline almost as soon as the notes were issued. By the spring of 1863, one greenback was worth only sixty-seven cents in gold. And not merely the federal government kept the presses busy—banks could also print money at this time.

Coloradans distrusted paper money. Gold dust had served as the medium of exchange since 1859, and the "miserable substitute in the shape of worthless paper currency" seemed unnecessary. Gold dust had a feel, a known worth, that paper money lacked.

Central City's *Tri-Weekly Miners' Register*, November 19, 1862, expressed this opinion: "And now come these well-dressed, fancy eastern gentlemen, saying to us: 'Here now, this gold dust is very INCONVENIENT as currency' and exchanging our trade dust for their new notes, borrowing our gold on their promise to pay without interest or proper security." Bank notes continued to fluctuate in value, whereas gold always rated a high premium over the best of paper money. The use of paper currency was viewed as a persistent effort on the part of bankers and speculators to rob this country of its precious metals. No one in Colorado could be sure of the value of this "paper trash"; that uncertainty bred apprehension.

Merchants shouldered most of the greenbacks' disadvantages. They had to take the notes in trade and then send them off for redemption at a possible discount. The inconvenience and time required for the transaction added to their woes. A group of Central City and Black Hawk businessmen finally took the bull by the horns and pledged not to accept any Iowa or other paper money for goods, except Treasury notes. Iowa, the nearest longestablished northern state, was apparently seen as the worst purveyor of paper. The State Bank of Iowa did a particularly large business in Colorado.

The *Register* launched a crusade against paper money and did all it could to halt its introduction. The editor charged that paper currency inevitably increased the price of every article, and laborers, unless they demanded a corresponding increase, would be the losers. With a paper dollar worth less than gold, Casey's miners and others rebelled when paid in greenbacks.

Shilly-shallying on the stock market between the prices of gold and paper money gave further evidence of the changing currency pattern. Prices generally moved in gold's favor, tempting speculators to jump in and the unwary to gamble on the price of gold. The nation's economy aside, currency speculation would probably stimulate interest in Colorado's gold mines.

It also encouraged Gilpin County miners to shop around in Denver for the bankers and brokers who would pay the premium price for their ore. In January 1863, for instance, the price per ounce varied from $18.50 to $22.00. Byers, never enthusiastic about speculation, continued to warn his readers that it only caused inflation, which would inevitably hurt everyone in the territory. As the second year of the war ended, the issue remained unresolved and promised further commotion.

Even with inflation, miners' wages stayed fairly steady through the year. In August underground miners received $2.50–$4.00 per day, depending on their skill; gulch miners, $2.50; and mechanics, $3.00–$5.00. Miners in the Nevada district earned $3.50–$4.00 a day in November but had to sustain their own board costs. In February, miners in the Gregory district received $2.50–$3.50, with some experienced men getting $4.00. Winter had put the placer mines out of action.

For those men being paid in greenbacks, wages actually declined. The miners suffered further when some owners decreed that Monday would be payday, in an attempt to curb the miners' tendency to "spree it" on Sunday, after a Saturday paycheck.

Central City miners perceived all these changes as grossly unfair, and anger replaced old-time amity. In March they privately discussed grievances and the possibility of a strike for higher wages. On April 5 the aroused miners called a mass meeting. They were angered by the suddenly complex world of mining and in no mood to compromise. Loud applause greeted each issue. The miners ultimately voted to strike, the first labor strike in Colorado mining history. No union action, this, just a spontaneous outburst of frustration against changing times and the confisca-

tion of treasured individual opportunity, which is what had attracted most of them to the territory. They had not intended to
be daily laborers, but sometimes that was the only option
available.

The demands of the men had a familiar ring to miners
everywhere: a set wage—blasters, $4; strikers, bucket fillers,
bucket dumpers, and all other laborers, $3 a day.

A day would consist of ten hours daylight or nine hours night.
Miners would not work until these demands were met. The
"blackleg," who did not endorse these resolutions or failed to
hold out until wages improved, was "justly entitled" to the contempt and scorn of the faithful. A committee that included John
Crumby, Michael Kelly, and others was selected to acquaint the
mine, mill, and placer owners with the terms. Threatening no
work and promising not to use any means inconsistent with law
and order to prevent others from working at the old wages, they
went forth.

The miners did not receive wholehearted newspaper support.
The Tri-Weekly Miners' Register stated that in a free country the
miners had every right to meet and pass resolutions. The owners,
however, also had the proper right and privilege to pay wages,
stop work, or employ other hands. So long as the strikers ab-
stained from violence, no one had any right to complain.

Crumby, Kelly, and their friends were doomed. Nothing went
right; they visited mines and saw that nonstrikers kept right on
working. Angered, they threatened violence against Jerome
Chaffee's miners on the Bobtail Lode, compelling them to quit,
which violated the strikers' earlier idealistic goal. A little
drunken rowdiness on Monday and Tuesday nights in town
worsened matters. Tenuous public support vanished, and the
strike died out. The miners returned to work at their former
wages with no strength, no solidarity, no union, and no real hope
of accomplishing anything beyond venting their frustrations.

The first fruits of corporate control and the impersonalization
that came to be a hallmark of the industry hit these Gilpin County miners unexpectedly. The difficult, dangerous work continued;
they found themselves mere workers rather than pioneers with
hopes of a fortune. The course of local mining developments

slipped out of their hands almost unawares. They did not fully grasp how this change had come about. Perhaps the explanation was similar to the one attributed to the death of Thomas Robinson of Davenport, Iowa. This miner, apparently in good health, was found dead in his cabin after a day's work. Such a puzzling episode necessitated an inquest, and the jury concluded that "the deceased came to his death by a visitation of God."

Absentee owner George Pullman seemed especially perplexed by the transformation of the mining industry. When he returned in May 1862, he found the once-promising business affairs of his firm "pretty badly mixed." He wrote his mother that in the course of a month he would be able to form a pretty correct idea about his prospects of making any money in Colorado. If prospects were dim, he would "leave the country in disgust and probably marry and settle down in Chicago." Colorado's glittering image had acquired some tarnish.

Meanwhile in Buckskin Joe, where things had quieted noticeably since last year's hubbub, Samuel Leach lived the life of a less-regimented miner, similar to that of a fifty-niner. Describing his quiet life and steady work to his brother, Leach wrote that he ate heartily, worked hard, slept soundly, and bathed in cold water, commonly with ice in the pail. No hoodlum element lived in Buckskin Joe, so residents witnessed no killings or lynchings, but, Leach hastened to add, that did not mean a monotonous life. Apparently he did not want his brother to think that without nefarious activity the West lacked interest! What surplus energy remained after a hard day's work was spent pitching quoits, wrestling, boxing, shooting, and riding horseback (when horses were available). Of his neighbors, he said that he had "never seen a cleaner lot of men, nor a more law abiding lot." Leach, addicted to the mining life, had learned by experience what it entailed:

There is always the element of chance that fascinates. But it is hard work just the same. You have to stick at it and keep your eyes open. And if you do get a good claim you had better keep still about it for if you get excited and tell your friends someone is sure to hear of it and jump the claim or make trouble for you in some other way.

Speaking of jumping a claim, William Dutt wandered over from

Buckskin Joe to Niggar Gulch, to do just that, getting lost along the way. His effort came to naught: "I came over here to jump some claims, but I could find none vacant, so I went to work at $1.50 per day and board." His years in Colorado had not been fruitful, and he told his sister he did not think she would own him as a brother, describing his "dirty, greasy, ragged, long hair with a face perfectly innocent of shaving for the last two years." In a June letter to her, he described the life he led in this "hard country":

Explosures of all kinds, though not often considered, continually stare a man in the face, and is every man's doom to meet, if he makes mining his business. Sufferings, privations and hardships of life, generally are more often realized than the object for which they are endured. A man's hopes to anticipate a fortune in the Gold mines often end in a broken down constitution, anticipations not realized, and an utter disgust for the country and gold mines generally. Few men make a fortune here but many never make anything.

This unusually insightful miner painted a grim picture. Restless, he returned to Buckskin Joe, and then gave up mining to join the army.

Buckskin Joe represented the contrast between a known past and an uncertain future. The need for mining laws and miners' meetings receded now that territorial courts were functioning. Decline in placer operations and increases in hard rock mining heralded a major transformation featuring new problems and new challenges. Milling operations were of great concern; at the moment, they seemed "more or less" successful, with experimentation under way to solve the loss of a startlingly high percentage of gold.

Buckskin Joe needed eastern investors with pockets full of money. Like Pullman, other easterners were finding that Colorado was a mixed blessing. The New England Mining Company in the Tarryall mining district, for example, had judgment rendered against it in June. As a result, its flume, sluice boxes, and mining claims were put up for sale. The company lost everything and received very little recompense—twenty-six mining claims went for $36, and 1,200 feet of flume for $25.

Precious-metal mining supplied only part of the action in the territory. Coal from Boulder and Jefferson counties was already being advertised in the newspapers. Small, one-horse family operations characterized the industry at the moment. Only inade-quate transportation frustrated the waiting market. The Middaughs mined twenty miles north of Denver and sold their coal for four dollars a ton at the mine, ten dollars in the city.

On a more exotic plane, the firm of Cassady and Company, after drilling at an oil spring northwest of Canon City, struck a "plentiful supply" (a barrel per day) at twenty-eight feet. Capitalizing on good fortune, the company sold refined oil to il-lumine nearby houses. By February samples had reached Denver and were burning with a "beautiful clear red flame." Byers thought this innovation to be of "incalculable advantage." Con-sidering that the first American oil field had been opened only four years earlier near Titusville, Pennsylvania, this feat was remarkable indeed.

When all was weighed, Colorado mining had experienced another solid year. Though not as exciting or prosperous as years gone by, this one had brought a maturation. Mining dominated the territory, and everything else depended on that industry. Miners sometimes carried their advantage too far, as in Spring Gulch, Gilpin County, when miners undermined roads and storekeepers' buildings to further their relentless search. The *Rocky Mountain News* (June 21, 1862) cautioned that "although their rights are paramount to all others," miners must realize that others had rights, too, and must take care that no injustice was done them. The warning carried little weight where "King Min-ing" reigned.

6

"Pick and shovel for sword and bayonet"

IN THE SECOND YEAR of the American Civil War, or as some called it, the War between the States, the conflict was reaping ever more vicious harvests as the two sides hammered out professional armies from the mobs that rallied in the spring of 1861. The titanic, bloody battles—Seven Days Around Richmond (Mc-Clellan failed, despite his vaunted reputation), Second Manassas, Antietam, Fredericksburg, and the opening of the Vicksburg campaign—caught and held the attention of Coloradans.

They looked on with horror at the holocaust: nearly 25,000 soldiers died in one day in the "awful tornado of battle," as a survivor described Antietam. Only later would Americans realize that this battle gained the melancholy distinction of the bloodiest single day's fighting in the war. They debated generals and strategies, fueled the controversy raging over emancipation in the political arena, and argued politics. On a more practical plane, Coloradans could donate to the United States Sanitary Commission (a forerunner of the Red Cross), buy government bonds, or volunteer for the army. In the eastern states, these momentous matters far overshadowed any territorial issues, but to Coloradans local matters took priority.

The big news politically was the arrival of the new governor, John Evans, on May 16, almost a year to the day after Gilpin had arrived. Again Byers hailed the appointee and could not resist taking a jab at the previous officeholder: "That his administration will be free from the blundering stupidity which has characterized that of his predecessor, we have an abiding confidence."

This tall, kindly, Ohio-born physician-businessman was welcomed at the now-customary reception at Tremont House, which included a band and three hearty cheers. Coloradans had again been fortunate, especially since Washington insisted on sending many of its political hacks west. (Byers's and others' opinions notwithstanding, Gilpin did not fall into that category.)

After graduating from the College of Medicine at Cincinnati, one of the best schools in the country, Evans moved to Indiana, then to Chicago, where he gained a substantial reputation as a physician and educator while on the faculty of Rush Medical College. Wise investment in real estate made him independently wealthy by the early 1840s, and he turned to other endeavors. One of the principal founders of Northwestern University and a crusader for higher standards in public education, Evans also dabbled in politics. Lifelong humanitarianism placed him in strong opposition to slavery and made him a natural candidate for the Republican party. Colorado's second governor seemed even better qualified than the first, according to Byers in the *News* of May 18: "Thank Heaven, Colorado has at last got A GOVERNOR!"

Evans's remarks on the evening of his arrival sounded just the right note. Enthusiastic applause greeted his statement that in "no distant day" railroad connections with the East would be completed. The governor harbored no doubts of the future success and prosperity of Colorado and its people.

With less fanfare, Samuel Elbert was nominated secretary of the territory. This twenty-nine-year-old lawyer, also Ohio-born and a Lincoln supporter, stood to give Colorado a strong governing team. The pair's honeymoon in Colorado politics lasted through the next twelve months. When Evans went back east in the fall, he devoted his efforts to promoting Colorado's interests, which pleased Denverites and Central City folks equally. The *Tri-Weekly Miners' Register* (November 5, 1862) expressed a common sentiment when it praised Evans as exactly the man for the territory. Colorado seemed "truly lucky" to have an individual of such high character and standing as its governor. Elbert, too, earned accolades for discharging his duties as acting governor with promptness, sagacity, and firmness.

Events favored the new governor. The July–August session of the legislature passed smoothly. The legislators, less busy than in the previous year, deliberated diverse issues: incorporating the Ute Pass wagon road; outlawing the carrying of concealed weapons in cities and towns; incorporating a free cemetery for Conejos County; and changing the name of one Lazarus McLain. Perhaps the touchiest issue they discussed, designating the capital, ended with William Loveland's campaign paying off hand-somely, and Golden's being chosen. Colorado City's one advan-tage, a beautiful site, failed to overcome its major drawback—isolation from trade, travel, and population. Jealousy and fear of Denver prevented that city from winning the coveted honor. "We must try and make the best of it, and do without the Legislature as well as we can," consoled that every-loyal booster, William Byers. Denverites never gave up hope for their destiny, however; someday they would capture the capital.

Legislators concentrated some of their attention on Congress and sent that harassed body a series of joint memorials and resolutions regarding territorial needs, as if Washington had not enough to worry about as the war dragged on without noticeable Northern success. Colorado asked that the Union Pacific Railroad go through one of its passes, that the Indian titles be cleared, and that triweekly mail be delivered to Boulder City. The territory also wanted funds to print the laws in Spanish.

Hiram Bennet, Colorado's nonvoting delegate, presented these resolutions to Congress. A congressional political eunuch, but an energetic one, he did surprisingly well with his limited power. Then, having finished his year's term, Bennet ran for reelection, as Colorado came into alignment with the biannual election pattern of the rest of the country, which voted in even-numbered years.

With a year's experience under their belts, local politicians had organized themselves. At that moment, though, not many prizes dangled to entice their efforts; if statehood could be achieved, the circumstances would change quickly. Already that idea was being openly discussed and the benefits weighed. Thomas Gibson thought it should happen; statehood would grant more freedom and independence and assure less outside governmental intervention. The majority of Coloradans were not ready to take this step, however, so statehood would have to wait at least another year.

Meanwhile the Republicans, dubbed the Union party for the war's duration, fell to bickering among themselves before renominating Bennet. His chief rival, the ever-optimistic William Gilpin, and Gilpin's backers promptly bolted. This inspired Dave Moffat to write his Buckskin Joe business partner, Irving Stanton, that the Gilpin party "are killed dead by bolting our convention." He advised Stanton to do all he could to aid Bennet. Not much could be done in that lightly populated district, but Stanton did "respectfully decline" to support Gilpin.

Rough-and-tumble Colorado politics often played to hostile audiences, who were inclined to express their views with groans and hisses. To "groan down" a speaker became somewhat of a political sport. In what eventually emerged as a three-man race, the Democrats had no hope—Bennet started in the lead and stayed there. Supreme Court Justice Moses Hallett asserted in late August that "Bennet is gaining ground every day and I think the prospects are flattering." The fact that he supported Bennet might have colored his view.

All the not-yet-forgotten blunders of Gilpin's administration were gleefully exploited by the vindictive *News*. Election day, October 7, passed quietly in Denver, the only question being which candidate would do well in Arapahoe and Gilpin counties; the rest of the territory had little political significance, unless the vote was close. Nearly a month passed before the individual ballots could be counted, the voting trend determined, the results certified, and the totals sent to the governor's office. Not until late November did all the precincts send in their returns. Bennet won, with Gilpin finishing in third place. Incumbent Bennet's victory was gained by carrying Arapahoe, Gilpin, Park, Summit, Lake, Jefferson, Boulder, and Conejos counties. Gilpin had fared well only in Clear Creek.

Either the election had not elicited strong interest or the Idaho mines had indeed cut seriously into Colorado's population, because the vote total came in lower than the previous year. Gibson, almost as much of a territorial booster as his rival, Byers, comforted his readers. They had nothing to fear—the total population still exceeded forty thousand.

John Evans, fortunately for his peace of mind, did not confront so active a Southern element as had Gilpin. Neither did he become as nervous about it. Coloradans were taking the war in stride now. They seemed more concerned, like Matthew Dale, about the secession's impact on investment than on possible invasion. Soon after Elbert arrived, he wrote William Seward that, as far as he could determine, the territory was "eminently loyal." Seward probably reflected on past events and hoped fervently that things would stay calm. More important matters, such as England's attitude toward the North, left him little time for Colorado as long as that precious gold kept coming east.

The News did not waver from its position, its editorial banner featuring an American flag with these words underneath: "We'll furl not our flag until over our nation all the stars blaze again in one grand constellation." Byers still saw Southerners lurking behind rock and tree and seemed driven to prove territorial loyalty. When some community or group of citizens met to support the war or pass patriotic resolutions, almost without fail a report appeared in his paper. Gibson's Commonwealth, not one to lose a patriotic step, followed suit. Gold Hill was commended for raising money to pay bounties for volunteers, and Larimer County residents living along Big Thompson River were cheered for the same show of patriotism.

Byers capitalized on the horrors of war, which had "sadly disarranged" business and social relations in the States. He knew just the place for people in search of quiet, peaceful homes: "For this class there is no better 'Land of Promise' than Colorado."

Daniel Conner did not see Colorado as a land of promise anymore. While mining in Georgia Gulch, that ardent Southerner found that "Rebel and Federal friends became Rebel and Federal enemies." Both sides showed the strain of war passions, sometimes releasing their feelings in an emotional way, such as when one of Conner's Reb friends fired both shotgun barrels at an American flag. Unable to endure hardened attitudes and increasing harassment, Conner traveled south beyond Pueblo in September to Mace's Hole, where he joined other Southerners rendezvousing to form a regiment. Poor leadership and the approach of federal troops caused the plan to fail, so Conner left Colorado.

Other, less fortunate pro-Confederates were seized by the provost marshal for uttering disloyal and treasonous statements. Though Colorado did not lie in a war zone where habeas corpus had been suspended, Southerners' freedom of speech had virtually disappeared. Byers's opinion on the subject became evident in February, when the *News* described an incident in the Methodist church. A Southern lady objected when the minister prayed for divine blessing for President Lincoln. She rose, gathered up her children, and then, with a "haughty toss of her head," stalked off. Byers hinted that any repetition of that act might necessitate the introduction of a mild Butler regime in Denver. Gen. Benjamin Butler, faced with similar recalcitrant ladies in New Orleans, had declared that any who by "word, gesture or movement" showed contempt for a United States officer or soldier should be "treated as a woman of the town plying her avocation." For his troubles the Confederacy declared Butler a felon, an outlaw, and an enemy of mankind who, if captured, should hang immediately.

February also produced a noisy row in Central City when one of Pat Casey's hands cheered Jefferson Davis and was promptly arrested by the provost guard. A general donnybrook broke out, featuring swearing, screaming, and firing of pistols before order could be restored. Liquor probably lubricated the free-for-all. Just enough agitation persisted to keep the territorial press, which stood unanimously in the Union camp, distressed.

The war engendered the expected interest and comments from armchair strategists. Amid preparations for Christmas came the shocking news of the "defeat and disgrace" at Fredericksburg. Coloradans blamed General Ambrose Burnside's blundering for the great loss of Union lives. Where, oh where, was "Peace on Earth, good will towards men"? Even during this nadir of despair, the *Weekly Commonwealth* saw "much more ground for hope than fear."

The Emancipation Proclamation attracted surprisingly little interest, with one notable exception, Central City's *Tri-Weekly Mining Life*. The outspoken editor, Sandwich Island native L. M. Amala, put his paper firmly in the Democratic party column in a December 30 editorial on the issues dividing the two parties; it contained some biting comments on blacks and emancipation:

That the white people of the North shall be taxed to feed and clothe the "Niggers" of the South, freed in violation of the Constitution and Laws. That the "Nigger" shall be placed on an equality with the white, and shall be competition for place and power, in every avocation of life.

We cannot but positively disapprove of the Proclamation, as unfortunate, illtimed, injudicious and alarmingly injurious in its every bearing; and regret the faulty judgement of the President, more in a spirit of honest censure than vindictive rebuke. (January 15, 1863)

Amala, whom Frank Hall considered disreputable, lasted another ten days as editor. Whether his views influenced his departure remains unknown. To their disgrace, other Coloradans agreed with him. Racism appeared no more dead here than elsewhere in the North.

More concern was generated for the draft, or conscription, and its potential effect on Colorado. The first effort in 1862, called the Militia Act, reinforced state systems. Even with its many defects and at best a limping effort, the draft had an impact on Colorado. Freighters in Missouri found it difficult to find bullwhackers to transport goods west. In March 1863 Congress passed a national conscription law, which greatly perplexed Coloradans, who wondered whether it referred to "all able-bodied male citizens" between twenty and forty-five, or simply to those living in the States. As the second year of the war drew to a close, the question remained unanswered.

War horrors took the blame for dampened enlistment enthusiasm and the resultant need for conscription. The excitement of 1861 waned under the thunder of battle and the boredom of camp. Ellen Williams wrote soaringly about the brave men who exchanged "pick and shovel for sword and bayonet" (her husband had joined the Second Colorado), but others weighed the matter less emotionally.

Now more than ever, men were deciding, or reaffirming their

conviction, to stay home. Samuel Leach wrote his brother that, were he anywhere else, in all probability he would "shoulder a musket." Loyal to the core, Leach had his hands full mining, which he believed aided a Union that needed Colorado mines and minerals. His neighbor, Irving Stanton, however, sold out his business and pleaded with Moffat to help him get a commission. He received one and also became part of the Second Colorado, spending the rest of the war in Missouri fighting bushwhackers.

In the meantime, the territory overflowed with recruiters. Coloradans had their choice of enlisting in the First, Second, or Third Colorado Volunteers, or in the New Mexico Volunteers. A recruiting war heated up in May, then diminished; few enthusiasts were left.

When the Second and Third marched east in February, Colorado again faced the prospect of a weak defense. This deficiency worried residents more than it did the army. Col. Jesse Leavenworth, who recruited the Second Colorado, wrote the commander of the Department of Missouri in March that, beyond the troops already stationed at Forts Lyon and Garland and Camp Collins, "there is no more necessity for troops at this point than at Syracuse, N. Y." The hue and cry for troops, he believed, reflected the desire for speculation: "All the rest retained are to protect new town lots, and eat corn, at $5.50 per bushel." Had Coloradans been aware of that attitude, their indignation would have known no bounds. The charge contained more than a grain of truth—Uncle Sam's military provided contracts, jobs, and business throughout the region, and westerners were loath to see the soldiers go. In the end, 1862–63 proved to be a peaceful year, and no more troops were needed.

Those who preferred to stay home and patriotically march and maneuver joined the home guards: Denver paraded its Governor's Guards, Montgomery mustered a company of Home Guards, and Black Hawk recruited the Elbert Guards, whose name honored the territorial secretary. They drilled, studied tactics, waited for uniforms and arms, and considered themselves part of the war effort, while scoring a hit on the local social scene. A dash of rivalry whetted interest. Denverites railed, "Don't let the Mountains beat the Valley." How dependable the militia might have been was open to question; Montgomery's boys met regularly in the Red Bird Saloon for "drill."

Regular army life bestowed both excitement and boredom, but usually more of the latter. Discouraged miner William Dutt joined a company at Buckskin Joe and marched off for a pleasant trip to Fort Garland. By the time the company reached the fort, six men had deserted and one had been discharged for a disability, leaving forty-nine soldiers. Having no duty, they drilled twice each day, except Sunday, and consumed large amounts of grub with little grumbling. They became Company M of the First New Mexico Volunteers and would be stationed in that territory.

Romine Ostrander of Company F, First Colorado, purchased a diary in February 1863. Several earlier failures to maintain a daily record spurred him to "see if I can't keep this one so here goes for a beginning." Stationed at Fort Lyon on the Arkansas River, he found it to be the "dullest kind of life." Entry after entry in the next month repeated this theme. Transferring to Denver gave no relief for this one-time miner from Ohio: "Monotony! monotony! monotony! every day just like the one that precedes it." A rare break from the routine came when a detail rode to Golden. Finding no stolen government property, they discovered instead brandy cocktails and whiskey, "upon which the boys got rather salubrious."

Ostrander was a member of the valiant First, heroes of Glorieta Pass, who returned to Denver in January, not as the "ruffians" who had left a year earlier, but as "bronzed faced, brave boys." Ostrander missed this parade but arrived in time for the anniversary of the battle and marched downtown on that occasion, listening to flattering and patriotic speeches by Evans, Weld, Chivington, and others.

The officers treated the company to three kegs of lager beer, which was drunk in toast to the memory of the "comrades who fell. May they never be forgotten."

The boys' "gallant colonel," John Chivington, preceded them to Denver by several months; in August 1862 he had given a detailed report of the regiment's career to a large, enthusiastic audience at the Platte Valley Theatre. No one emerged a greater hero from this campaign than the ambitious, respected

Chivington, who aspired to the rank of general and command of the Colorado district. Already, though, his actions were arousing jealousy and conflict within the regiment. Samuel Tappan, who had recruited a Central City company, felt particularly aggrieved and accused Chivington of undermining his fellow officers:

> I understand that you have in the presence of several [people] threatened if the officers of our regiment meet together to take into consideration the affairs of our regiment and I am among them I shall be put in irons. . . . I confess that I am exceedingly annoyed and excited to anger when I hear that you in my absence threatened me with this and that you speak of me with contempt. I most earnestly and sincerely protest against such proceedings.

Interestingly, Tappan had waived his right to promotion and command in favor of Chivington.

Professional jealousy, though not unheard of in armies on either side during the war, caused widespread comment in so small a territory as Colorado. The disputes went deep in the First, back to the recruiting days, and intensified during the campaign and the slow months that followed. Tappan concluded his January 23 letter by blasting Chivington: "Do not exercise the power conferred upon you to gratify your personal spite and sacrifice the interests of our country for the gratification of your political ambition."

Certainly Chivington was ambitious. Although he did not become a general, he was appointed to command the Eleventh district, Colorado Territory. In appreciation of his "gallantry and courteousness," the officers of the First, most of whom obviously did not agree with Tappan's sentiments, presented him with a $550 saddle and bridle. Chivington responded by hosting a "most elegant" dinner at Tremont House for the officers, Governor Evans, and others. Ned Wynkoop's toast to Chivington and the regiment's commander, John Slough, brought harmony to the evening. Not just the officers appreciated this "kind friend, unassuming gentleman and . . . gallant soldier," John Chivington. Ovando Hollister wrote that the love and respect the men held for their colonel required him only to lead in order for them to follow. This show of esteem gladdened Evans, but the animosities ran deep. John Chivington's antagonists awaited only another day to take their revenge.

The governor also was pleased that, aside from a few annoyances, the Indians remained peaceful. Trying to govern a territory while simultaneously taking charge of Indian affairs trapped Evans in a nearly impossible role. He could avoid difficulties only if matters stayed calm and he could avoid taking a stand favoring one or the other.

The Indians themselves tried to maintain their traditional way of life. This task proved hardest for the Cheyennes and Arapahoes, as settlement pressures were already crowding in on them. Prairie land and buffalo disappeared before the settlers' advance. Problems loomed less pressing for the Utes to the west. William Dole, Commissioner of Indian Affairs, reported that they continued their wild, warlike, independent life. Most Coloradans could not understand why they were considered intruders by the Utes, but Dole warned that a treaty was needed to avoid a fatal collision. To the detriment of both, neither culture sought to understand the other.

Even during this time of apparent peace, Evans heard reports of harassment by Indians. A complaint from Boulder County in July reported stolen horses, a house rifled, and oxen killed. Locals blamed Utes, but no one seemed absolutely certain. Newspapers, of course, latched onto these incidents to justify emotional editorial comments and a call for more troops or for moving the Indians away from the settlements. An Indian camp could almost always be found somewhere near Denver. In June, a war party of Arapahoes and Sioux had arrived triumphantly, swinging fresh Ute scalps from spearheads and herding a number of captured ponies. Such proximity threatened to put the town in a sideline seat during any retaliatory raids by other "Native Americans," as Byers occasionally called them.

Susan Ashley, who came to Denver as a bride in November 1861, was no admirer of "Poor Lo," as she and others called the Indian. The sight of Cheyenne and Arapahoe Indians on the streets almost every day disturbed her. After being assured Indians would not open a gate, she insisted on having a fence built around her home—alas, to no avail. While working or sitting quietly reading, she would suddenly be seized by an uncanny feeling of being watched. Looking up, she would see in one or more windows the "stolid face of an Indian." On one occasion, Susan forgot to lock the outer doors and entered the front room to find three Indians there and others entering. "With assumed bravery I cried out 'Puck-a-chee!' (which I had been told was the Indian way of saying be gone!) and I put my hands against the nearest Indian as if to push him out." Her method worked; they left without resistance and resigned themselves to looking through the windows.

The unexpected Sioux war in Minnesota sent chills down Coloradans' spines. In this August outbreak, which neither side really wanted but both provoked, over seven hundred settlers were killed. This violence could lead to a general Indian war, warned the *Tri-Weekly Miners' Register* (December 29). "No quarter or kindness or liberality is shown by them. They simply kill and steal," the *Weekly Commonwealth* had railed a few days before. Coloradans agreed and hoped for the best.

Westerners had a pretty good idea of how to contain the barbarities. They cheered in late January when Col. Patrick Connor led his troops to victory in a battle at Bear River in what would become southern Idaho. Raiding, stealing, and killing by both sides prompted his campaign. Connor made clear his intention not to take any prisoners. Estimates ranged from 224 to 300 Bannock and Shoshone Indians killed, many of whom were reported to be women and children. Threats to the trails and settlers in that region diminished, and settlement of the land continued. The *News*, on March 26, supported an editorial from the *Santa Fe New Mexican*, which called "red skins . . . a dissolute, vagabondish, brutal and ungrateful race," who "ought to be wiped from the face of the earth."

More rational thinkers hoped to avoid that kind of bloody end. They trusted that the Ute leaders headed for Washington in February would agree to a new treaty, thus peacefully opening up more territory in accordance with Coloradans' wishes. No one seemed to care what the Utes wanted to do. They, meanwhile, came into town, had their pictures taken, attended the theater, and seemed to enjoy themselves immensely.

Disquieting to those who cherished a dream of peace was a survey of the Cheyenne and Arapahoe Indian reservation in southeastern Colorado. Given to them because of its generally desolate appearance, the region now was found to contain coal, iron, limestone, and fine grazing land.

That was Colorado in the second year of the war, with new faces and old, nagging problems, and another year's maturity. Reviewing his months as chief justice, Benjamin Hall had written William Seward in April 1862 to describe both his joys and his frustrations. He felt pleased that he had helped restore peace in "this once turbulent territory" and planted the seeds of higher civilization. His salary of eighteen hundred dollars merely defrayed his "personal expenses here," leaving him with nothing to support his family. He further revealed that he had "come to this rugged, ill remunerated post more as a matter of duty than of interest." Hall, the ever-loyal Unionist, and others came and stayed despite their misgivings and continued the process of carving a territory out of the plains and mountains.

7

"There is no such thing as can't"

Twenty-two-year-old Ellen Coffin, an Illinois resident since the age of four, endured the same weary miles and long days that the fifty-niners had experienced, before she caught her first glimpse of the Rocky Mountains. Things had not changed much in three years.

A few days after entering the region, she arrived at her brothers' cabin near future Longmont. Ellen had come west because of their encouragement, not to find gold. Her health had been precarious in Illinois, and she hoped to benefit from Colorado's dry climate.

This crisp November day bestowed its benefits on one of the newest of Coloradans, as it did on others suffering from the fevers and ague that seemed to stalk the Midwest. Ellen had much to offer her new home; she immediately made her brothers' bachelor quarters more livable. Hard work, without much of the frontier's "romance," characterized the life of women in Colorado. Cooking for the boys in a fireplace using a bake kettle explains why:

This bake kettle business, I remember, I did not like very well. It was a whole day's job to bake a panful of cookies and a few pumpkin pies, as only four cookies or one pie could be baked at one time. The lid had to be lifted and the hot coals removed very often. If your hand should suddenly lose its grip, or someone jostled your elbow, down the lid would come and the coals more often land inside the kettle. The fronts of my

117

dresses would be scorched, the toes of my shoes burned, and my face nearly blistered in the process.

Ellen remembered her social life as quite circumscribed. Young women were few and their outlets limited.

Just how scarce women were, in the mountains as well as on the plains, Daniel Conner explained. An old lady came into Georgia Gulch to start a "deadfall" in connection with a hotel. She was accompanied by her daughter, affectionately known as Sis, the first young woman to appear in these diggings. Sis waited on customers and proved quite a business draw:

Miners would come from neighboring mines quite a distance to get to buy a drink from Sis. The common remark of the miners, when meeting friends was first, "Boys, there is a gal in the gulch." "When did she come?" "Oh, I don't know, but she's there." Hurrah! Hurrah for Georgia Gulch. . . . And off they would go to see Sis, with as much curiosity as boys who go to see the monkey.

Sis and Ellen, worlds apart socially, brought something to Colorado that it needed—feminine mystique. The honor and respect they merited for their courage in simply being there did not preclude their undergoing sore trials. Samuel Leach feared that the boys at Sterling would overwork the one poor woman there when she came to start a boardinghouse. Sam thought it no place for a woman, but a friend ecstatically saw the coming of civilization, with women "to darn our hose, cook our meals and keep our houses."

Clara Witter journeyed to Colorado from Indiana in the spring of 1862 to join her fifty-niner husband in Hamilton. Traveling through the mountains to the camp brought her into contact with bright sun and snow, and the possibility of snow blindness. She recommended the common method of blackening the cheeks under the eyes with charcoal as a preventive. Few remedies could keep her skin from aging under such an onslaught.

The Witters's two-room cabin, with a trundle bed for Clara's daughters, was not what she had left behind, "but it was home." She found most goods and food expensive. Staples back east— bacon, ham, and potatoes—were now luxuries, when available: "Our living was not rich enough to hurt our health." Husband

Daniel had to curb his wine making because, as Clara explained to her mother, "we can not afford to use so much sugar as it is thirty-five cents a pound."

Being part of Colorado's frontier epoch did not impress five-year-old Jessie Witter. With her mother's help, she described to her grandmother in Indiana what excited her about Hamilton. Every day she got to go to Mrs. Jackson's for milk, a highlight worth mentioning. A book brightened one day, and Mrs. Case gave her a slate pencil and several little papers with hymns. An apron and a "new dolly" were much more important than mining success or gold. She asked Grandma to send the words to "Oh I love to come to my Sabbath school" and "I want to be an angel." Grandma undoubtedly beamed over such youthful piety.

Most women lived in the larger camps and towns, and they continued to enjoy more freedom than their sisters in the East. Divorce in Central and Nevada became so prevalent that the *News* chided in October that folks on mountaintops must "marry in haste and repent at leisure." Mollie Sanford spoke to this new freedom and its problems for her. Living with her husband at Camp Weld outside of Denver, she observed:

I presume I am too impulsive and make friends too easily. I take it for granted that everyone is just what they pretend to be. I am commenting on this subject because I found out today that a woman whom I thought so good and pure, had run away from husband and two little children to live with one of the officers. Such things, altho of common occurrence in this country, shock me dreadfully. I hear vague whispers about several more of the women here.

Fannie Moffat exemplified a much more typical life as the wife of one of Denver's rising young businessmen. The couple enjoyed their prestige and social life as members of Denver's growing upper middle class. With his business prospering, Dave Moffat was able to send his wife home in the summer of 1862 to see the "old folks." Her departure made Moffat a temporary "grass widower," a condition he survived through a lonely summer. Before the year was out, Fannie's husband received honors befitting one of Denver's young lions. First, he was appointed acting postmaster, and then Governor Evans designated him adjutant general of the

Colorado militia. Moffat's budding career illustrated a real Colorado success story.

Other aspirants met with less success. Irving Stanton ran a bookstore in Buckskin Joe, hoping to emulate his friend Moffat. His site did not prove out, and throughout 1862 transportation problems, mislaid shipments, ruined merchandise, and a small market burdened his business hours. In December, as mentioned before, Irving called it quits, sold out, and joined the army. For everyone who quit, someone else lay in wait to try his luck. Someone named Johnson bought Stanton's store on credit, as Stanton had done before him; Dave Moffat handled both notes. Credit kept Colorado going.

Charles Desmoineaux hoped to make his fortune by operating a bakery in Spring Gulch, near Central. When his business proved less than successful he tried mining, which failed to pan out, so he returned to baking—all in the summer of 1862. Denver merchant W. M. McMahan, on the other hand, could not face failure and skedaddled in October, leaving behind creditors, a wife, and three children.

Samuel Leach provided insight into what a mining-camp merchant had to do to succeed in business. He noted that the men in Sterling liked strong, serviceable articles that were made to wear and endure, not for fashionable display. Blankets and playing cards, in great demand, moved rapidly off the shelves. Boots dominated the footwear market—no one cared for shoes. Little variety in staple goods, especially groceries, limited customers' selections. Samuel observed that few things could be profitably transported in wagons.

For enterprising individuals, Colorado could be a road to wealth and respect. William Loveland continued to prove that in Golden. This merchant, miner, untiring road builder, and politician now served as treasurer of Jefferson County's School District No. 1 and remained as prominent a social figure as ever. Also successful was the widely "celebrated pilot" of the old Planter's House, James McNasser, who in August opened a new Planter's House in Denver with appropriate fanfare. Just what the young city needed, Planter's House provided the very best billiard tables in the territory, a "spacious and noble" dining hall, elegantly furnished bedrooms, and a tonsorial department run by one of "Africa's choicest sons." The establishment far surpassed anything else of its kind in Colorado.

Every community aspired to its own Planter's House to demonstrate its progress to visitors. Most towns, however, including Central and Black Hawk, had to settle for less imposing hotels and boarding houses. Eastern visitors were variously intrigued, shocked, and amused by the territory's striving for respectability. They probably did a double take when they saw Central City's milkman bringing milk into town in cans on pack horses.

Nothing better evidenced this striving than the emergence of a public school system; women dominated teaching, one of the few acceptable professional outlets for them. Such educational enthusiasm might have been spurred by a legislative act that specified that the number 3 claim on all lodes be sold to benefit schools. Central Citians busied themselves organizing a district in October, selecting versatile David C. Collier (newspaperman, lawyer, and real estate promoter) as superintendent. Arapahoe County and Russell Gulch followed suit in December, joining Boulder, Black Hawk, and Pueblo. Soon newspaper reporters poked their heads into the schools to see how things were going. Black Hawk's *Miners' Register* found its school to be in flourishing condition (excellent for community esteem), but it had only one teacher when it needed two, the room was cold, and the benches were uncomfortable for the young scholars. A lack of uniform textbooks plagued everybody. When each student used a different book, how could a teacher develop a lesson? Woolworth and Moffat had the solution—they were publishers' agents for textbooks of all subjects, from elementary spelling to advanced orthography and moral philosophy.

The fact that miners agreed to be taxed and allowed further governmental organization, ideas they generally abhorred in non-mining matters, showed growing maturity. Byers became so enthusiastic that he recommended in March that Denver schools be kept open all summer so that immigrant families' children would have access to the facilities. No one asked the children what they thought.

Private schools provided an alternative to public education in some of the larger communities. Ella Kendall opened a school in Central City in September; "small" scholars paid fifty cents per week, advanced scholars seventy-five cents. Highly praised for her work, abilities, and pleasing manner, Ella exemplified the perfect teacher. When another private school opened, the editor of the *Colorado Mining Life* advised people to "send along your brats." Considering the times and the struggle over slavery, it is interesting to note that Denver opened a private night school for "colored" boys, girls, and adults in March 1863.

Coloradans, never known to be in the forefront of the struggle for racial equality, far too often treated blacks as second-class citizens, both in print and in practice. Occasionally, comments were blatantly bigoted; the *Colorado Democrat* seemed to propound the worst remarks. The Democratic paper printed letters from readers critical of Republicans: "Let the 'nigger organs' and nigger worshipers rant, paw, howl, and gnash their teeth in their impotent rage, for their day is short."

An attempt at humor in the police court notes when a black couple, George and Nancy, tangled in a domestic scuffle—a "vi et armis," as the reporter described it—displayed both a racial stereotyping of individuals and insensitivity. On the other hand, when restaurant owner David Millen, carefully described as a "colored man," died, the *Weekly Commonwealth* took time to hail him as a much-respected, good citizen. Byers was equally praising of this forty-one-year-old Georgia native, an enterprising Coloradan since 1860. Denver had already become the heart of the territory's black community.

Denver still reigned as the number one community in Colorado. Although the city endured its dull moments, most of the residents would have wholeheartedly agreed with Thomas Gibson in his editorial on October 30, that "Denver City has become the most important point in the far west."

While mulishly feuding over the site of the capital, Denver was beginning to take a more positive attitude toward its mountain rivals. "What would Denver be without the mountains?" Byers asked. "And what would become of the mountain folks if there was no such an entrepot as Denver to occasionally come to and supply their many wants?"

Central and Black Hawk winced at that idea and assumed they had enough merchants to satisfy their own residents' needs. A mild building boom erupted in both towns, and it was believed to be just a matter of time before the urban cluster of Central, Nevada, and Black Hawk surpassed Denver. Golden, too, awaited the moment when it would be a formidable rival. Its beautiful location, natural resources, and "perhaps the most salubrious climate in the Territory" merely awaited capital to be developed. Golden, only a brisk, fifteen-mile ride for the "dust covered denizens of Denver" (parched and panting from the hot sands of that location), offered the lure of the Colorado mountains.

Montgomery and Trail Run, quite to the contrary, were "dull as a mule" when spring came to the mountains, but that condition rated ahead of abandonment. Throughout the year, Coloradans watched engrossed as camps became ghost towns. At various times the newspapers reported Hamilton as a deserted village and Tarryall with grass growing untrodden in the streets, "a sad change from last year." Missouri City's houses were being moved to Black Hawk, and Silver City had dwindled to six houses, one family, five miners, and half a dozen dogs and "purps." The placer-district camps in the Blue River region resembled a graveyard.

The mining frontier ebbed and flowed. Yesterday's glamour evanesced into today's gloom; today's dream evolved into tomorrow's metropolis. Bobtail, near Central, held out great expectations in the winter of 1862–63. A town for the working classes, it stood ready to increase in wealth and size. "Success to Bobtail," hailed rival Central City. At Tarryall City the roof of the *Record* office had collapsed, destroying the last remaining monument of the once-lively paper.

Like the communities they represented, newspapers came and went, always feuding and promoting with zest. Some editors, such as Mat Riddlebarger, always seemed to pop up with a new paper; his latest publication was Buckskin Joe's *Western Mountaineer.* It lasted only until December, when once more Mat found himself unemployed.

Thomas Gibson, on the other hand, stubbornly continued his fight with Byers in Denver, changing his newspaper's name to the *Commonwealth and Republican.* For a while William Gilpin bought in as his silent partner, and Gibson loyally backed him in the 1862 election. Byers, however, remained the premier newspaperman and carried on in his flamboyant manner. Even though he enjoyed pricking the ballooning reputation of Colorado's chief mining rival, Nevada, with stories of killings, gunfights, and other violence in the Comstock district, Byers honored a contemporary of like stature when William Wright visited Denver. Better known as Dan DeQuille, this talented writer, outstanding mining journalist, and correspondent dominated (along with Mark Twain) Virginia City's newspaper pages with his "gifted art of shoving the quill" for the *Territorial Enterprise.*

Virginia City returned the shots, describing Denver's and Colorado's strange goings-on, all of which helped build the legend of the Wild West. Of course, neither Colorado nor Nevada thought of itself as a lawless community or territory, but rather as a paragon of respectability. Easterners had no way of knowing the truth, except by personal observation.

The truth could be hard to discern; rumors and exaggerations eluded verification even then. The *Republican,* for example, reported on May 22 that two men had recently been killed in Gregory and that three others were killed within the past month on the Arkansas, and one or two in the southern mines. Only for the first two deaths was there any tangible evidence; one man had been shot over a claim dispute and the other in a fight between two "game cocks" at a sporting house.

Charley Swits, for one, discovered that western gunfights were not what easterners supposed them to be. Swits and Central City theater owner George Harrison nurtured a bitter grudge dating back almost a year. (Both, coincidentally, had been called to testify in the Charles Harrison trial in September 1861.) Swits had been so rash as to brag on July 30 that "he would have to kill the damned son of a bitch, that [George] Harrison dare not kill him anyhow." Harrison dared and did. When Swits stepped out of Barnes's billiard saloon the next evening, Harrison opened fire from the balcony of his theater, first with a pistol, then using a double-barreled shotgun for the coup de grace. Swits proved a poor prophet and died on the spot.

Harrison promptly surrendered to the sheriff. Discharged following a lengthy hearing in the Justice of the Peace Court, he promptly created a tempest of short duration when he opened his National Theatre on Sunday, thus violating territorial law. A poorly written statute gave Harrison a victory in the case.

Dissatisfaction with the original court hearing led in November to a Gilpin County grand jury's indictment of Harrison for murder. The floor of the crowded courtroom began to sag several inches, and Sheriff Jessie Pritchard immediately ruled the room unsafe and ordered the court adjourned, ironically to the sturdier and larger National Theatre. After several days of "exciting testimony," the jury took a few hours to acquit him.

All this publicity did little to encourage business. Harrison sold his theater and left the territory. Six months later the *News* reported that he had opened a theater in the Confederate capital of Richmond. True blue Unionists nodded knowingly—to them, all Southerners were ruffians, murderers, and worse. Harrison's escapades had not done much to enhance the theater's image, either.

On the other hand, the Langrishes lived in Central City and maintained their respectability. Surveyor and next-door neighbor Hal Sayre found them to be excellent neighbors, and he thoroughly enjoyed Jack's performances. His facial expressions alone could keep an audience in an uproar for several minutes. The Langrishes and others occasionally played to a rowdy audience, but disruptions were becoming unfashionable. Thomas Gibson scolded the "scoundrels in the gallery" one evening for their vulgar, slang phrases and cat calls; he admonished them to stay home if they could not behave themselves.

Life upon the stage was tenuous at best. The National Theatre was renamed The Montana after Harrison left, and a month later it closed. Small houses almost every night doomed it to failure. Byers could not resist pointing out that Denver was having its best theatrical season ever.

Coloradans still preferred comedy mixed with drama, such as *Colleen Bawn, or the Irish Beauty,* or the London and New York stage hit, *Our American Cousin.* Colorado, not to be outdone by those theatrical centers, was producing its own culture. None other than Mike Dougherty had introduced a new song, "Pat Casey's Night Hand," to continued "rounds of applause." In Denver and Central it became a great hit, Casey being a local celebrity in his own day.

So had been Charley Swits before George Harrison dispatched him. Swits had audaciously claimed to be the boxing "Champion of Colorado Territory," which angered the legitimate champion, Con Orem, enough to bring him out of retirement. In June and early July the two exchanged long-distance punches in the newspapers, with Orem getting the upper hand. In his opinion, the "indecent, ungentlemanly whipping of a few drunken men" by Swits did not constitute a ring champion. Harrison ended that issue once and for all, but Orem reappeared in the ring, putting retirement behind him.

After a few exhibitions, Orem left Pike's Peak country in October for New York, sporting a "magnificent prize belt" of solid silver and gold, the champion's belt of Colorado. It had cost three hundred dollars and carried with it the sports pride of the territory. Denver papers were pleased to chronicle the interest created by "the Pike's Peak pugilistic champion" in eastern sporting circles that winter and spring. Orem upheld the honor of Colorado.

Baseball did not fare quite so well. The spring of 1862 had rekindled interest, and in late April Byers crowed that the boys would soon be able to challenge the New York and Brooklyn clubs, then the country's best known. Alas, the challenge never came to pass. Two months later the *News* conceded that "things aint as they used to was." As soon as the mining season opened, a good share of the players went to the mountains, and the baseball club was consequently "tabled for the summer." The "lazy" boys in town received one of Byers's tongue-lashings.

Interest did not revive in the fall, and a lack of baseball news in the papers indicates the sport had died. Undoubtedly, the war also helped bring about its demise, as many young men volunteered and marched away. The eastern teams suffered as well.

Attention to the red-light district was decidedly not tabled. Brother Dyer's warning that the "evils of dancing were such a curse to community that no man could say too much against it, or against the sin creeping into their neighbors' houses and leading silly women away from their families" went unheeded. The reference to "silly women" begged the issue. Saloons, dancing and gambling halls, and prostitutes fared well as part of Colorado's entertainment and business life, aided and abetted by the men they served.

Byers rejoiced in July when Denver passed an ordinance prohibiting houses of ill repute. The legislation had, he observed, a magical effect upon the cyprians, who left singly and by twos for the mountains, which would "soon know them no more forever." Forever lasted only a few weeks. Soon again the police court saw Jennie Ausman, Kate, the mysterious Miss A. B., and other fair-but-frails brought up on a variety of charges, including keeping an ill-governed, disorderly house. Annie Burnett and Kate paid fines for wearing male apparel, for what reason no one seemed to know. In November, a few overly zealous souls tried to burn the brothels, apparently to remove this "abscess from the fair face of society." Though they believed they were "doing God's service," they failed on all counts.

Scandal occasionally contaminated the respectable community. Lumberman J. J. Haman worked out a cozy relationship with Lucy Ohmer, alias Lucy Simpson, until his wife and children arrived in June. Both women wanted the magnetic Haman, but Lucy conceded and departed after an uproar. The strain proved too much for Haman, who shot himself "through the heart" on the evening of July 13, 1862. Byers was moved to moralize about the "prevalence of reprehensibility among many of the 'lords of creation' here."

Those lords of creation could imbibe in a saloon without fear of social ostracism. Even in that male bastion, times and manners had changed; the saloon bands were now relics of the musical past in Denver. Some saloons sold native wine from Pueblo, a breakthrough for Colorado agriculture that took a steep toll on the consumer's pocketbook. Native wine sold for $30 per dozen bottles; wine from Cincinnati cost $10-12.

For ladies and gentlemen, Central City provided the Cabinet Saloon. Here Coloradans of style and discernment could find lemonade, a dish of ice cream, a fragrant Havana, or a glass of Catawba. Dan Doyle and Tom McAnally ran a more traditional establishment, a convivial hangout for the Irish. In neighboring Russell Gulch, Federal Hall was the rage: "Any Saturday night you wish to 'drop into' a gay crowd of hard working men and beautiful women, make it a point to visit Federal Hall." For those devotees of Federal Hall not light of foot, popular Charley McDuffie opened a dancing school every Saturday night and, in his spare moments, furnished music for a dancing school in Central. Women and men were instructed in separate, three-hour sessions for the first three or four lessons, after which they met at the same hour.

Unmarried men and those without families favored spending their holidays at saloons. The spontaneity and rowdiness of earlier years had been replaced by more gentility and orderliness. Christmas epitomized this progress in many ways, from the variety of gifts available—toys, photographs, books, and clothes—to the bill of fare at Tremont House, which tempted gourmets with roast beef, turkey (with cranberry or oyster sauce), corned beef and cabbage, and pork, and all surrounded by heaping servings of potatoes, carrots, beets, green corn, squash, and relishes. For dessert came mince, blackberry, and peach pies, pudding, pound cake, charlotte russe, and jellies. A good selection of wine was available to toast the season and conclude the feast. Dickens's "ghost of Christmas present" would have felt right at home.

In Denver, Christmas morning brought a nippy, snowless, twenty-five-degree day. The Witters, who moved to Denver for the winter, passed a pleasant holiday. Cora and Jessie, hanging up a pair of their mother's stockings, found Santa had arrived: "You should have seen them & heard them when opening their little treasures." Candies, apples, raisins, teakettles, and "new calico dresses" made it an occasion to remember. Ten days later, a new baby girl, Hattie, joined the Witter family. The older girls welcomed their "pretty special" new sister.

Coloradans were reading more, another sign of the changing times. Dave Moffat said he had sold more bound books during the past summer than in his whole sojourn in Denver. This development spoke well for the territory's citizens, exulted Thomas Gibson.

Maum Guinea, the tale of a mysterious slave woman, never supplanted *Uncle Tom's Cabin* in popularity and soon was over-shadowed by other current favorites. The author, Metta Victor, attempted to entice Coloradans with one of Beadle's dime novels, *The Gold Hunters*. How could it fail with scenes laid on the plains and in the Rocky Mountains after the discovery of gold? Colorado's legendary Buckskin Joe strode across the book's pages, the hero of some "wonderful adventures." Moffat stocked the book, believing it would be particularly appealing to Pike's Peakers.

As March turned into April, Hiram Bennet, in war-engrossed Washington, found time to spend Congress's $2,500 appropriation to purchase books for a territorial library. Grousing that the amount was only half the usual appropriation, he did the best he could with what he had. It seemed likely that before long Colorado would be the literary mecca of the Rocky Mountains.

The territory was already destined to be the agricultural heart of the region. Despite the commonly held belief that Colorado was "eminently a miners' region," an increasing number of people saw it becoming an agricultural and pastoral land capable of exporting commodities. That belief required a leap of faith, because self-sufficiency was not even close to being attained.

Isaac McBroom exemplified such faith when, in the spring, he imported the first colony of bees across the plains by ox team. He was selling honey in Denver by October, thanks to his industrious, pioneering bees. Homegrown cotton and tobacco also reached local markets. An article in the *Weekly Commonwealth* (August 21, 1862) expressed this view: "Let us have no more of this nonsense about 'can't do it.' There is no such thing as 'can't' in the vocabulary of a good farmer."

After a bad siege of grasshoppers in May, June, and July, some farmers might have disputed that statement, but crops survived and reached local tables. Sylvanus Wellman, still living in that "vast, most beautiful farming district" of Boulder, was one farmer who prospered. A full year of activity for Wellman and his hands began with plowing, then moved through planting, irrigating, weeding, and harvesting to sorting squashes and cleaning and sacking corn in January. Wellman returned home on a particularly windy January 5 (1863) to find wheat stacks blown over, fences down, and "things upside down generally." Boulder was already acquiring its windy reputation.

Wellman and other Boulder Valley farmers shipped corn, wheat, potatoes, onions, turnips, and every variety of garden vegetables and dairy products to Denver and the mountains that season. Eighteen sixty-two had been a good year for them. Improved transportation to cut freighting costs and time would have made it even better.

The steam wagon again chugged into newsprint, if not into Denver's dusty streets; it had fallen victim to another accident near Nebraska City. "Where is the steam wagon?" queried the *News* on October 30, "We Peakers are getting anxious to see it." When the inventor said he needed a well dug every five miles to furnish water, and trees set out and cultivated to furnish fuel for the "voracious" engine, the dream exploded. The steam wagon never rumbled into Denver, sparing the city's horses the inevitable panic it created. The railroad connection had also proved elusive, though it would come in time.

Coloradans were left to the mercy of freight wagons and stages that lumbered over roads not noticeably better than the previous year, or the year before that. The usual weather problems only raised tempers higher and made delays longer.

The expense of freighting did not do much to soothe tempers, either. Susan Ashley brought her piano from Ohio to enliven her days in Denver, and paid $200 to freight the Steinway from the river. Competition sometimes drove local stage rates down to as low as $2 between Denver and Central. Spring's natural elixir was tainted when the rates rose to $4. (The fee was $12 to Buckskin Joe, seventeen hours from Denver over 109 tortuous mountain miles). It cost $75 to return to Atchinson, Kansas; $100 to visit the Mormons in Salt Lake City; and $150 to go see the wonders of the Comstock. Most people forwent traveling by stage as too expensive. For those who stayed put, life provided much less excitement than in previous years. Colorado was being tamed; maybe the time had come to bring out the wife and family.

The church began to play a larger role in the community, and Methodists in Central showed particular faith by purchasing a lot on Eureka Street and planning to construct a brick building in the spring. The pastor, William Fisher, also advocated honoring the Sabbath by not working. A committee of three women sent out to secure assistance in stopping the "growing evil" of the "desecration of God's holy day" was greeted with a noticeable lack of enthusiasm. The prospect of a building pleased merchants, because it symbolized a growing respectability, but they strenuously objected to tampering with one of the week's best business days.

Dyer and Billingsley, meanwhile, continued their rounds, trying to save souls and promote Christianity. Dyer, in the mountains, had great difficulty making ends meet; he prospected during the day (with little success) and preached at night. He also carried the mail and served as a county officer (deputy assessor, Lake County) to bring in additional income. Never wavering in his mission, Dyer pushed on, pleased that he and his preaching were treated with respect. The miners occasionally enjoyed teasing him, as they did one Christmas evening: After dinner, his host's wife and other ladies invited Dyer to stay for a dance. That, of course, he could not do and rose to the situation by replying, "You're a lady, but not quite handsome enough for me to dance with." Amid laughter, he succeeded in escaping to his cabin.

Amos Billingsley found little success in the mountains during several jaunts to Montgomery and Buckskin Joe. He preached, distributed tracts, and enjoyed the scenery, though the air was "so light I can't speak without stopping to breathe." After three months at Buckskin Joe, Billingsley finally received some money: "It don't pay pecuniarily, yet it does pay *spiritually.* The Lord will reward."

Buckskin Joe seems to have been well preached over. Samuel

Leach described one Methodist itinerant, however, who missed the mark. Leach and his friends, so well secluded up in the wilds, resented the preacher's admonitions against wine, women, and song. His strong plea for salvation fell on deaf ears. Leach summed it up as an appeal to the emotions that "left us nothing to think about afterwards."

More agitated was the Reverend Learner Stateler, who arrived in Denver to find that the church building he had been promised had been sold to the Episcopalians. In disgust, he moved on to the "little village" of Golden. With slight success there, this Southern Methodist turned to a circuit, received only fifty dollars for a year's work, and wondered why he had come to Colorado. Eliza Ann Petefish also immigrated west with her minister husband. At age twenty-five she was dead, a victim of the relentlessly rugged life of early Colorado.

The war did not affect the personal lives of most Coloradans, who pursued their routine (and not so routine) activities. Mollie Sanford did something she never expected to do, "*played cards!*" Furthermore, she confessed, "I find it fascinating for myself." She might even have sampled John Robinson's "tip-top, A No. 1" sarsaparilla, "a pleasant and healthy beverage for summer consumption."

Flies and bedbugs, those "persevering, vindictive 'creeturs' [that] *bite!*" tormented Coloradans, particularly during the summer months (one of the few phenomena that made people wish winter would hurry back). Winter, for all its cold and snow, proved a blessing in another way. The odious, lingering stench of putrid garbage wafted around cabins and down alleys until winter's freeze. Neither the smell nor the health hazard kept Coloradans from trashing their towns—they thoughtlessly littered, as did other Americans. Even burning rubbish, though somewhat more sanitary, left an annoying smell.

Many drawbacks frustrated Central Citians. They fussed about high rents: buildings on the main streets cost $300-400 and houses $100-175 per month. "There is no reason for this exorbitant exaction." They feared that the cost would drive trade from Central. Extravagant milk prices, eighty cents per gallon, engendered more hostility. Others were more concerned about lung fever in horses as winter wound down; several fine steeds died in Denver in March.

At least one woman fretted about her wayward spouse, notifying "all women not to harbor or have anything whatever to do with" him. The mysterious cause for such an admonition remained unspecified, and the newspaper failed to follow the story.

Fire continued to pose a significant danger, but most people ignored it and trusted nothing would happen to them. A positive step to alleviate the danger, organization of a fire company, stirred little interest in Central, to the horror of *Colorado Mining Life*.

Weather, unlike fire, always attracted attention. Sylvanus Wellman, with a practiced farmer's eye, jotted down such terse comments as "heavy rain and hail storm, day very windy, warm and pleasant." Denverites were startled when Cherry Creek suddenly rose in June. Large crowds gathered at several bridges to witness this "wonder of wonders." The water eventually receded, along with concern about flooding.

Aches, pains, and other common ailments plagued Coloradans. Despite the variety of illnesses, Dr. William Grafton found too few patients to satisfy his practice and had moved in the past few years from Nevada to Central to Denver. Perhaps Grafton ran up against the still common suspicion of doctors and the prevalence of home remedies. Alexander Toponce received such treatment when he froze his legs after falling in a stream during forty-belowzero weather. When he reached his cabin, his partners gave him a shot of whiskey and heaped snow in a tub with a bucket of water to start it melting. Putting Toponce's legs in the tub, they held him there despite his excruciating pain (another cup of whiskey helped alleviate it), adding more snow until the tub was filled with ice water. The cure nearly killed him, but it saved his legs and feet. Even had a doctor been available, there was no time to contact him.

Health became an issue in January when Central City's *TriWeekly Miners' Register* reported that smallpox was prevalent in Denver. Byers labeled the report an attempt to malign Denver and keep people away. His attack was countered by a charge that the *News* had been reckless and heartless in spreading a rumor about smallpox raging in Central.

Consumption appeared to be on the increase, in spite of the prevailing belief that Colorado's climate could induce a cure. Un-doubtedly, a number of sufferers arrived too late to derive any benefits from the health-enhancing air.

Lawyers also encountered their share of problems. The law, sometimes seen by outsiders as the royal road to wealth, did not always prove profitable in Colorado. Henry Teller did well, con-sidering that he was one of at least eight lawyers practicing in Central. Debtor cases helped keep the wolf from his door. He handled the famous, such as the *Casey v. Burroughs* imbroglio, and the ordinary, such as the case against Alevin March. In 1859 Alevin signed a note for $175, which he still had not repaid in February 1863. A letter from the worried Omaha creditor to Teller said, "I have about given up all hope of getting it except I do so by a suit."

In another matter, Joseph Loughridge lamented the difficulty of collecting debts. Philosophically, he noted, "I often think of what I heard a certain Dutchman say one day in speaking of the disap-pointment of men in that country. Say he 'Such is life in the Rocky Mountains.'" Philosophy gave small consolation to the lender who wanted his money plus interest.

Handling estates also occupied lawyers' time. Charley Swits, for example, left a log cabin worth ten dollars in Leavenworth Gulch and half ownership in the Colorado Varieties in Central City, valued at four hundred dollars. Property was leveling off in value; a house and lot in Central went for six hundred dollars, and in nearly abandoned Mountain City, fifty dollars.

The value Coloradans placed on their animals did not fluctuate as much as real estate. When Cub, a venerable, well-known horse, disappeared, it made the *News*, as did his return. A small, shaggy, dark brown dog with some white around his face and forelegs also came up missing. Whether Jupiter ever returned, and whether someone claimed the liberal reward, went unreported. Surplus dogs posed a persistent problem; most were not valued so highly as Jupiter. Unless they were treasured pets, dogs, like some people, led a miserable life.

One of Denver's funniest commotions occurred when out-on-the-town porkers lived up to the adage "drunk as a hog." Few

people had actually seen a drunk hog until three good-sized pigs
rooted into "a lot of brandy cherries" thrown out as spoiled:

Forthwith they proceeded to enjoy a good spree. For a while their antics were very ludicrous, but at length the fun became very dull and
heavy. One old fellow, before losing all discretion, beat a retreat, and
was just able to navigate by taking both sides of the street. The other
two were still reeling about in the neighborhood of the cherries when
dark came, utterly unable to get away.

Coloradans could be cruel to their animals. Daniel Conner
crossed the pass to Georgia Gulch in April 1862 and saw
numerous dead horses and mules that had fallen off the trail and
been left to die. Only small burros could be lifted back onto the
beaten path.

During these years game and fish were still plentiful in the
foothills and the mountains beyond. The *News* reported that a
fishing party of five men landed "700 of the fattest finny fellows
that flop" in two days up Bear Creek. Both Conner and Samuel
Leach recalled encounters with mountain lions; Leach, however,
called rats the greatest pests around, the largest he had ever
seen.

A couple of names from the past briefly regained the spotlight.
Mlle Carolista, of tightrope fame, performed her walking
wonders in Detroit between buildings four and five stories high.
She had never been able to perform that stunt in Denver's two-
story skyline. Later in the year, she starred at the Varieties
Music Hall in St. Louis in an "exciting equestrian drama of Kit
Carson." Of more permanent artistic value was the completion of
Emanuel Leutze's fresco on the wall of the west stairway in the
House wing of the capitol.

Charley Harrison, last year's Confederate diehard, was
variously reported as having been captured by Union troops,
having *not* been captured, riding with the notorious Quantrill
gang in Missouri, being dead and, finally, being once more alive.
How fleet his fame: Harrison was now described as the
"notorious thief, gambler, and murderer of Denver and Leavenworth memory."

Coloradans had the usual words of wisdom, humor, and wit to
beguile their time:

If a man has a shrew for a wife, is he a SHREWD man?

Scandal, like a kite, to fly well, depends on its tale.

Who are the most dishonest people? Hardware merchants; they sell iron and steel for a living.

Galloping Consumption. Cavalry foraging in the enemy's country.

If a young woman's nature is gunpowder, the sparks should be kept away from her.

Those ever-popular homemaking hints assisted both bachelors and housewives. For those who could not procure yeast, it could be made at home by boiling one pound of flour, a quarter pound of brown sugar, and a little salt in two gallons of water for an hour. When "milk-warm," it was bottled, corked, and allowed to sit for twenty-four hours before it was ready to use.

Surveying the year just past, Coloradans sensed progress, though they believed the eastern part of the country did not really appreciate or understand them. A comment appearing January 6 in the New York Times reinforced this opinion when the writer estimated that probably half of the people of New York were as yet unaware of the territory. Even those who had heard of Colorado, the author concluded, simply had a cloudy and undefined idea that it lay somewhere beyond the Great Plains in the region of the Rocky Mountains. Another report placed Auraria (long since part of Denver) near the scene of the Minnesota Indian troubles, "of no more interest than any other of the many little villages which dot the Minnesota prairies."

Optimistic residents believed that Colorado was changing for the better, whether or not the East took any notice. They pointed to myriad changes, many positive, a few indicating the negative impact of civilization. One cause for concern was that very little game was now seen in Gilpin County. On the other hand, the editor of the Colorado Mining Life saw morality improved over the early days, and "social relations more in accordance with usages of civilized life." Byers observed steady improvement in transportation and communication; news reached Denver within forty-eight hours, the mail came regularly, and by stage a traveler could make Denver in four to five days (with exceeding luck) from the river.

Progress aside, a certain longing for the "old days" was reawakened. When editor Byers heard a string band playing at Chase and Heatley's new saloon on an April evening in '63, it reminded him of the fall of '59 at the old Denver Hall or Dick Wootton's.

In the words of a favorite poet of that generation, Alfred, Lord Tennyson:

> *The old order changeth, yielding place to new,*
> *And God fulfills himself in many ways,*
> *Lest one good custom should corrupt the world.*

Part III

A TIME FOR ACTION: 1863–64

8

"GLORIOUS NEWS! Richmond is ours! We Hope!"

As the third year of the war began, Coloradans found themselves increasingly caught up in the conflict. *Harper's Weekly* and other eastern publications had steadily improved their war coverage and now hit full stride. Reporters and artists marched with the armies, and Coloradans were provided with articles and pictures that portrayed war activity at the front and behind the lines.

Far from the battlefront, fact and rumor intertwined, alternately raising and dashing hopes. Because of the eastern press's bias, news from the front centered on the long-sought capture of Richmond. The war in Missouri, of course, generated the most local concern; Colorado troops fought there, and the fate of overland transportation rode on the outcome.

Readers had become cynical after having had their hopes dashed so many times, and as George Kassler explained to Maria, the glorious news that Richmond had been taken (which reached Denver on May 13) seemed "too good to be true."

I am going to believe all the news we got today fearing that tomorrow's dispatches will dispel the general good feeling that now beams out on every man's face.

Indeed, it did prove too good to be true; Richmond's fall lay far in the future. The Army of the Potomac's advance had sustained a shattering setback at Chancellorsville a week before, and the soldiers now limped back toward Washington. At least Kassler, who had grown "so accustomed to hear[ing]" that dulling phrase, "all quiet on the Potomac," could take heart in the new military season. Now, if Lincoln could only find a general to turn words into deeds.

Many excuses were proffered to justify the latest failure. Irving Stanton, who was stationed in Sulphur Springs, Missouri, analyzed for his friend Moffat where he thought the trouble lay:

> This damn political influence will ruin our country if we are not careful. If we get a good Gen., one that is trusted and has the confidence of Loyal men and the army, A set of miserable Political hacks must be set upon his track and follow the President around until they accomplish their end by having him removed. I wish the Politicians were all in h——l we have no use for them now unless they will shoulder a musket.

Ex-civilian Stanton had become quite the military authority in so few months.

Fortunately, Stanton's ideas were not implemented. The President knew better than most of his generals what the Union needed to do: go after the armies, deplete Southern manpower, and use Richmond to hammer Lee's forces out of existence (the capture of the city being only incidental to the main goal). Then came the news of victories at Gettysburg and Vicksburg. "Our cause is in the ascendant. It will triumph in the end," cheered Thomas Gibson. He was right on both counts, and in Central City the "grandest gathering" that ever took place in the mountains hailed the Union's success with rockets and roman candles, cannonades, patriotic songs, resounding cheers, and a torch parade. By year's end, Kassler could tell Maria that Denver's great hero was Gen. Ulysses S. Grant; meanwhile, quiet again descended on the Potomac.

Colorado duty offered few opportunities for the soldier who aspired to glory. Romine Ostrander of Company F, First Colorado, persevered with his diary, although "it is pretty hard to have to write something every day whether one has anything else to do or not." During the early summer, Ostrander patrolled in South Park, where he guarded the stages, camps, and trails. Lawlessness in the park, aside from war-related conflict, had made the populace uneasy. Until finally run down and killed in September, Vivian Espinosa, along with his brother and cousin, had gone on a rampage, killing about thirty people in the park and farther south. Only the isolation and distance from Denver's newspapers kept this slaughter from creating a general panic. Ostrander found time to be in a play, nevertheless, which netted the soldier-actor fifty-one dollars at Fairplay; the production had gone in the red at Buckskin. When ordered back to Denver in mid-July, Ostrander was sorry to go. He and his fellow soldiers had "been treated as gentlemen here and behaved as such."

Patrols swinging out of Denver to the north and south enlivened otherwise slow days (described by Ostrander on August 22) by "lounging about camp talking about the war, the new mines, the old mines, politics, reading the papers, playing cards and blowing off our extra gas generally, as usual." A week later the First lived up to its original reputation when Ostrander, on patrol near Pueblo, spied a melon patch. He signaled some of the other boys, and they promptly carried off four watermelons.

Out on the plains, the troops visited the Comanche camp of Ten Bear, who had recently visited Washington. He told the soldiers that "he [Ten Bear] and his tribe are good men but the other indians are bad men." Such statements made it difficult for Ostrander and his comrades to determine just who was friendly and who was not. Ten Bear spoke the truth—he used his influence for peace.

Several weeks later, on October 4, Ostrander speculated on his future: he had entered his last year of enlistment. "I have all along calculated to go home . . . [but] I, like a great many other young men, do not like the idea, after leaving home to make a raise, seek my fortune, or whatever it may be called, of going back empty handed." He hated to admit that the promised land had not proved out. Army life had seemed less than glamorous, and he did not know what to think about the problem of the Plains Indians.

Ostrander did, however, recognize the basic issue, the land's potential: "I have not a doubt but it will be settled before many years in spite of its being on Indian reservation." Farmers and ranchers, attracted by mining, moved into the valleys. The same thing was happening that summer in the Owens Valley in California. The Paiutes battled to maintain their way of life, but they ultimately became victims of the mining rush that produced Aurora and eventually Bodie.

The Plains Indians gave Coloradans the jitters: the Minnesota Sioux had fled westward to their cousins' villages, bearing all their hatred and resentment. Evans wrote Commissioner of Indian Affairs Dole in November that he feared a general outbreak in the coming spring. He also hinted that a "great many Mexicans" from New Mexico lived with the Indians, urging war and promising aid. He recommended that all persons furnishing ammunition to the Indians be barred from the territory. That simple solution came too late; onrushing events precluded peace.

In December the now-alarmed governor wrote Secretary of War Stanton that he foresaw an alliance among the Sioux, Cheyenne, Kiowa, Comanche, Apache, and a portion of the Arapahoe Indians that, come spring, might turn several thousand warriors loose on Colorado. The result could be worse than the bloodbath in Minnesota.

Ovando Hollister, whose book on the history of the First Colorado received complimentary reviews in the Central City and Denver press in April, agreed. Now proprietor of Black Hawk's *Daily Mining Journal*, he wrote in a January 15 editorial, "Exterminate the Sioux," and that "every white man in every part of the West should consider them as his deadly enemies, more vengeful and dangerous than the scorpion or the panther." Less emotionally, George Kassler had complained to Maria several days earlier that "Mr. Indian" was again amusing himself by attacking stage stations. He hoped that this would finally prompt the government to take proper measures.

As spring neared, bringing warm days and increased fear of the Indians, Evans again stressed to his agents the utmost importance of preventing an outbreak of hostilities; he wished to avoid the butchery and horrors of Indian war. Evans wanted spies planted among the Indians to report on their plans and activities, but he did not specify how that should be done.

The ultimate responsibility for protection actually lay with the army. Troops were thinly scattered from Camp Collins and Camp

Weld to "the southeast key to this Territory," Fort Lyon (two cavalry companies, one infantry) and Fort Garland (two cavalry companies), with detachments in between. Chivington was in command, and he faced a multitude of trouble, including the government's attempts to move his troops to what seemed to be more threatened areas. When it was suggested in September that a regiment could be spared from his district, he irately wrote Maj. Gen. John Schofield, commander of the Department of Missouri, that whoever so advised could not know whereof he spoke, nor did he care about Colorado's safety. Inferior supplies and food also hampered Chivington. Scurvy broke out among the troops at Fort Lyon and Camp Filmore in March and lasted for several months before fresh potatoes and antiscorbutics finally arrived.

Despite his failure to check what seemed to be a mounting Indian threat, Chivington retained his popularity. When he spoke at the July 4 celebration in Empire, the former minister received frequent outbursts of applause. A listener remarked that the speech "was full of good hits and scathing rebukes of traitors." The same person, however, made this confession: "I would rather have him shoot at me with his pistols than to have him shoot his mouth off." The Methodists, meanwhile, kept Chivington active by appointing the colonel to their Rocky Mountain Conference Committee on Missions. He also received national attention when *Frank Leslie's Illustrated* featured the "universally esteemed, fighting preacher." The article included a very good likeness of him. The one-time presiding elder had come far since joining the army two years earlier.

The boys of the historic First also garnered their share of praise, and not solely from comrade Hollister. When New Mexico's legislature passed a resolution praising the troops who helped free its territory from the Confederates, Coloradans believed their soldiers and support had been slighted. A yearlong tempest in a teapot ensued, which climaxed on November 12 when Evans asked for "justice to her [Colorado's] brave and patriotic soldiers." A new resolution the next year settled the matter. When it came to pride in its military, Colorado ranked with the best in the East.

That sharp-eyed Englishman, Maurice Morris (a summer

visitor to Denver), noted that veterans of the First boasted of themselves as the "toughest cusses" in the western army. He agreed, further believing that they might even be superior to eastern troops. One substantiated fact supports that claim: Colorado led all territories in furnishing volunteers that year.

Although hostility was increasing toward the Plains Indians, Evans had better luck with the Utes. Although one of their delegation died, the rest returned safely from Washington. The trip had been a revelation for Ouray, their up-and-coming leader. Never before had he seen so many whites; nor had he imagined their armies so grand as the one he observed near Washington. In other ways, the capital proved somewhat boring. The Mississippi River ferry crossing made the Utes sick, and passage through the land of their deadly enemies, the Arapahoe Indians, endangered their lives.

The visit did some good from the governor's perspective, however, and in October he was able to negotiate a treaty with the Tabeguache Utes that ceded the San Luis Valley and gave them land to the west, plus annuities and rations. Ouray and Evans got along famously, which contrasted sharply with strained relations on the eastern plains.

Lt. Col. Sam Tappan, commander at Fort Garland, faced a different problem: Ute Indians were trading Navajo women and children to New Mexicans. This practice had been going on for generations and had some basis in Mexican law. But in 1863 it violated government policy by perpetuating slavery. Fort Garland, so far away and with so little impact in Washington, would have to wait for help in eradicating the Indian slave trade.

Chivington and his troops did not need the additional problems that 1863 brought. Rumors of imminent Confederate attacks raged through Colorado, and the troops checked out these reports to calm nervous civilians. Denver's old friend, Charley Harrison, was a principal figure in the most notorious of these intended raids. He and a group of followers planned to ride west, raise Confederate troops, and seize gold for the South's waning fortunes. Unfortunately for Harrison, his group ran into the Osage Indians, and was ordered off the land. Someone fired a shot, a fight ensued, and Harrison and all but two of his men were killed in Kansas, far from their mountain destination.

"Our citizens will all rejoice to hear of the death of this noted desperado, who once boasted that he had enough men in hell to form a jury," wrote Thomas Gibson, who remembered Charley from the old days. Thus died one of Denver's early legends, his fate left, one assumes, to that jury in hell.

Whereas Harrison had represented a genuine threat, the varied stories of Texans invading or inciting the Indians never materialized. Chivington and Evans could not afford to ignore the rumors, however, and patrols rode out, probing and seeking. At least one officer, Maj. A. H. Mayer, became greatly upset with Byers and his stubborn persistence in reporting every rumor about marauding "Texians." Such remarks, he believed, threw disbelief on the military effort and "cast a damper on the military ardor of the people preventing recruiting, God Knows we want every man we can get." The much better known Union general, William T. Sherman, would have concurred; he did not get along with the press either.

One of the army's most important tasks, to keep the transportation lanes open and the wagon trains safely moving, occupied much of its time. Although a few people still envisioned an overland steam carriage, its day had come and gone; most Coloradans sneered at the idea now and coveted railroad connections.

Innovative travelers occasionally managed to pick up the pace. Tom Barnes and his party raced from the States in fifteen days with mules in March 1864. Others, like Peter Winne, joined slow-moving wagon trains. After a "sad time parting with our dear ones," Winne and his wife, among others, left Wisconsin for California, only to decide en route to go to Colorado instead. They merged with a larger party and reached Denver in a month and two days. The only disquiet during the trip came from the violation of an agreement not to travel on Sundays. Angered but unwilling to travel in too small a party, Winne's group was forced to comply. After a bout with fever, Winne, who "always had a desire to go farther west," arrived on June 13. Another newcomer had achieved the promised land.

Although Winne's party encountered no hostile Indians or unexpected problems, at the end of the year the *Weekly Commonwealth* reported one wagon train missing and overdue by several weeks. The wagon train's fate was never reported; it probably arrived late in the freighting season.

The army protected all travelers from early spring until winter shut down freighting. The troops also attempted to protect the telegraph lines, which the Indians delighted in tearing down. The line between Julesburg and Denver was completed on October 14; it reached Central a month later. News now reached Colorado from the East in mere minutes (at worst, hours) instead of days or weeks. Increased speed translated into extra expense: a ten-word dispatch to Omaha cost $4.00 and to New York $9.10; each additional word cost sixty-three cents. Coloradans relished the "characteristic progress of this century" and patted themselves on the back for its advent in their territory. The poles and wires framing the prairie landscape tied Colorado more tightly to the Union and marked the triumph of American progress over the frontier's isolation.

Lost wagon trains, stranded pioneers, downed telegraph lines—the army took them all in stride. Occasionally, though, even the seasoned veteran was caught by surprise. Soldiers at the forts and on patrol gawked in disbelief when turkeys trotted past in late spring. The flock, from Iowa and Missouri, managed twenty-five miles a day with tail winds, considerably less with head winds. The birds ate grasshoppers, when available, and shelled corn their owners had brought along when live feed became scarce. The turkeys trotted through Nebraska City in late April and reached Denver on May 30. A pleased William Byers reported that they, along with some geese, had arrived safely stowed away, "like animals in Noah's ark," in a mammoth coop perched over the wagon. The "pilgrims" asked the modest sum of four dollars for each gobbler.

Colorado agriculture had taken firm root, and Byers promoted it as enthusiastically as ever. The novelty had worn off, and Colorado farmers now had a fair idea of what might be grown profitably and what yield should be harvested. They no longer saw the area as the "great American desert," and prudently acknowledged that irrigation proved helpful. Farmers in Jefferson County constructed a system of ditches to water their fields.

Farming and ranching moved steadily eastward, along the river bottoms out onto the plains, portending unlimited future growth. The unblushing Colorado booster, Edward Bliss, concluded from New York that the territory possessed advantages even over Texas, which had "a world-wide reputation in this respect." This encroachment enraged the Indians, however, and gave the army more isolated farms and ranches to protect. The fuse hissed toward a dangerous climax.

Even with all its progress, Colorado was by no means agriculturally self-sufficient. During the snow-locked winter months, food and grain prices soared. Hollister, on January 15 in Black Hawk, commented on the prices—corn, $6.00 a bushel; butter, $1.25 a pound; and hay, $160.00 a ton. "That people still live in Colorado and do business and pay them should convince the most skeptical of the unlimited capabilities of the country." Residents *did* pay, and the farmers prospered enough to keep try-ing to surmount a variable climate, grasshoppers, loneliness, and drought.

John Evans watched over his territory with pride and per-plexity. He understood the conflict with the Indians only too well; less clearly defined was a movement within Colorado to remove him. Dissident parties were attempting to stir up trouble, Evans wrote to Dole, by spreading a rumor that difficulties ex-isted between the two men and with the secretary of the in-terior, John Usher. In an editorial on November 11, an ex-asperated Byers lashed out against the "busybodys" who, through "bigotry, jealousy, prejudice or malice," had been accus-ing Chivington and Evans of forming a "Methodist Clique" to try to run Colorado. Byers, who did not belong to any church, called the accusation "baseless, groundless, unjust, ungenerous and undeserved."

The opinionated editor may have been right, but feelings of an-tipathy persisted. The problem was undoubtedly aggravated by the political climate; the question of statehood was heatedly debated throughout the year. An overabundance of would-be officeholders jockeyed for political plums that would come with admission to the Union.

The shenanigans might have amounted only to academic wool gathering had national Republican leaders not been concerned about the outcome of the upcoming 1864 election. Electoral votes for their presidential candidate and senators would be needed to pass Republican legislation. Congress thus bestirred itself and offered statehood to Colorado, Nebraska, and Nevada. When Congress passed the enabling act in March 1864, the question leaped from the academic realm to the front page. Coloradans had only to frame a constitution and submit it to voter approval. Once done, the political plums became available for plucking. Geographical jealousy resurfaced instantly. Mountain communities aligned themselves against Denver, and newspapers fanned the fires of envy. Golden and Denver squared off, and various groups pushed their favorites for senators, representative, and governor.

Evans, meanwhile, returned to Washington to oversee Colorado's interests, trying in particular to ensure that the transcontinental railroad would go through the territory. The governor, who had a life-long love affair with railroading, marched in the vanguard of those Coloradans who appreciated what the railroad could mean to trade, growth, and promotion. He did everything within his power to win those iron rails, and his determination and energy augured well for Colorado.

Realizing that he needed his own spokesman in the wild world of Colorado politics, Evans (like Gilpin before him) became a silent partner in Gibson's *Commonwealth* in December. To defend themselves and their cherished aspirations, Colorado's political leaders could not afford to undervalue the importance of a friendly press.

Chief Justice Benjamin Hall, however, faced an increasingly hostile press. His overly enthusiastic actions and rash statements during the war's early days, combined with his weak knowledge of mining, alienated Coloradans. In the summer of 1863 this sincere patriot resigned and returned to Auburn, New York, to practice law.

Most Coloradans wore their patriotism a little less pugnaciously than Hall. Many of them, along with Evans, Byers, Chivington, Jerome Chaffee, and Ostrander, joined Union League lodges for an initiation fee of one dollar. According to Ostrander,

. . . every union man should belong to it for there are undoubtedly a good many copperheads in this Territory and all union men should be able to know each other when they meet.

The men held meetings and promoted Union causes. Coloradans, like Americans elsewhere, were willing joiners.

The more enthusiastic ones, especially young men with eyes for young ladies, enrolled in local guard units and mustered and paraded right at home, a preferable alternative to enlisting in the regular army and marching off to war. No unit was more socially prominent than Black Hawk's Elbert Guards, which elected its members! John Ingraham promised, "I shall endeavour to do my duty as a soldier and permit me to say that my motto has been and always will be 'Our Country, may she always be right; but our country right or wrong.'"

Even with that kind of enthusiasm, or perhaps because of it, the guards encountered difficulty in adjusting to military discipline and procedure. The simple matter of arriving at drill on time created a problem. Capt. Frank Hall warned his recruits that talking in rank was strictly prohibited and that they could not enter or leave rank without permission after being mustered in drill. The armorer, Josh Bales, complained that the men took very poor care of their guns and other accoutrements, "all very dirty and some very rusty," and that they continually misplaced bayonets and equipment.

Some recruits resigned from the guards, citing a variety of reasons. Charles Leitzmann said his business made it impossible for him to attend to his duties, and J. V. Jewell worried about the "peculiar state of my financial concerns" (he also complained about being afflicted with frozen feet). H. Pool intended to leave the territory in a day or so. Those who stayed enjoyed their first annual ball in November, the highlight of the year. Black Hawkers mixed war and good times in winning fashion.

The draft, though, continued to cause nightmares. When the federal government passed a national conscription law, it appeared finally that Coloradans would be enrolled. Capt. John Wanless, provost marshal for the First district of Colorado, planned to start the job after attending to organizational details.

No qualifying males (able-bodied citizens, between twenty and forty-five) would be exempt, nor would it be necessary to claim an exemption until after receipt of a printed draft notice.

Knowing full well what had happened back east, Wanless anticipated opposition and made several arrests in July to forestall it. A. F. Freeman, who bragged that he would shoot any Union officer who attempted to take him, promptly ended up in Denver's jail; Wanless went personally to Clear Creek County to arrest him. The captain had no doubt of his ability to enroll men in every part of the territory, once a surgeon and commissioners were appointed and the enforcement of the draft ordered.

Colorado troops, it turned out, were not needed. Fear of the draft quickly subsided as autumn settled over the mountains. Volunteers and draftees in the East alleviated the need to institute conscription in this territory, with all the cost and time outlay the process would entail. Easterners grumbled that the western territories were havens for draft dodgers.

As the cold winter gave way to the spring of 1864, the war in the States entered a new phase. On March 9, President Lincoln handed Ulysses Grant a commission as lieutenant general, a rank newly restored by Congress, and gave him command of the Union armies. Lincoln had finally found his general and proceeded to develop a modern command system to fight a modern war.

Almost immediately, the final grand strategy of the war began to unfold. Grant, backed by numerical superiority, growing economic strength, increased recruiting, and his own willingness to deal sledgehammer blows, plunged ahead against a weakened and reeling Confederacy and its main army, led by the redoubtable Robert E. Lee. Grant's trusted lieutenant, William T. Sherman, made plans to launch a campaign against Atlanta, which was defended by the other major Confederate army in the field. The beginning of the end seemed at hand. What role Colorado would play in this grand strategy was as yet unknown; Colorado Unionists saw only bright days ahead.

9

"To take things easy . . . and live comfortably"

"SUCH EBB AND FLOW must ever be, Then wherefore should we mourn?" wrote Wordsworth a generation before Colorado emerged as a territory. The English poet could not better have summarized circumstances in 1863-64 had he been at Central City among his fellow Englishmen digging out the gold.

Coloradans alternately brooded and bragged that year as mining enthusiasm plummeted from early-decade excitement into valleys of despair and back out again. The dominant downswing showed no favorites; mining district and camp, miner and prospector, buyer and seller—all took their lumps. Maurice Morris, curious to see the country beyond Denver, traveled over to Middle Park. On his way he visited Mammoth City, once the dream of Boston investors, now, in consequence of bad management and poor mining methods, a "failure absolute." Everything salable had been carted off by creditors. On his return trip, Morris stopped by Gold Dirt, which in bygone times had promised great things; now it lay all but deserted.

As much as they would have liked to accentuate the positive, more experienced Colorado observers returned with similar opinions. William Byers, who visited Clear Creek Canyon in September, was struck by the "air of desertion" that surrounded so many villages of "pioneer magnificent expectations." Denver's editor did not have to look far for the apparent cause: Too many people crowded in during the early days, building houses, mills, and towns before knowing whether paying mines existed.

Byers's Black Hawk rival, Ovando Hollister, concurred in this opinion, further noting that in his district people abandoned the outlying camps and concentrated in Central, Nevada, and Black Hawk. A resident of Empire, identified only as Toughcuss, observed that places of "pretentious greatness" only a year or two ago were now so depleted in population and resources that no one remained to bestow reverence.

These reports came from the north and south forks of Clear Creek, the heart of Colorado mining since 1859. The change could be seen everywhere. The legendary poor man's diggings and placer gold, or at worst a windlass and shallow mine, had disappeared. In their place came quartz mining, which was grow, ing ever deeper and more water troubled, becoming increasingly expensive in labor and equipment, producing more complex ore almost by the day, and requiring skills the fifty-niners rarely possessed.

Some of the drifting crowd wandered off to chase their rain, bows elsewhere. "Bannack-on-the-brain" affected many of them as Montana's placer mines took the headlines away from Idaho's Salmon River diggings. Gibson labeled it a "bogus Eldorado," and Byers could only lament, "When will the world grow wiser?"

The answer was probably never. George Kassler explained his motivation to Maria:

I am becoming somewhat infected with what they call here the "Ban, nack Fever," that is the desire to go to some new mines. . . . I rather like the busy activity, and *go ahead aliveness* of a new country and see men grapple with nature in all her wildness, build towns, cities, and open the way for New States.

Kassler did not yield to temptation, but others did.

Former Denver merchant William Kiskadden put philosophical jottings of this kind into perspective when he returned from Ban, nack with seventy-five pounds of gold dust, the profit from a train of goods he had hauled up there. He should have warned about the hard work of finding and developing paying claims, because Colorado miners, down on their luck, could see only his gold.

Colorado's boosters happily noted that "pilgrims" kept coming in the spring and summer of 1863. The numbers never reached those of previous years, but they certainly helped offset the immigration to new discoveries. Coloradans could not shake the haunting idea of "grow or die," and it did not take great perception to realize that the territory's rate of population increase had dwindled to nearly zero percent.

Circumstances changed in other ways, too. The boys of 1859 and 1860 were being replaced by hard-rock miners, investors, and the picket line of corporation mining. Jerome Chaffee and Eben Smith symbolized this trend as they bought, developed, and sold mining properties on their way to building a tidy fortune. From England, via the copper and lead mines of Michigan and Wisconsin, migrated the world's best hard-rock miners, the Cornish. Morris met a "large influx" of his countrymen, "free lancers of the profession." He confidently expected them to improve mining practices.

The Cousin Jacks (as they were nicknamed) and Chaffees of the mining world spoke to the changing times and the future. Pat Casey, on the other hand, personified the fading past. He still mined in the spring of 1863 and typically managed to land in trouble socially when he threatened to pelt Mike Dougherty "with eggs, stones, etc.," if the actor should "attempt to sing the 'Night Hands' at my benefit this evening." Dougherty responded by requesting that Capt. Frank Hall's company of the Elbert Guards attend the event, "armed & equipped prepared to quell any disturbance." On a stormy April evening, the Guards and an overflow crowd attended this farewell benefit for the popular actor.

Casey, back in the States by fall, sold his properties and realized some $50,000. Byers lauded the well-known miner: "He helped business in Nevada and other Gregory towns, during the past two years, more than a regiment of your old fogy order of miners." Casey's hour in Colorado was nonetheless finished. In February a report circulated that he had gone into the tobacco business in New York City, a story possibly designed to pull someone's leg. Edward Bliss, previously of the *News* and now a New Yorker, related that "Mr. Casey's wealth does produce airs." Parlaying his notoriety and in keeping with the tenor of the times, Casey plunged into a successful business in stock and gold speculation. The enterprise fit more precisely his image of himself, as did owning one of the city's finest "turn-outs," which he proudly drove about the streets.

Colorado mining never marched at an even tempo. Casey could have related to the life Samuel Leach led in Sterling City; he had been through it back in 1861. Casey would have been chagrined, however, since Leach never used tobacco in any form. A monotonous diet, especially molasses, did little for his appetite: "I hope I shall never have to use it again when I leave these parts." Burning the candle at both ends, Leach still operated a store for Denver merchant John W. Smith and did "backbreaking work" at a mill when needed.

Sunday gave Leach his only break, and he occasionally walked over to Buckskin Joe to spend the day with his friends, the Tabors. One afternoon he and Horace speculated about their future. "Sam, twenty years from now I shall have enough money to take things easy three months in each year and live comfortably at hotels in New York or Washington." Augusta asserted that they ought to work and save as long as they were able, to provide for their old age. Horace, she added, liked his leisure too well and did not exert himself as fully as he might. One barb led to another, and a full-fledged argument eventually erupted, during which Leach wisely kept his mouth shut.

Despite their frequent combativeness, the Tabors were well liked by Leach: "Each of them has fine qualities and they are good company." Horace, who enjoyed fishing simply for the diversion, was full of fun. Thrifty, hard-working Augusta (a "driver," Leach thought) provided the perfect balance. Even though the men laughed at her, Augusta planned a garden, arguing that she had read about vegetables being raised in the Alps and saw no reason why they could not be raised here. Whether her plan succeeded is uncertain, but a garden undoubtedly would have enhanced her prestige among her boarders. She already raised chickens, two cows (she churned her own butter), and a litter of pigs.

Leach and the Tabors did as well as possible in their district, which was now a year past boom. They dreamed and worked, ordinary people living out their lives in quiet obscurity. Nestled against the backbone of the continent, they strove to make ends meet and, if possible, get ahead.

Inactivity characterized many of Colorado's mining communities. Cache Creek dwindled to three families that winter, and a local resident feared the "horrors of dullness," as winter closed in around him. Wolfe Londoner, still living in almost-abandoned Oro City, expressed hope that the Red Mountain district to the southwest would continue to show promise. Until winter shut down the hydraulic operations near Gold Run and Delaware, miners muddied the Blue River in their efforts to make a living. This form of mining was gaining support among placer miners, and Summit County miners pointed out that if only Denver merchants would stock more hose and pipes, hydraulic mining could take off next season. Still looking backward, A. Hunk, from Parkville, pointed out that "glory hath to a great extent departed" from Georgia Gulch.

Morris was startled when he observed mining's environmental impact on Clear Creek and the surrounding mountains. The landscape looked as if rival armies had disputed every inch of territory and thrown up small earthworks. Stones and debris marked the banks of muddy Clear Creek, and stumps stood in memory of "former tenants." Coloradans had no time for cleanup operations and spent little time worrying about them.

More important issues dominated their thoughts. Would the Tenth Legion Mine continue as a famous producer? Would the bustle and business of 1860 return to Russell Gulch? Should production be reported in cords (a four-by-four-by-eight-foot stack, weighing roughly 7½–10 tons depending on the kind of ore), or simply by tons? Cords had been used for years; newspapers and the general public preferred tons. And what would be the role of coal in Colorado mining? New beds had been reported as far away as the Arkansas River Valley, but the price had jumped to $30 a ton during the winter, before dropping back to the $18–25 level. A sudden January fuel shortage prompted the increase and also led to the gradual disappearance of nearby wood sources.

Romine Ostrander, who took time from soldiering to supplement his income by working as a miner in the Fairplay area, wondered why he had done so. Stiff and tired (softened by the military life), Ostrander found mining every bit as laborious as it had been nearly two years earlier when he quit to enlist. Other miners in Gilpin County feared the bad air that came with deeper shafts and workings. Better ventilation, a simple but somewhat costly and time-consuming solution, threatened profits; owners almost always put money ahead of mine safety.

These attitudes widened the gap between management and labor. Low wages and payment in greenbacks created the most tension. (Blacksmiths in Central City called two short strikes for higher wages, winning one and losing one.) At Gold Run, fiercely independent placer miners struck the ditch company's high water prices of ten to fifteen cents per miner's inch. A compromise was reached of four to eight cents, although some miners pressed for nearly half that amount.

The impetus for curing mining's tedium before the territory suffered irrevocable damage came from the war, in combination with the maxim, attributed to showman P. T. Barnum, that a sucker was born every minute.

Coloradans identified capital as their greatest need. To be successful, a mining region required plentiful ore deposits, good transportation, and money for investment. Colorado provided the natural resources, but money was needed to buy suitable machinery, improve transportation, and solve the riddle of refractory ore. Colorado miners found themselves "pretty generally tied up with a short string," as the saying went; they needed cash.

Money became available, not from the experienced mining state of California, which had invested in the Comstock, but from the East. Easterners were prospering. Seldom in this century had times been so good, thanks to a war-honed economy. Government contracts enriched all segments of the Northern economy, and profits needed to be invested. Paper money and inflation threatened to eat away some of those profits—unless a dependable, safe, and profitable investment could be found. Nothing appeared safer than a gold mine to naïve easterners.

Colorado had plenty of mines, especially around the well-publicized mining community of Central City. In the summer of 1863, as Union armies slogged toward the victorious turning point of the war, Colorado mines increasingly competed with war-front news for readers' attention.

Yet another blessing was bestowed upon this territorial Garden of Eden. The price of gold, though it fluctuated, eventually rose to its highest point in the nation's history. What more could an investor ask?

Speculators promptly forgot the war in favor of gold. Greenbacks declined in value, and one paper dollar was worth approximately thirty-five cents in gold. New York's stock market heated up; speculation in gold and mining stock had become the royal road to wealth. Buy low, sell high, make a killing. Before the frenzy subsided, New York brokers had organized a gold exchange, with a gold exchange bank as its adjunct.

Coloradans welcomed eastern capital, and some miners even sold out their operations and turned them over to outsiders. Men who had little ready cash of their own were finally able to realize their dreams of 1859.

Easterners fell right in with the plan, a perfect marriage of cash and mines. With science, suitable machinery, and efficient business methods, they could solve the problems that had daunted these unenlightened westerners. Pat Casey, who arrived on the New York scene in August, helped cement the image of the rather artless Coloradan.

As summer drew to a close, more and more Coloradans and their agents ventured east to test their luck at tempting investors. Easterners listened, sampled, and leaped. Suddenly any hole in the ground had become a bona fide gold mine. Every claim marker hid the next bonanza. Residents of Central City and Black Hawk had never before had such good luck. They didn't need Santa Claus that Christmas—the Gregory Lode was selling for $400 per foot, and some investors paid up to $2,000 per foot.

Cagey Ovando Hollister foresaw bogus companies emerging among legitimate ones, yet even he could see no lasting harm in the new system. Subsequent problems would be the fault of the operators, not the mines themselves.

Thomas Gibson surveyed the mountains a fortnight before the

holidays and noted with great pleasure the manifest desire on the part of eastern capitalists to invest: "We are safe in saying that capital and labor is all that is required to prove, not only Clear Creek County, but Colorado, to be one of the richest mineral regions yet developed." Coloradans, who had envisioned this development for so long, were overwhelmed.

New York and Boston investors clamored to buy property in Colorado and eagerly devoured the numerous mining pamphlets that flooded the market. Easterners were convinced of the abundance and inexhaustibility of Colorado's gold reserves and believed that ore grew richer with depth. They were confident that they could solve all of Colorado's mining problems, and phrases such as "easily worked," "favorably situated," "first-class property," "very promising," and "high assays" suffered from overuse. Nearly identical testimonials from so-called mining experts sometimes appeared in two or more pamphlets; they were read and trusted.

Samuel Barlow, in New York, received private communications refuting much of the published material. Rotund, *bon vivant* Barlow, one of the best corporation lawyers of the day, had invested in mining and, being the shrewd businessman he was, had determined to keep abreast of local developments. His Colorado agents warned him about bogus claims and titles not "worth a damn," which were being offered by "infernal rascals." At least one agent pointed his finger at investors for pushing up the price in their rush to wealth. "I can assure you that they all tend to enhance the *prices* of lode claims if it does not enhance their value." As he digested these reports, keeping the information secret, Barlow must have watched with barely suppressed amusement the activities of some of his uninformed, overly cocky rivals.

Bela Buell, Gilpin County clerk and recorder, hired a large force of clerks to work day and night recording claims, abstracts, deeds of transfer, and other related documents. The telegraph wires nearly burned up as mining messages flooded the office and the keys seldom fell silent. Individual bills of fifty to three hundred dollars showed how far the mania had carried frenzied investors.

On the stock exchanges, Colorado-based companies found investors eagerly subscribing—even oversubscribing—their stock. And the price of gold against greenbacks kept rising.

More claims were located or refiled upon; miners who thought their claims worthless now discovered them to be hot items. Full-scale mining and prospecting awaited only the coming of warm days. Gold speculators had a ravenous appetite, and an anticipated feast of such magnitude attracted scoundrels from all directions.

Frank Hall (who had gone to Black Hawk to mine) gave up mining and joined Hollister in the *Daily Mining Journal*. They were alarmed by March over the potential for fraud.

Those who have the true interest of Colorado at heart, will uniformly frown on all attempts to swindle parties in the East by selling at enormous figures property which has no known existence, outside the Recorder's Office.

They trusted that wildcat speculations would "stick to the fingers" of those who tampered with them, to "burn like Greek fire."

Edward Bliss, in contrast, saw only good times coming and jumped on the bandwagon by publishing a pamphlet, *A Brief History of the New Gold Regions of Colorado Territory*. He promoted the idea that sturdy muscle, prompted by intelligence and common sense, was necessary to win a fortune in Colorado. Of more importance, he stated that since the war began Colorado had produced a steadily increasing amount of gold, from one million dollars to six million, then to fifteen million last year, and he estimated twenty million dollars for 1864. And these figures represented returns only at the Philadelphia mint. He hinted that the numbers were lower than what was actually mined, because not all the gold was sent to Philadelphia. Bliss was probably right, since Governor Evans complained that same March to the mint's superintendent that Colorado gold had been credited to Idaho, a practice he wanted stopped. The figures more than evened out, however, because the enthusiastic Bliss overestimated production. More conservative estimates later placed total production at 9½ million dollars for these three years.

Bliss opened an office to facilitate immigration to the territory.

When an unenthusiastic Colorado legislature refused to appropriate money for his endeavor, he closed shop.

By April agents had inundated Gilpin County, buying anything
and everything. The *Journal* (April 5) had this to say:

Never in the history of the country did the excitement of mining
speculation run so high as at present. Men are every day receiving
windfalls in the shape of receipts from the sales of claims to Eastern
capitalists.

Hollister and Hall warned that this "state of things is unhealthy."
Others were not so pessimistic, especially since the price of gold
had broken the $170 barrier ($2.70 in paper money purchased
$1.00 in gold).

The *New York Tribune* warned would-be stock buyers to find
out who was selling and managing the enterprise. The admonition did little good. The next morning, April 7, the demand for
stock exceeded any previous demands on Wall Street. When the
New York Gold Mining Company of Colorado opened its books,
it was oversubscribed within a few minutes by forty thousand
shares. Property changed hands in frenzied activity. The Bobtail
Lode brought one thousand dollars a foot. Stock was frantically
sold and purchased as companies started sending machinery west, along
with managers to oversee their investments. In these overheated
days, Colorado was making its first major impact on the eastern
stock market.

George Kassler could not believe the fabulous prices that gold
was attracting. On April 11 he wrote Maria that a few days
earlier a poor private in the army had received six thousand
dollars for his share of some property sold.

Colorado and New York waltzed to a speculative dance of
wealth as the third year of the war closed. This was the West
most Coloradans had imagined.

Back in August 1863, before the current frenzy had begun,
Nathaniel Keith had written his parents from Black Hawk that
the gold was there; "they dig this 'root of all evil' out of the
ground." Colorado had the gold ore but, as Keith intimately
knew, had not yet developed the process to mill it successfully.

Perhaps it was with prophetic insight that Keith saw gold as the "root of all evil" for Colorado. At the moment, most of his contemporaries heartily rejected his gloom. Their philosophy consisted of sitting back, enjoying, and prospering—the day of the jubilee was at hand. No, not the day, but as Henry Clay Work's popular tune suggested, the "Year of Jubilo." Prosperity had finally come, and with it the prospects of a glorious 1864. Talk of ebbing fortunes and threatening rivals was forgotten as Colorado rushed toward a long-promised future.

10

"The money is not in the hands of Christians"

BY THE SUMMER of 1863 the full reality of living in Colorado with her brothers hit Ellen Coffin:

I would sometimes have such a longing for my eastern home and friends that I could hardly overcome the weakness, if it can be called such and prove myself a worthy pioneer. I was careful that the boys should not know how homesick I really was, but there were many days when I would begin to cry as soon as they left the house in the morning for the field and keep up my weeping until I saw them coming for dinner when I would wash my eyes so they would not know.

Ellen's homesickness was shared by many. Life on the frontier, even four years after the rush, still meant a lack of most of the amenities enjoyed in the East. And for Ellen, life on the farm in Colorado differed not a whit from life on the farm anywhere in the Midwest or West: early rising, long hours of hard work, and loneliness for the women. Mining's urbanism and increased tempo had little impact on her daily routine.

Ellen eventually broke out of her farm-locked life by accepting a teaching position in Boulder in September. Warned by the outgoing teacher, who felt sorry for her enthusiastic replacement, that this was a very difficult school, Ellen did not flinch: "I was full of courage and eager for the work I loved so well." She needed all that courage and more to deal with the conditions she recorded in her diary on the fifth: "The school is undisciplined, the schoolhouse dirty, window lights broken, blackboards nearly paintless, and almost every pupil has a different kind of book."

Standing firm, she persuaded the boys and girls to remain after school to clean the premises and believed she had made a good start with her twenty-five pupils. As winter approached, more of the older boys came to school, bringing enrollment to nearly fifty. Some of these latecomers, older and larger than their teacher, proved harder to manage than "Hottentots of Africa." For this endeavor, Ellen received one dollar a day and board at the homes of her students' parents, the usual custom of the time. She enjoyed herself as she had not since coming west, "I found so many friends."

Boulder's school term lasted until April 1; Black Hawk's ended a couple of days later with a "charming exhibition." Proud parents sat through three hours of original compositions, selected readings, songs, declamations, and short comedies in the first of what the reporter trusted would be many "long and successful school exhibitions in our thriving mountain village." Nothing but praise rained down on John Schellenger and Miss Batchelder, the teachers, who received $55 and $44 per month, respectively.

Not only was Miss Batchelder not identified by a first name, but neither did she receive equal pay, the fate of most women in American society. Each year a few women broke out of the mold, which was always easier to do in the West than in the more tradition-bound East. Sarah Slate was assistant principal of the Nevada school ("one of the best in the mountains"), and Ada Laurent, a danseuse at the Montana Theater, opened a "select" dancing school in Central. With some years of teaching experience behind her, she guaranteed to "perfect" in twelve lessons. Denver's Miss L. E. Miller was the sole Colorado agent for Wheeler and Wilson sewing machines and advertised a thorough education in the use of them, gratis, to all purchasers. Husbands could buy one for their wives for $65, $85, or $100, according to size. In June, Henriette Brenner promoted herself as a midwife, but by January she informed the ladies of Gilpin County that she could provide the professional services of an *accoucheuse* (midwife) and ladies' nurse. She proudly claimed to have studied at Heidelberg University.

Most women labored as housewives and mothers. Their activities outside the home were usually limited to the church.
Margaret Evans and the Methodist women of Denver raised
about four hundred dollars for their Sunday school by staging a
program that featured tableaux and recitations. Charity and
church constituted two acceptable outlets for women's efforts.

Lively and pretty Maggie, as her husband John called her, had
arrived in November 1862. She was in a "family way" and gave
birth to her second son in June. The Evanses lived in a small,
brick house at the corner of Fourteenth and Arapahoe. The
house was nothing like the ones Margaret had known in Evans-
ton, Illinois, the Evanses's former home. Determined to make the
best of the situation, she worked to smooth the rough edges of
her adopted home.

Although some people still complained about a shortage of the
"fairer sex," women seemed to be more abundant now. Romine
Ostrander, who had been in the territory for several years, noted
in his diary (July 26) that Denver projected a much more cheerful
aspect now that he met women almost as often as men on the
streets. The same held true in Central, where Leob and Hatten-
back opened a Ladies' Ice Cream Saloon opposite the People's
Theatre. They promised it would be second to none in the territory for ice cream, confectioneries, and other refreshments.
Calling ladies the "real ornament" of Central, Maurice Morris
tipped his hat to them for making "these rough places of the
earth" feel the power of refinement and civilization.

The fashion writer of the *New York Express* recommended that
ladies wear short dresses (the "style") scalloped around the edge
and worn over "balmorial jupens" of sufficient length to display
kid boots. An alternative was a skirt looped up, at every seam,
nearly to the knee and showing a colored petticoat of mohair,
cashmere, or silk; one should definitely *not* wear a trailing dress
or long petticoat, which were "out." That the *Weekly Commonwealth* (October 15) printed such an article showed how far
Colorado had progressed since 1859. Even Byers got into the act
in March, describing how skating hats appeared to be the
fashionable rage. Pity there "isn't a Central Park," he noted.

Denverites were becoming fashion conscious, and Clara Witter wrote her mother that "they dress here the same as in the States. . . . There are a great many aristocrats here that put on a great deal of style." Women had not left their fashion instincts behind, and now, for the first time, Colorado's life-style allowed them to indulge themselves in the latest trends. To a lesser degree, men could do the same, though their styles simply did not change much during the war years. Now that fashion had arrived, other social refinements could not be far behind.

For Nancy Hezlep, the changes came too late. She died on the fourteenth anniversary of her wedding, that day when she had "jumped over the broom stick," as the event was described. Nancy left behind a sorrowing husband and three "bright and beautiful little girls."

New mother Sara Hively repeated often in her diary her thankfulness that sickly baby Arthur was improving, though slowly. She had feared he might die from a bout of chicken pox, followed by a sore throat. Although the boy rallied, he remained a constant worry to his mother, who prayed, "dear father in heaven help me to bring up my little one aright."

Parents could not protect their offspring from childhood ill-nesses, and when sickness struck, they relied on medicine or home remedies. An "infallible remedy" for that terrible "child destroyer," diphtheria, recommended that ice be administered in small pieces. Sometimes nothing helped; the Jell family, in Nevada, lost two children in a couple of days and barely saved two others.

On a cheerier note, Nathaniel Keith wrote his parents that his wife, Anna, and their daughter had joined him. The family did not enjoy the luxuries of the East, but they were making themselves very cozy and comfortable, especially appreciating a climate that was too cool for flies, "mosketoes," or bedbugs. They wanted no more of the sweltering summer days of Penn-sylvania; the new environment had done wonders for Anna's health.

Daniel Witter was equally determined to provide his growing family with the comforts of life, now that they had moved out of the mountains to Denver. They occupied a new house, "larger and better furnished" than they had ever lived in before. Sound-

ing a familiar refrain, he wrote his mother that it "cost me considerably more than I intended to spend on it when I commenced." Daniel paid about $1,100 for the house and lots.

Edward Seymour thought so highly of Colorado that he
brought his family out in the spring, despite the fact that he had
not achieved much success back in 1861. The family journeyed to
Oro City, now a greatly depressed community. Seymour's ten-
year-old son, Bennett, reveled in his new surroundings, even
though few other children lived nearby for him to play with. His
parents kept Madison House, and Bennett learned to play crib-
bage, becoming, in his words, an "expert for my age." The only
dark cloud to shadow his youthful life came when his pet dog
died after eating some poisoned bait left out for wolves.

The Seymours never recaptured the life Edward remembered
from an earlier time; Oro City had long since passed its prime.
The days of prospecting were fast disappearing in camps and mining districts throughout Colorado. A wistful affection for those
"young days" (one might be tempted to call it nostalgia) had
already begun to soften images of the past.

The boys of 1860, wrote a miner from Bull's Bar in Clear Creek
County, were an unpoetic lot, except for the names they left
behind on sites and structures. The perturbed writer wanted
more respect for those "ancient {man-made} land marks," many of
which were disappearing, Denver's Cibola Hall being a case in
point. Fondly remembered as a "female buffalo" hall, the building
was sold and moved. The famous Criterion became a boardinghouse. Mlle Carolista, once a star performer there, thrilled
crowds in St. Louis with her lofty tightrope ascension on
September 4, 1863. It seemed like only yesterday she had performed in Denver. The notorious George Harrison was now
rumored to hold a position on Robert E. Lee's staff. So the old
order gave way, merging into history.

Following his destiny, William Crawford raced to Colorado to
save souls. A field agent for the American Home Missionary
Society, Massachusetts-born Crawford settled in Central City,
where he organized the first Congregational church in the territory and reconnoitered for other potential congregations.

Fervor collided headlong with reality. Dedication alone saved poor Crawford from his moments of despondency. He observed dejectedly that "very few intend to make a permanent residence. They mean to get their 'pile,' they say, and then go back to 'the states.'" This fact of frontier life made Crawford's work that much harder. Fated to learn from experience, he sadly concluded, "we depend on nothing but uncertainty."

Crawford informed his home office that it would "have to pay a large portion of their [the missionaries] support. We cannot live here on a small salary, and the people cannot pay us a large one. The money is not in the hands of Christians, and we cannot get it from others." The people had no conscience with respect to their obligations to a minister, Crawford lamented. Amos Billingsley, after all his troubles, would have empathized; he went back east to become a military chaplain.

In his inexperience, Crawford sometimes despaired unnecessarily. The Christians had funds and, more important, the determination to put down roots. Black Hawk and Central had Episcopal, Presbyterian, Catholic, Methodist, Congregational, and Universalist services. And Black Hawk proudly watched as the Reverend George Warner, formerly of Rochester, New York, guided his people through a building program; by October they had the only church with a steeple in the territory. These Presbyterians had done well. William Muir, editor of the *Colorado Miner*, praised them: "Nothing speaks so well for the financial prosperity and morals of our people as the erection of a church."

Methodists, meanwhile, had difficulty getting their church off the ground in neighboring Central. They paid for the lot and graded the foundation, then fell to wrangling about how donated money was being used. Pastor William Fisher finally wrote a letter to the paper explaining the expenses and pointing out that church books were open for inspection. Methodists had more fun in Quartz Valley at an "old fashioned" camp meeting in mid-July, which included preaching by Bishop Edward Ames, one of the most "able public orators in America." Ames lived up to his advance billing.

Methodists in Denver endeavored to raise money to establish a seminary, which they at first envisioned as more a high school than a college. Other churches made do with whatever was available. The former deputy postmaster general of Jamaica, Maurice Morris (who seemed to venture everywhere) went one Sunday to an Episcopal service at a theater in Central. The location surprised him, though not as much as seeing "sitting in the conventional sofa of the stage . . . my Lord Bishop magnificent in his robes, and with him of course an assistant priest." The choir sang extremely well and the sermon, a temperate and charitable defense of the "formulas of the church," was delivered to a fairly well-filled theater.

For Central Citians who did not attend church (to hear ministers tell it, that meant the majority), Sunday bore no resemblance to the traditional Sabbath. Main Street and the red-light district thrived on the business of customers whose only day off was Sunday. Entertainment challenged hell fire and damnation for men's attention; although women had made inroads, it remained a man's world.

Criticism did nothing to diminish the lure of the red-light district, which continued to make a profit and generate news in the police courts as *nymphes du pavé*, drunks, and others paid their fines. Mollie Martin anted up for keeping a house of ill fame, and several of "Aunt Betsy's girls" paid the price for fighting. Aunt Betsy, who had been driven out of Atchison the previous summer, ran one of Denver's most disgraceful establishments. After a soldier was killed there, a large crowd gathered, set fire to the house, and allowed nothing to be removed. Civic morality, disguised as a vigilante outburst, temporarily curbed the district's worst elements.

Most establishments did not descend to Aunt Betsy's level. Saloons flourished everywhere in Colorado without social stigma. In one respect, they even got better—the rotgut sold to customers in early years gave way to liquor improved in variety and quality. Black Hawk's John Warner and Company, for example, served bourbon, rye, Scotch, and Mon'gehela whiskey, as well as St. Croix and Jamaica rum, champagne, wine, brandies, bitters, and gin.

Public drunkenness, or being "on it," was frowned upon by a growing segment of the community as being a bad example and detrimental to the local image. Those who drained the intoxicating cup were admonished to remember "the home and friends they have left behind" and to consider the consequences should a "report of their debaucheries" reach there. Woe, too, to the saloon keeper who did not take out or renew a license—a grand jury indictment might await him.

These temptations only added to the difficulty of raising children in a frontier environment. Boys appeared to be more susceptible and required more watching. The carrot-and-stick approach prevailed as the approved method of keeping them in line: "But who would not prefer to have her child influenced to good conduct by the desire of pleasing, rather than by a fear of offending." Parental example and encouragement of good behavior sometimes had to be supplemented by the rod. Yet even in the best-regulated young lives, a monotonous day could tempt beyond resistance; a slingshot and an inviting target often brought out the worst in the "little shavers."

If youthful antics became epidemic, the sheriff had to intercede. A good scolding or spanking usually ended the trouble for the moment. Gilpin County Sheriff William Cozens probably wished that children's misbehaviors were the worst of his problems. His more pressing duties included serving judgments, checking out complaints of bogus greenbacks, corralling drunks, curbing the dog surplus, arresting speeding drivers and riders, seizing attached property, and pursuing accused criminals.

Gilpin County actually faced only two serious law-and-order problems that year, one a riot, the other a murder. The riot started harmlessly enough with a broken window. The owner complained and an officer tried to make an arrest—the ordinary procedure in such cases. Unfortunately, the officer was the only one involved in the dispute who was not Irish. Friends of the guilty party "beat and bruised" the lawman severely, which prompted others to jump into the fray, including some nearby soldiers. The riot exploded.

Pat Casey, watching all the action, shouted that the Irishman should not be taken, and in mounting anger bellowed he could "whip any d——d soldier son of a b——h." Not satisfied, he roared over the rising din, "I don't care a d——n for Uncle Sam's soldiers or for United States laws." Perhaps he envisioned himself back in Ireland and thought the hated British had reappeared. His taunts inflamed the soldiers, and they promptly seized Casey, who yell-ed to a bystander to fetch his mining hands to "liberate" him.

Sheriff Cozens attempted to take Casey, but Lt. Sam Peppard, the officer with the troops, refused to give him up, claiming this to be a military matter. When it looked as if civilian and military justice would come to blows, calmer heads prevailed and the mat-ter was dropped.

Casey's men, meanwhile, hied themselves down from Nevada in a surly mood and arrived with mayhem on their minds. Less than a week ago they had been bluffed out of preventing Mike Dougherty from singing his "Night Hand," and they planned to avenge that embarrassment. Finding that their employer would not be released, the men took to the streets, behaving riotously, according to the paper. Over the uproar shots were heard, and one of Casey's men fell wounded, another killed. Attracted by the noise and shouting, locals flocked to the scene, and the fracas threatened to turn uglier. To defuse the escalating crisis, all saloons were ordered closed. The Elbert Guards mustered to pro-tect the jail posthaste and finally, at dusk, the people were told to disperse and clear the streets. Grumbling and issuing threats, Casey's "nocturnal employees" wandered off.

When Peppard again refused to turn over either the prisoner or the key to the jail, a judge ordered Cozens to arrest the officer. Fortunately, Chivington happened to be in town, and he and Peppard discussed the situation. Those who hoped he might bring sanity to the situation misjudged their man; the colonel ap-proved Peppard's actions and recommended a promotion. An ac-ceptable compromise was eventually worked out, and within twenty-four hours, after all his bombast, Casey took the oath of allegiance and was released.

The newly freed rabble-rouser requested that the *Tri-Weekly Miners' Register* print that he did not say "son of a bitch," claim-ing he never used such language, and that he had never said he "did not care for United States laws." The reporter countered by stating that though he had not personally heard Casey's words, he had received his information from a reliable source.

In the aftermath of the donnybrook, Dan Griffin was given a memorable funeral. His friends formed a procession a quarter mile in length on the way to the cemetery. The inquest a week later justified the killing as self defense. The *Register*, hoping to avoid a recurrence of the violence, stated, "Who was most to blame, it is not our province to say." In a sense, this event marked Casey's farewell to Central City.

The other cause célèbre occurred without Casey's help. Passion, jealousy, and greed prompted William Van Horn to kill Josiah Copeland in a dispute over Nancy Squires on October 17. Van Horn and Squires were partners in the Bobtail Exchange at Gregory Point, where she ran the house and he kept the bar. Nancy, who left her husband in Kansas to come west with Van Horn, had been out walking with the well-respected Copeland, either as a lure for the age-old badger game or in actual friendship. Van Horn intercepted them, an argument ensued, and Copeland was shot. Caught up in the tragedy, Nancy pointed to her paramour as the murderer.

Emotions heated and Cozens barely kept his prisoner from being lynched. Hollister believed that only the high personal regard in which the sheriff was held allowed the law to prevail. The trial took place; Van Horn was found guilty and sentenced to death. Moved to Denver after his friends tried to smuggle a knife into his cell, Van Horn was returned to Gilpin County on December 17, escorted by a squadron of Company D, First Colorado. The next day, in front of two thousand or so people, he "died game," refusing to confess, dying as he had lived, "a hardened man."

Nancy, not implicated in the murder, had boarded a stage late in November and returned to the States. Public opinion had already convicted her, however, and her escape to freedom was deemed highly unfair. Despite her faults, she must have possessed considerable personal magnetism. Even though her confession put him on the gallows, Van Horn remained "perfectly infatuated" with her to the last. Reviewing the whole sordid affair, David Collier described a positive aspect when he wrote in the *Daily Mining Record* (December 19) that the trial and hanging proved law had gained ascendancy in the territory. Henceforth, mob or lynch law must end. A few weeks later, Van Horn gained a certain infamy by having a likeness and a sketch of his life published in New York's *Police Gazette* tabloid.

Publicity of that kind did little to enhance the territory's reputation. Nor did morbid public interest in the Van Horn case. One Central City youth of eight or ten summers built a scaffold and played hangman, using a piece of wood for the condemned!

These episodes aside, Colorado had matured into a more lawabiding territory. The newsworthiness of violence created a false impression of its significance and frequency. Minor crimes did not disappear, but robbery (such as an incident at Joe Block's meat market in Black Hawk) and Saturdaynight rowdyism simply did not attract headlines and public interest the way murder and horse stealing did.

Fire, not crime, created headlines in Denver. Around 1:00 A.M. on a windy Sunday morning (April 19), the longfeared catastrophe struck. Cries of "Fire!" soon awoke most Denverites, who fought "like heroes" to stop it. The "great fire" did at least $350,000 in damage, consuming the heart of the young city and leaving scores of homeless and ruined businessmen. A heartsick George Kassler described the scene as "desolute" the next morning; a number of people had lost almost everything they owned. Undaunted, Denver rebounded "like a tiger."

Temporary buildings were moved into the burnedout district within twentyfour hours, and Byers saw, through the smoke, better quality buildings emerging from the ashes. Amid the ruins and desolation, a new downtown was destined to arise.

Denverites exhibited their spunk and determination in rebuilding. Although few people carried insurance, Kassler proudly noted that, unlike "most any other place," no one begged for assistance or accepted money raised at two benefit concerts. Unfortunately, talk of creating a fire company died faster than Denver rebuilt. Byers fumed when the "Rip Van Winkles of the City Council," six weeks later, still procrastinated in purchasing muchneeded fire equipment. Denver folks, in general, soon forgot the "great fire" and the lessons it should have taught; by fall newspapers were again warning them about the consequences of their astonishing carelessness.

Kassler, Byers, and other dedicated Denverites saw nothing in curably wrong with their budding gateway metropolis. Others complained incessantly about the muddy streets, the too hot summers, and the isolation from the civilized world. William Crawford blistered the locals and town, charging that "some of the Denverites think they have found the best spot on earth. Poor, deluded mortals!" Denver, he wrote to his board, reminded him of a Watts hymn: "Lord, what a wretched land is this, which yields us no supply, no cheering fruits, no wholesome trees, no streams of living joy."

The news in Black Hawk, Nevada, and Central was dominated by a movement to unite the three towns. Central Citians favored the plan, but Nevada responded, "We neither want nor will have it." A group of Black Hawk citizens met and vehemently opposed the idea as being unjust, inexpedient, inconvenient, and simply a ploy by Central to ruin Black Hawk. Needless to say, the idea was squelched.

Still enthusiastic about organizationalism, Central City then moved to incorporate and adopted a city charter in March that established a council and mayor. This step showed a refreshing willingness by the city's residents to be taxed, a growing faith in the permanence of their community, and the intent to put down roots near their plunging mine shafts.

Black Hawk moved in the same direction, albeit more slowly. Crawford dismissed the mountain towns as merely places to make money and went about his business. Ed Bliss, on the other hand, visited those same towns in August before leaving for New York and saw only progress, change, and the "promising and dazzling future of Colorado."

Visitors' preconceptions about Colorado commonly conflicted with their on-site impressions. Empire, which had been such a hit the previous year and continued to be newsworthy, did not impress Maurice Morris on his travels. The only signs that a city existed, according to him, were about a dozen mean log huts and a few frame houses. He did not like Golden either, a wooden town raised by speculators. Gibson concurred somewhat with Morris, commenting that Golden was noted for its "brilliant expectations." Part of his attitude reflected resentment that Golden had stolen the capital away from Denver.

Coloradans relished having their territory mentioned by the outside press, even if only briefly, which was usually the case. Whenever a reference was made, residents were convinced that the corner had been turned and the great day of recognition was at last at hand. Except for the gold excitement, the territory had warranted little news during the past few years. Coloradans were better informed about their neighbors in Utah than the Mormons were about Colorado, if the few items in the *Deseret News* can serve as a guide.

But Utah did not have a boxing champion. Con Orem's exploits continued to attract attention from the East, even though he lost a fight or two (one to a "dirty poltroon, a dastard, and a thief," who did not fight honestly). The popular sporting journal of the day, the *New York Clipper*, followed Orem's tour and matches. The return of the "Colorado Champion," now the "American Champion," was hailed in April by the "town of his pioneer adoption." Even though the *News* still opposed prize fights, John Condle Orem earned the paper's accolades. Young Colorado could match the best of the East when it came to Con, a gentleman and "old citizen."

The *Clipper*, besides covering boxing, billiards, rowing, horse racing, cricket, and baseball, provided a look at the seamier side of life. Among its advertisements were "curious books for curious people [books on love and mock love], Parisian Cartes de Viste, Love-A-La-Mode [catalogues of books, etc.] and Seekers of pleasure—'La Decalcomanie.' " The less sensually inclined could purchase cures for chewing and smoking tobacco ("to be saved from emaciation & insanity"), an unguent guaranteed to grow whiskers or moustaches in six weeks, and dogs and game fowls. In addition, the *Clipper* was a profitable weekly seller for local businessmen. The public paid 6¢ per issue, wholesalers paid 4¢, and retail agents were charged 4½¢, a nice markup for the seller.

Whether Moffat sold the *Clipper* in his improved and enlarged store is not known. He did, however, help George Kassler open a business similar to his own in the summer of 1863, apparently not fearing inroads into his profits. Kassler, who longed to marry Maria, still considered himself economically unready. He had lived with his friends, the Moffats, since soon after their marriage and had grown tired of boarding and "batching." When the Mof-fats went east for a visit, Kassler wrote Maria in April 1864 that again he had fallen to the mercy of hotels for his "grub."

William Loveland also traveled east that April, going to New York and Boston to lay in a stock of goods and, coincidentally, to seek a market for some of his "valuable gold claims." To furnish proof of Colorado's wealth, Central City's Joe Thatcher sent 430 ounces of gold to Denver on December 7. A Coloradan since 1860, former Kentuckian Thatcher now worked at the branch banking house of Warren Hussey and Company; he had formerly been in the mercantile business. His gold shipment not only created a stir in both communities but also helped fuel the East's growing interest in Colorado mining, perhaps even helping Loveland's sales pitch. Thatcher did not concern himself with promoting the mining speculation, however, and continued about his banking business.

Another persevering go-getter, X. Beidler, ended his freighting business to California Gulch and left Colorado for Bannack City to try his luck in the new mines. Trying to freight to Washington Gulch the past couple of seasons had nearly "busted" him. Jerome Chaffee, moving steadily ahead in mining and politics, suf-fered a personal setback when his sister died in Denver. So it was that during this, the third year of the war, some found success, others disappointment, regardless of the fortunes of the battle-field.

Coloradans welcomed the June arrival of noted artist Albert Bierstadt, who reportedly planned a great painting of Colorado. He sketched in the mountains above Idaho Springs, then moved on to Salt Lake on a trip that would take him to the West Coast. A few Coloradans grumbled about the coming of Fitz-John Porter, a former Union general. Porter had recently been court-martialed, found guilty, and dismissed from the service. A Democrat and friend of George McClellan, Porter had become embroiled in the intrigue and political crosscurrents of Washington and the Army of the Potomac. Now, militarily ruined, he had come west to examine mines and mining opera-tions as an agent for Easterners.

Much to the chagrin of Hollister, Frank Hall, and others, one of

the superpatriotic territorial legislators introduced a resolution
giving Porter thirty days to get out of Colorado. Though it attracted some attention, this "piece of buncombe" was pigeon-
holed, to Hollister's immense relief. Bliss, in New York, warned
that such a resolution would not injure Porter and might even
deter investment. That possibility disturbed Coloradans more
than any moral indignation over what Porter might or might not
have done.

Other individuals and institutions, including the once-thriving
Colorado theater, had their troubles, too, which reflected as
much as anything the end of flush mining days. Despite rumors
that they might be breaking up, Langrishe and Dougherty continued to bring the best theater to the territory, though they had
to reduce the size of their troupe. The popular *Our American
Cousin* and *Hamlet* continued to draw praise from the public and
press, but the applause was waning, and by spring Langrishe was
considering a move to Idaho.

Then came the announcement that Artemus Ward, the man
who made Lincoln and most other Americans laugh, was coming
to Colorado. Ward was "a comic cuss wet or dry in public or private." He packed them in at a dollar a seat in Central and Denver
for better than an hour's presentation that featured several
topics, "but nary topic was dwelt upon to any alarming extent."
Then, in March, he boarded the stage for Atchison and the
world beyond, leaving Coloradans in a somewhat happier mood.
Those who missed his performances could read his comic stories,
which appeared regularly in the newspapers.

Thirty-seven-year-old Alonzo Boardman missed most of these
diversions during his brief sojourn in Colorado. He did, however,
convey to his wife, Nancy, back in Wisconsin some interesting insights into life around him. Working in Lump Gulch at Quartz
City, some six miles north of Central ("nary a house except one
miner's cabin"), he found himself far from the focus of Colorado
happenings. Nevertheless, this perceptive Pennsylvanian observed much of interest.

Boardman arrived tired and sick with rheumatism on July 3.
But because he was "just from the States" and one of the proprietors of the Lump Gulch Mill Company, he became an instant
attraction at the July Fourth celebration in neighboring Gold

Dirt. He went to the ball and danced "with a dozen mountain maids—all married," he reassuringly wrote Nancy, adding that he "suffered tremendously."

Unlike most of his contemporaries, who thought only in terms of mining, Boardman looked to lumbering for his fortune. "As good as money," he believed it to be, despite the time-consuming, hard work involved. Boardman oversaw the entire operation, from cutting to sawing to hauling into Central, where the company had a lumber yard. It "takes all my time and attention to keep everything in running order," he lamented; breakdowns and repairs monopolized his waking hours in July and early August.

He liked the country, he told Nancy, yet did not think it would do for his family: "If we only had schools here I should think very strongly of bringing you all here next spring." In a couple of August letters, Boardman observed:

We are nearer heaven than you poor souls in the lower states, but I can't say that we are any more spiritual. Indeed I fear that religion here is very much diluted. . . . Sunday at 11 A.M. the stores are all open, trading brisk, the billiard rooms & lager beer saloons are in full blast.

Mrs. H. has been indulging in her intemperance for months past until like a Dutch Uncle I told her to discard morphine and if she must get drunk anyhow to take whiskey as it less injury to mind and body, and she has finally broke off again, but she had a terrible time of it and made everybody miserable in the house.

Few of Boardman's contemporaries mentioned drug problems, a topic genteel Victorians did not discuss. Pushed under the rug as it was (along with alcoholism among women), the problem did not go away.

Unfortunately for Boardman, lumbering profits did not materialize, and his partner proved untrustworthy. Finally, in November, he returned home to Wisconsin and Nancy. He hoped, when all his Colorado property was sold, to have enough money to pay his debts, which was why he had gone west in the first place.

One anxiety of Coloradans this year was resolved advantageously—the long-awaited branch mint swung into operation, though for the time being it only assayed and bought gold, shipping it elsewhere for coining. A stir was created in February

when an employee stole gold bars and treasury notes worth approximately $37,000. The theft especially astounded Denverites,
because James Clarke, the guilty party, came from a good family,
had the highest recommendations, and was well thought of in
local society. Gambling lay at the root of it all. Clarke was
ultimately arrested, and most of the treasure was recovered.

Keith's glowing accounts of Gilpin County notwithstanding,
mosquitoes and bedbugs thrived in Colorado's rarefied atmosphere and were a continual source of aggravation. One resident
of Empire swore that mosquitoes there weighed a pound!

Ascertaining the correct time posed another problem for Coloradans, and missed stage connections and late meetings sometimes resulted. In Denver alone, fifteen-to-thirty-minute time dif-
ferences handicapped the punctual. Some folks ran on Chicago
time, others on Leavenworth, and there were always a few rugged individualists who followed their own.

Byers drew attention to another frustration—Denver's buildings remained unnumbered, and the streets were rarely identified
by signs. This, he decried, reflected badly on "a city of our size."

A cool drink of sarsaparilla or lemon soda (both beverages were
manufactured locally) could help soothe nerves frazzled by the
city's deficiencies. A trip to the "fitted up" hot springs near
Idaho might also do the trick. The waters were said to possess
"fine medicinal qualities," and convenient buildings for bathing
were available. "A speedy cure or no pay asked" was guaranteed
by Dr. E. S. Cummins. He owned and developed one of
Colorado's first health and tourist attractions.

The Masonic order provided a social outlet for some. In the
fast-changing world of Colorado, lodges opened and closed with
abandon, and members backslid with impunity. Grand Master
Henry Teller encouraged members to read more Masonic literature and expressed concern about lodges making "Masons on
sight." Masonic growth, following the territorial trend, peaked,
stabilized, and declined. Some lodges did not m t for months on
end.

A minority of Coloradans was becoming aware of civilization's
impact on the environment. Newspapers in both Central and
Denver published letters on the subject. On September 3, Byers
wrote an editorial about the wanton destruction of trees. His fear

was legitimized in November when a "wood famine" hit town, thanks to the "storm king's" closing the roads. With nearby sources exhausted, chilly Denverites relied on wood that came in from farther and farther away. When the crisis passed, Byers's warnings, as usual, were quickly forgotten.

Another serious warning went unheeded—that the war was being fought for a reason more profound than mere freedom from slavery. The enslaved sought equality as their ultimate goal, a concession many Coloradans and other Americans seemed averse to granting. Maurice Morris noted, "Woe even here to the fairest of Ham's descendants" who venture to intrude rashly on Denver society. A ban as "strong as ever" against equal rights for the so-called inferior races remained in place. The few who supported minority rights were accused of "nigger-on-the-brainism."

The prevailing attitude revealed itself in a variety of ways—the establishment of a "colored" church and a "contraband" grocery, labeling of blacks as "the bone of contention" (by George Kassler), and disruption of a "colored citizens social party." Morris saw only one solution for an end to prejudice—the accumulation of wealth by blacks. Barney Ford, who achieved just that, marched straight down the road toward acceptance. Most blacks in Denver, however, never achieved materialistic success and accepted their unfortunate place in society with little protest.

Coloradans nonetheless prided themselves on a rough-hewn, frontier egalitarianism, at least for Anglo-Saxon whites (it helped to be Protestant, too). Morris observed this phenomenon in his travels and noted that there generally existed a strong feeling against social distinction, a somewhat shocking discover for this proper Englishman.

Coloradans, at the moment, would not tolerate many social airs. They had also become confident enough in themselves and their territory to endure a little teasing without taking personal umbrage and issuing sharp rejoinders. After Denver's fire a wag commented, "Blessed are the poor that have nothing, for they have nothing to burn up." Referring to rival Montgomery, a letter writer from Buckskin Joe observed:

In that town there are now 62½ men, 37¼ women, 41¾ children and 193 dogs. The women—or most of them—support the men and children, while the men support the dogs.

Their efforts might not as yet have reached Artemus Ward's level, but they were a start. Coloradans laughed at such ditties as these:

A gentleman whose father had been hanged was accustomed to say of him "He died suddenly upon a platform at a large public meeting."

"Why do you keep yourself so distant?" said a fair one to her bashful lover. "Because" said he, "distance lends enchantment to the view."

What is the difference between a legal document and a cat? One has pauses and the end of its clauses, the other has claw-ses at the end of its pawses.

The weather continued to amaze and bewilder Coloradans. Spring sometimes left no visible record, any day could prove fickle, winter was always contrary, and Boulderites feared being blown away. Outspoken William Crawford thought the climate highly overrated, neither as salubrious nor as healthful as claimed. Bliss proclaimed the climate "blissful," and most Coloradans supported his view. Cool summer days and chilly fall nights were invigorating.

The territory had successfully survived the third year of the war. Certainly aware of the struggle, Coloradans found it directly affected their lives in many ways, but physically the conflict seemed to be occurring far away, almost in another land.

One morning David Collier, looking out the window of his Central City newspaper office, was startled to see a string of little burros, each one carrying a large pack box painted all over with the Stars and Stripes. The obviously Union owner of the string called his outfit the "Central City, Idahoe, Spanish Bar and Trail Creek Jackass Express." He displayed his loyalty in public, as did most other Coloradans, and all went about the business of building a Rocky Mountain empire in the midst of national tragedy.

People and Places

Once, up in Gilpin County, Colorado
When a long blue afternoon was standing on end
Like a tombstone sinking into the Rocky Mountains,
I found myself in a town where no one was.

—Thomas Hornsby Ferril, "Magenta"

Unidentified Gilpin County mines and miners awaiting the big bonanza discovery (Courtesy Denver Public Library, Western History Department)

Urbanization: Main Street in Central City (Courtesy Colorado Historical Society)

Placer miners using a sluice near Central City (Courtesy Denver Public Library, Western History Department)

Log cabins in Buckskin Joe (Courtesy Colorado Historical Society)

Wagon train transporting a boiler on Denver's Larimer Street
(Courtesy Denver Public Library, Western History Department)

Mlle Carolista walking a tightrope in Denver, July 18, 1861 (From
author's collection)

Black Hawk's brass band, 1862 (Courtesy Denver Public Library, Western History Department)

Detachment of the First Colorado in Empire, 1862 (From author's collection)

The New York Gold Mining Company and Enterprise Mill, near Black Hawk (Courtesy Colorado Historical Society)

Hard-rock mining produced environmental disorder at the Tenth Legion, 1864. (Courtesy Colorado Historical Society)

Central City in 1864 (Courtesy Amon Carter Museum)

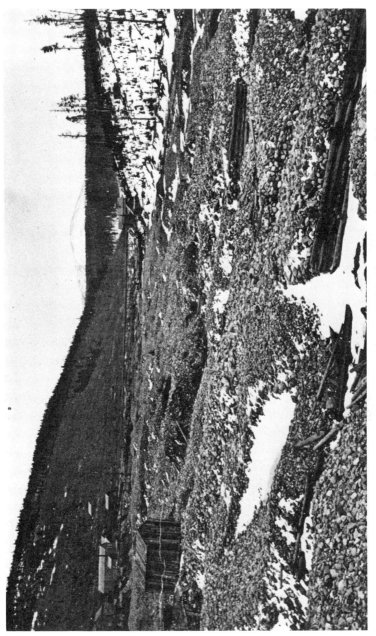

Mining's impact on abandoned California Gulch (Courtesy Amon Carter Museum)

Denverites inspect Cherry Creek the morning after the great flood,
May 20, 1864. (Courtesy Denver Public Library, Western History
Department)

Boulder after the war, spring 1866 (Courtesy University of Colorado,
Western Historical Collections)

Part IV

A TIME FOR PEACE: 1864–65

11

"Assumption and Jack-ass-ical presumption"

GOLD! GOLD STOCKS, GOLD CLAIMS—Easterners craved them, and Coloradans, suffering from "claim-selling on the brain," hastened to assuage their countrymen's appetite. A gold-buying epidemic seized America from Wall Street to Eureka Street and threatened to become international when one Denverite planned to return to his Canadian home to organize a Colorado gold company. The gold price soared in the meantime to 188½ ($2.88 paper money for $1.00 in gold) on April 15, an all-time high.

Both the New York and Rocky Mountain highs collapsed three days later on "blue" Monday, April 18. A chaotic scene ensued; according to a *New York Times* reporter, "abusive epithets were lustily interchanged" and "lively pugilistic exercise indulged in" during the "slaughter of the innocents." Before the exchange closed, contracts were repudiated, margins wiped out, and principals mercilessly sacrificed by their brokers. By the close of the day's "festivities," lame mining ducks were a drag on the market. The reporter could offer little consolation: "They have sowed the wind and have reaped the whirlwind." Colorado's year of the jubilee had come to an abrupt end, well short of twelve months.

Reasons for the debacle had developed over a period of time. Investment in Colorado mining stocks had been based on speculation and fueled by greed. When the price of gold declined, those on the inside decided to sell quickly and take their profits. Waning interest accompanied falling prices. A telegraph dispatch reached

Central on the nineteenth: "The bubble is burst—mining stock has gone to the devil. Can't sell any more; can't even give it away."

In the aftermath of the collapse, Coloradans surveyed their ruined hopes, firmly convinced that they still had the gold and tangible prospects to assure future prosperity. That conviction did not prevent a devastating loss of interest. What once had been a hot topic for bulls and bears now slumped on the market. Within a fortnight the *Tribune* recommended that its readers not buy gold or silver stocks. Front-page news focused on the emotional aftereffects of the infamous Fort Pillow massacre. Northern newspapers embellished this brutal Tennessee battle and the alleged refusal of the Confederates to give quarter to surrendering black troops. By late June a vendor of Colorado property wrote home that he was treated "with derision and contempt."

An angry easterner, John Wetherbee, explained this change of heart. After contemplating what had taken place, he pointed the finger of blame at Coloradans: "That was a new vein that paid well, and it was worked with vigor—no one knowing how soon it would run into *cap*." Burned investors agreed that the westerners were at fault, but Wetherbee also criticized the gullibility of the buyers, who often paid "sums that made the seller smile in private at the prodigality of eastern people." Black Hawk mill man Joseph Kenyon described the situation more bluntly when writing to a friend in June:

I have seen so much assumption and "Jack-ass-ical" presumption displayed by some of the "old residents" taking "advantage of fortunate circumstances," during the last three months . . . The fortunate circumstances are those which make better "digging" in New York than in Colorado.

Colorado had not fared well with easterners and its reputation was now besmirched. How fleet the hopes!

Deeper investigation revealed the underlying causes of the collapse. Purchases of newly issued government bonds had increased the stringency of the money market in April. Mounting criticism of gold speculation as unpatriotic was another factor. Secretary of the Treasury Salmon Chase publicly commented that if Grant destroyed Lee's army that summer, a cooperative effort of all the speculators on Wall Street could not keep the price of gold from falling for a single week. Doubt crept into the minds of the "innocents," quickly unnerving those who had assumed gold prices would continue ever upward. All these elements conspired to produce "blue" Monday.

Coloradans, who saw their glory turn to ashes over a weekend, could not be consoled; many blamed easterners for their ill fate. A few bit the bullet, attributing some of the panic to locals who had sold worthless claims and forced stocks on the market prematurely. Frank Hall agreed and asserted that many purchasers of mines were never even able to find them!

Both Hollister and Hall, with the advantage of hindsight, criticized easterners for expecting too much, sending out unfit managers, purchasing useless machinery, and exercising little prudence or sagacity in operations. Though right on all counts, their explanation did nothing to brighten Colorado's tarnished mining reputation.

In truth, Coloradans had had little effect on Wall Street beyond providing the means for speculation. Investors were looking for stocks to buy; they had money and wanted to spend it. Colorado mines and companies appeared on the market at just the right moment—Coloradans needed the money, and easterners wanted a "safe" investment as a hedge against inflation. In no way was the territory master of its own fate. The only harvest would be that inevitable whirlwind.

To avoid the worst, it seemed prudent to pick up the pieces and move ahead. The prospecting mania came to an abrupt halt, and serious mine work resumed without wildcat speculators looking over miners' shoulders. The needed machinery would soon be coming or was already at hand for development. Coloradans worked hard, never losing faith that gold stock would rebound once people realized the mines remained rich "beyond parallel."

Interest in gold did not revive as expected, even though $1.00 of the "yellow stuff" could purchase $2.40 in paper money during September and November. Bliss, still in New York in December, wrote his friend Byers that the mining business continued to be depressed. Some of the existing companies would have to pay liberal dividends before the economy revived, certainly not before "another summer." Bliss and Byers were both wrong—the war would be long over when the revival came to pass.

More than one Coloradan came out of the financial wreckage smiling. Bela Buell parlayed his Gilpin County clerk's position and investment in mining ventures into an annual income of $40,000—not bad for a young man in 1864 and second only to Governor Evans in the territory.

As full repercussions of the collapse became apparent, Fitz-John Porter returned as mining superintendent and engineer for the New York Gold Mining Company, one of those organized earlier. No one barred Porter's way this time; the superpatriotic tempest had died away.

Some ill will might have remained had Coloradans known that Porter blamed the current problems on locals who had intentionally sold claims that existed "in the air as is the case with almost all high numbers." Undeterred, Porter set out to run his operation, warning Samuel Barlow not to anticipate much initial return on his investment. By late June, Porter had his mill running and had sent a gallon can of retort east to be refined. Investors and Central Citians approved his initiative.

Local curiosity about Porter's activities irritated him, and because the "telegraph leaks here badly," he devised a secret cipher. While putting his property in order, the superintendent stressed to Barlow and others that they should send someone west to ascertain the facts, rather than placing their trust in New Yorkers, who could easily foist off worthless mines as valuable. He further warned them to buy no more stock; he knew of only one company that currently had prospects of a dividend.

Whether through purchase or as one of the original investors, Porter operated the Gunnell Gold Company. Hollister approved this operation and the faith Porter showed by starting a "mammoth mill" in July. Five buckets kept the water from flooding the works in a losing fight that saw the water rise about a foot each week in the lower diggings. Porter ordered a Cornish pump to stem the tide and refurbished the neglected machinery left by former owners. Trials and expenses notwithstanding, Porter managed to send gold east every week. The shipments whetted his investors' appetites for more.

In September Porter traveled to the Red Mountain district to check out the rumored "biggest thing in the mountains." Miners there had been industriously organizing a mining district, digging out a road, and entertaining visitors with stories of their discoveries. They also found time to pick out some splendid samples to be assayed. In mining-depressed Colorado, Red Mountain became big news.

Porter did not like what he saw. He tersely advised Barlow's friends to have nothing to do with Red Mountain, unless they merely wished to sell undeveloped property. The isolation, high elevation, and short mining season caused Red Mountain's prom-ise to fade, and the encouraging assay returns evaporated as the veins pinched out. (Not all was lost, however; Wolfe Londoner found a last bonanza in Oro City. As Lake County clerk and recorder, he netted about $10,000, admitting that "fees were pretty high in the early days.")

Porter returned to Gilpin County and worked at developing the properties there. He sensibly advised Barlow that it would take enormous expense and at least a year to turn undeveloped property into a paying proposition. He also instructed easterners to be wary of milling processes: "Those who do work to the most advantage are not those who boast the most."

Cagey Barlow received abundant advice regarding Colorado mines and mills from Porter and other agents in the field. As did all absentee owners, he suffered from having to rely on others for information of activity. Barlow worked his vaunted unerring judg-ment overtime to keep abreast of developments. To make matters worse, Gilpin County seemed to foster an atmosphere of intrigue. As C. Blakesley wrote in December, "The principle here appears to be that your right hand should have no faith or trust in your left." Porter was trustworthy, but Barlow was warned that another man was "unscrupulous, dishonest and intriguing."

Barlow received a variety of advice but what was needed was a continued infusion of eastern money to turn Colorado mining around. The search for a profitable milling process dominated much of the correspondence. Barlow invested in the Kenyon Company, which planned to solve the riddle of refractory ores by using the Bartola process and an improved pan amalgamator (for mixing mercury and gold) invented by Joseph Kenyon.

Circumstances seemed to conspire against Kenyon as he tried

to get his mill running. First came freighting delays caused by Indian troubles on the plains, then unexpectedly high living costs, thanks to the plains warfare. The collapse of the mill's roof and the early arrival of cold and snow further complicated matters. Out of money and facing an overdraft of eight thousand dollars, Kenyon despairingly inquired of his New York investors what course he should pursue. An encouraging response reassured him, and he persevered.

The *Mining Register* hailed a trial run and forecast success. Unfortunately, extremely cold weather froze Kenyon's shaking tables and water supply. In January Porter wrote that the Bartola process had not worked successfully on many local ores, and cold weather had closed down Kenyon. Porter had no faith in the Bartola process and warned Barlow a couple of months later that it would prove ruinous to all who used it. He begged his friend not to invest one penny in the process or machinery until Bartola came to Colorado to revise the procedure.

Joseph Bartola did not go to Colorado that winter. His mysterious chemical process lay in ruins. Porter was not the only one who disparaged it; Rossiter Raymond later wrote, that

it is difficult to reconcile the history of this invention with the hypothesis of honesty on the part of the inventor. The secrecy with which its manipulations were conducted, and the readiness with which, after failure in one place, it was revived with the same splendid promises in another, and the immense prices exacted for its use, in advance of all practical success, were not the usual signs of a sincerely proposed improvement in metallurgy.

Desperate Coloradans nonetheless grasped at the straws offered by Bartola.

Various other attempts were made to develop a successful process. James Lyon, George Pullman's erstwhile partner, took ore to a smelter in New York City and saved more gold than Central City's mills did. He decided that smelting might furnish the answer and as winter dragged on, he made plans to build a plant at Black Hawk. Keith, meanwhile, was getting nowhere with his desulfurizing process and could only claim it to be "more or less" successful at the Mammoth Company's mill. Thus, in April 1865,

Colorado milling technology languished, not far advanced from what it had been four years ago. The profitable reduction of ore, after years of effort and expense, remained elusive and was the major barrier to success, one that had to be mastered if the ter-ritory hoped to become a premier mining region.

Kenyon was not easily discouraged: "I am still strong in the faith & hope for final triumph." Others had similar faith, includ-ing a group of Rhode Island investors, who hired Brown Univer-sity chemistry and science professor, Nathaniel Hill, to go to Col-orado to check on investment opportunities. "Very liberal com-pensation" induced thirty-two-year-old Hill to accept the offer. He told his wife, Alice, that the West offered one of the "finest opportunities to make not only some money, but also fame." Leaving his beloved family in Providence, he set out with an eye to investing in mining properties himself.

With a thriving consulting business and a well-earned reputa-tion in academic and business circles, Hill was no naive easterner. He arrived just in time for the exhilarating days of June 1864. Nothing pleased the lonely Hill more than to find a family from Providence in Denver and learn that they subscribed to the *Pro-vidence Journal,* receiving it only eleven days after publication. Colorado seemed not so isolated after all.

While the *Journal* might be an "old and dear friend," and Denver "hospitable and agreeable," they distracted Hill from his primary purpose for undertaking the long journey—to inspect Gilpin County mines. Getting down to the business at hand, he headed for the mountains. Hill early encountered what the natives called "a cloud burst," and the damage it could do in so short a time amazed him. He then traveled with ex-governor Gilpin to examine his grant to the south in the San Luis Valley. Gilpin had not changed a bit; Hill described him as the "most un-practical man I ever knew," who talked incessantly and seemed to know every man in the territory. "He is kind-hearted & highly respected by everybody in Colorado; but his mind is filled with great abstractions." As a sideline to Alice, apparently answering her question, Hill added this about old bachelor Gilpin: "I think any lady who takes stock in him, will get small dividends."

A devoted husband, Hill wrote a steady stream of informative

letters to his wife, describing a potpourri of subjects. He mentioned a universal notion that no man could live in Colorado
without liquor (he was a nondrinker). Nathaniel also chuckled
over the fact that Colorado City and Pueblo called themselves
cities; only in name did they qualify for that distinction, in his
opinion. One hotel in Pueblo seemed "to be kept for the
accommodation of bugs." After taking a room at the best hotel in
Golden, he prayed that God would "deliver us from the worst"
and told Alice she could "imagine the worst you can."

Returning from the San Luis Valley, which did not impress him,
Hill visited Sugarloaf in Boulder County, riding through wild and
broken mountain country. He examined the claims of Mr. Blake, a
graduate of an Ohio college who had come out in 1860; his wife
and children stayed in Iowa to run the farm. "Think of his life.
For more than four years, he has lived nearly alone in the mountains. Sometimes for two months, he has not seen a human
being," wrote the already-lonely Hill to Alice. Overcoming one
discouragement after another, Blake planned to go home in October, but not before making his fortune. Newcomer Hill was
becoming familiar with this dogged determination and the life-
style, which included the mountain custom of retiring soon after
finishing supper. Upon completing his examination, Hill hurried
back to Denver, believing Blake would realize his hopes "quite
probably now."

His side trips notwithstanding, Hill was most impressed by
Central and Gilpin County, and the refractory ore riddle intrigued him. Prospects of fame and fortune beckoned. The thrifty
Hill, tired of paying high rents, purchased a home and lot for
eighteen hundred dollars; he would rent the house out when he
went back east. Following a few more exploratory journeys and
after reassuring his nervous wife that travel would be safe, Hill
started home in late October.

The observant professor described how little Colorado had progressed from its rawest frontier days. Travel beyond Denver
resembled conditions of 1860, with all the attendant passenger
discomforts. "I have 'roughed it,' " he said, using a Colorado ex-
pression he had picked up, and "I am sufficiently toughened for
anything."

The general mining situation had not changed much, either. Discouragement, hope, decline, revival, slow times, good times—the cycle continued in various districts. Hollister de-scribed California Gulch:

The relics of former life and business—old boots and clothes, cooking utensils, rude house furniture, tin cans, gold pans, worn-out shovels and picks and the remains of toms, half buried sluices and rifle boxes, dirt roofed log cabins tumbling down and the country turned inside out and disguised with rubbish of every description, are most disagreeable and abundant and suggestive.

The promise of 1860–61 lay in ruins. Even a more recent marvel, Empire, was now rated "dull," and its Tenth Legion Lode offered only a "good reputation." Over at Sterling, one "Musquito" moaned that nothing but money would resuscitate business or dispel the gloomy apathy that had fallen upon "in-habitants hereabouts."

Miners, too, had their complaints, citing the high cost of living and the fact that their wages failed to keep pace. Management was disgruntled because of the difficulty of retaining a crew; men were eternally being tempted to go prospecting elsewhere. Porter blamed the problems on an overabundance of speculative, under-financed companies; wartime unrest; and "greenback inflation": "Truly we are between hawk and buzzard."

These tribulations generated more strife and a restless May 1864 for Gilpin County, including several wildcat strikes. Man-agement won that particular round and another one in October, protesting heatedly that raising wages would be suicidal to con-tinued operations. Wages nonetheless increased from July's $4.00 to $4.25, to February's $5.00 to $5.50. Paid in inflated green-backs, miners knew they were not coming out ahead.

In the midst of despair, the discovery of silver near Georgetown boded well for the future. Hill took samples to Providence that assayed 575 ounces to the ton. Ore from Belmont Lode assayed from $200 to $500 per ton in Central City in early November. Vi-sions of a silver rush were quickly conjured. Mining fever permeated Clear Creek Valley and Gilpin County, but the boys would have to wait out the winter before attempting to realize

their dreams. Silver, it was hoped, would be the answer to mining's woes.

Governor Evans wanted the best for the territory. Dabbling as
he did in mining, and president of the uniquely named Hope Gold
Company of Gold Dirt, he fully understood prevailing conditions.
Mining, however, was not the only major topic that occupied his
thoughts; Indians and the possibility of statehood also vied for his
attention.

Evans, in fact, would be one of the leading candidates for
senator if statehood should be approved. Others aspired to the
honor as well, and the fight started soon after Congress passed
the enabling act. Petty quarrels and vigorous mudslinging became
commonplace, and an acrimonious war between the *Mining Journal* and the *Rocky Mountain News* brewed further ill will. Evans
and the others found themselves entrapped in a statehood
morass.

Following local caucuses in early July, a constitutional convention met first in Golden, then adjourned to Denver. Statehood
proponents were in complete control, and a document was quickly drafted; September 12 was set as election day. The supreme
confidence of the delegates (William Byers was one) led them to
schedule an election for state officials on the same day.

The pro-statehood group, which included Byers, Chivington
(congressional nominee), Teller, Elbert, Evans, and, belatedly,
Chaffee, campaigned confidently. The men argued that statehood
would give Colorado the voice it needed to control its own
destiny, help elect the president, strengthen the Union cause,
provide more power in Washington, and inspire confidence at
home and abroad in the permanence and value of the region. The
unpopuular federal appointment system would be eliminated, and
the location of the transcontinental railroad could perhaps be
favorably influenced. Greater numbers of investors and immigrants would certainly come to the state, which would bring
additional benefits.

Hollister and Hall in Black Hawk formed the outspoken voice of
the anti-state faction. They rebelled against the prospect of increased taxes, believing the people to be overburdened with
"county taxes, city taxes, school taxes, militia taxes, special

taxes, road taxes, license taxes, poor taxes and income and postage taxes." Their argument swayed voters. Black Hawkers, already in the midst of a nasty local squabble over taxation, were in no mood to hear about any more. They also pointed out that the military conscription law would surely apply to the new state, which created more converts for their side.

Those aggrieved souls who were overlooked for nomination to state office either joined the opposers or sat on the sidelines and watched. The Spanish-Mexican population in the southern part of the territory feared for their rights in a state in which they would be a decided minority. Rumors drifted north of a possible secession to New Mexico, and the seeds of opposition were sown. The ultimate emotional issue revolved around the personalities of Evans and Chivington. In the 1860s, Colorado's rather abstract political issues failed to generate the emotion that individuals did, particularly in rallying the opposition.

Democrat Porter, who had no love for Republicans after his recent treatment, explained his view of the two controversial men in a letter to Barlow. He accused both of stirring up the Indian question to further their own political careers, and charged that Coloradans had "been afflicted with imbecility in the management of civil affairs." He described Chivington as a "preacher and pretended soldier" who relied on the military vote, the troops "being compelled to vote for him or be removed beyond the polls." Evans was depicted as being a weak coward, fond of bombastic dispatches. What Porter said in private, others aired publicly or in the press. The attacks did not stop, even after the battered Evans announced he would not be a candidate.

Rallies, letters, editorials, articles, accusations, slander—all flew fast and furiously in the weeks before the election. Porter saw it all hurting Colorado's future, and fellow Democrat Joseph Kenyon believed the "state organization scheme the most outrageous thing one could conceive."

Most Coloradans agreed, and statehood was defeated by a vote of 4,672 to 1,520. More than anything else, the election results reflected apathy; based on the 1860 census returns, less than thirty percent of the eligible voters bothered to go to the polls. Although the percentage might have been slightly higher if the 1864 male population had been known, the numbers still represented a pitiful turnout on such a critical issue, if one were to believe the pro-statehood argument. The *Mining Journal* congratulated voters on their honesty, good sense, and independence. "We trust the recent defeat of the rascals who had secured control of the Union party in this Territory will be the salvation both of the Territory and the party." Editors Hollister and Hall looked with pride on Gilpin County, which had almost singlehandedly defeated the proposition. "The issue was fairly made up between the honest laboring mass of the people and place and plunder hunters of all styles and complexions."

A bitter Byers, who had suffered a severe setback, blamed the Democrats for engineering the well-managed, anti-state campaign that duped the voters. His wrath against the *Journal* could hardly be contained, and he blasted "the anti-state organ, a vile, hissing snake-in-the-grass—a copperhead."

Years later, a mellower Frank Hall wrote that the people were not strong enough to support an independent commonwealth, "and they knew it." His analysis explained the outcome as clearly as anything. Colorado would never have been offered statehood had it not been for the exigencies of the war and the worries of the Union party in a presidential election year. Nor were people in general as interested in or concerned about the issue as were the politicians and would-be politicians, who saw their plans collapse.

The fallout from the election continued for months. The damage to Evans and Chivington by the scurrilous, unscrupulous attacks could not as yet be measured. At the moment they were trying to avert conflict between Coloradans and the Plains Indians. Despite rumors to the contrary, they had not manufactured the issue to benefit their political ambitions. The threat to the future of Colorado was real.

Although unable to vote because of their territorial status, Coloradans exhibited a lively interest in their first presidential campaign. While some (such as George Kassler and Joseph Kenyon) supported the Democratic nominee, George McClellan, most probably supported Lincoln. A couple of enterprising Black Hawk businessmen utilized the earlier split in the Union party over potential nominees to back "the Incorruptible Patriot," Salmon Chase, and "the truly honest man," Abraham Lincoln, in cleverly worded advertisements. Whether such piggyback promotion boosted sales remains unknown.

By the end of 1864 political interest had burned out, and Kassler wrote only that the legislature had "honorable members." The legislature still faced the touchy issue of where the capital would be, but for most Coloradans that seemed of little significance as they looked toward the new year.

12

"All Quiet on the Plains"

SPRING 1864 confounded Colorado's military and governing authorities. Conflicting stories and ever-present rumors bedeviled their days and haunted their nights. As summer approached, their anxiety only worsened.

Evans and Chivington saw about them an unnerving array of threats. Unable to distinguish between fact and fancy, they could not ascertain the true circumstances. Without the knowledge of hindsight, these two respected leaders found their choices extremely difficult and circumscribed.

Reports of Confederates, outlaws, and Indians were plentiful. Were Southerners stirring up the Indians? Would the Utes remain peaceful? Was that robbery by outlaws for booty, or was it an attempt by Confederates to strengthen their position? Might warmer days bring a renewal of raiding along the trails? Had the Cheyennes, Arapahoes, and other plains tribes formed an alliance? These difficult questions required immediate responses.

Short of troops, equipment, and accurate information, the governor and the district commander groped for answers. One vexation received quick dispatch. Ex-miner James Reynolds, the same James Reynolds who had been arrested when the Miller party tried to flee south in 1861, returned to Colorado in late July with a band of followers. Whether they were Southern guerrillas, who threatened to deal with Denver as "Quantrill had dealt with the town of Lawrence, Kansas," or outlaws looking for plunder was unknown. Denver had no wish to be sacked and burned, and South Park folks did not welcome a stage holdup.

Five members of Reynolds's gang were captured by local volunteers after the robbery. Under heavy guard, the prisoners, including Reynolds, "tried to escape" and were shot. The rest of the gang scattered, leaving behind a legend of buried gold. Their departure relieved the minds of many in Denver and South Park and ended rumors of Confederate activities in Colorado.

The Indian problem did not go away so easily, nor with such finality. Reports of suspicious Indian movements and depredations started in April and continued throughout the year. Accounts were heard along the mountains and out on the trails, and trouble on the plains seethed once more. The Cheyenne and Arapahoe Indians were identified as the guilty parties.

Unfortunately, in all the hubbub, little attention was paid to the Indians' point of view. They had ample reason to be angry. Resentment over treaties and the government's failure to fulfill agreed-upon terms dated from years back. Pushing and shoving of Indians by whites on native lands reached new heights after the Pike's Peak rush; harassment mounted in direct proportion to increased settlement. The pattern that had characterized the westward movement was being repeated. Not naive, the Indians knew well enough who would eventually have to give way.

Coloradans ignored Indian rights and rejected compromise; they thought in terms of extermination. Byers and the *News* were convinced of the rightness of their cause. Other papers joined the call for action, adding fuel to a fire that had been lighted in 1859. The Indians' will had to be broken or, better still, they must be removed from the territory. Nervous Coloradans pleaded with the governor for adequate military protection; one constituent, H. M. Fosdick of Booneville, warned that "fear and danger run riot." Evans, however, did not have the troops to respond. It seemed to be 1863 all over again.

What troops Chivington had available spent their spare time trying to distinguish rumors from hard facts. Chivington and Evans became even more discouraged when they heard seemingly reliable reports that the Indians were joining forces to wage war for plunder and to drive whites out.

An actual attack was far worse than mere rumors. When the Nathan Hungate family—father, mother, and two daughters— was slaughtered and mutilated on a ranch southeast of Denver, that city's residents panicked. Sara Hively heard the gory news on June 12 and observed, "The people of Denver fear that they [Indians] will attack this place and are preparing means to defend it." When the Hungate bodies were displayed at the post office, she did not venture out to see them, "but those that did said that they was a sight to behold." Nathaniel Hill was appalled that so many men, women, and children gathered to view the corpses. He privately accused the authorities of trying to incite retaliatory action.

No push in that direction was needed—excitement had already reached fever pitch. On the evening of the fifteenth, Denver experienced its first scare. Even Hill grabbed his pocket revolver to join in the defense against what proved to be a herd of cattle. Bells rang, dogs barked, shots were fired and meals left uneaten as women and children raced to prearranged shelters. Men thronged the streets and were given guns from the armory, companies were organized, and scouts were sent to investigate.

Lurid details of the massacre glutted newspapers in Denver and Central City, spreading fear and calming no one. Some Central Citians panicked over rumors coming from the valley. Irving Howbert reported that the news reached Colorado City about June 20, making the residents "exceedingly uneasy" and thereafter constantly on the lookout for "savages."

Evans called upon "patriotic citizens" to volunteer for militia companies; any help from Washington would, at best, be too late. Boulderites promptly organized a company and built a fort four miles east of town. A short time later, former schoolmarm Ellen Coffin Pennock, now a farm wife, hastened to the stronghold to escape a rumored raid, leaving behind a corral full of unmilked cows. She wondered whether she would ever see her home again. At the fort, Ellen's friend Mary Kinney slyly opened her pocket to reveal "a little bottle containing white powder marked 'Strychnine'. 'If we are taken prisoners,' she said." The women did not suffer "a fate worse than death," but the terror mounted.

George Kane, superintendent of the mint, pleaded with Evans

for twenty muskets and ammunition to defend the mint in case of a hostile invasion. Women and children sought safety there, and Kane could not protect them. Evans had no arms to spare. A month later the superintendent implored army authorities for rifles with bayonets.

Coloradans were not alone in their anxiety. Henry Bacon, after arriving in July, telegraphed Samuel Barlow that several of the stage stations he had just passed through had been attacked. "Under the circumstances one could not help raising his hand to the top of the head to see if the scalp was still there."

After four years in Colorado without finding his longed-for success, Edward H. Edwards decided to return home. He retained his faith in "the glorious future of the Territory," but it took more than faith to survive. His ill luck held out when his August departure had to be aborted; he concluded that travel was too dangerous and returned to Denver to await a safer day. The Denver Edwards came back to was in an uproar, with people "calling in god's *name for somebody* to go to do *Something* for the protection of the town, and the women & children, and their own 'Har' in particular from the imaginery ten thousand indians that would be there to destroy them that night."

Fresh stories of the horrors visited upon white captives had already reached the streets of Denver. Lucinda Ewbanks was the victim of an August attack by Cheyenne Indians on her house on the Little Blue. Traded from man to man, Lucinda learned why white women chose death over captivity. She never again saw her daughter, who had also been captured. Her account, when it appeared months later, confirmed the worst. By then, Lucinda's life and that of many other Coloradans had been irrevocably changed.

The results of all this turmoil, beyond mere threats and panic, translated into lost dollars, inconvenience, frustration, and rising prices. Direct communication with the States stopped; mail again had to be sent via San Francisco and then overland. The telegraph lines went down. Wagon trains stopped running. Flour and other goods rose in price, and paper nearly disappeared—editors made do with what they could scavenge. Badly needed mining machinery sat in river ports or corralled in wagon trains. Stages stopped running, and easterners could not help but question how wise an investment in Colorado might be. Farmers and ranchers retreated to the safety of foothill communities, com-pletely disrupting Colorado's agriculture just at a time when homegrown food was desperately needed to fill shortages caused by the missing wagon trains.

By August the state of affairs had evolved into the worst crisis Colorado, Evans, or Chivington had ever faced. Edwards had been right—Coloradans wanted someone to do something *now*.

The governor had been trying to do something. A year ago he had attempted to meet with Cheyenne and Arapahoe leaders, but the conference never materialized. The Indians refused to at-tend, having no desire to "settle down and live like white men." Evans was caught in an impossible predicament, between the desires and life-styles of two cultures. He left no question about his beliefs: "They [the Indians] had a right to hunt on the land, but that right must be subject to the higher occupation of the land, for a larger population and for civilization."

Now pressured by even more hostile Coloradans who, as the summer dragged toward fall, saw few redeeming merits in the "noble red man," Evans tried again. When such normally sane men as Nathaniel Hill and William Crawford called for the exter-mination of the Indians, peace faced long odds.

Evans considered various strategies. Using friendly Utes to at-tack their traditional enemies seemed an ideal solution to the problem. Though it proved impractical, the idea never died. With only limited backing from the commissioner of Indian affairs, the governor in June issued a proclamation to the "Friendly Indians of the Plains." The declaration called for them to assemble in designated camps, the Cheyennes and Arapahoes at Fort Lyon, to be issued food and offered protection. The Indians ignored the order.

Evans again appealed to Washington but with no luck. Secretary of War Stanton had more on his mind than what he considered an insignificant western sideshow. To his credit, however, Evans kept the War Department well informed about Colorado's "desperate" situation. He finally resorted to the dual approach of dealing directly with the Cheyenne and Arapahoe while also asking for authorization to raise a regiment of Colorado troops.

Then, at this highly inopportune moment, the statehood issue arose to muddy the waters and embitter feelings. In a no-holds-barred campaign, the anti-staters, led by the *Daily Mining Journal,* rancorously attacked Chivington and Evans. Joseph Kenyon, writing Barlow in October, noted "the fact that our late troubles are due chiefly to the perfidy & ambition of Gov. Evans & Col. Chivington our *Military* dictator." With a caustic press ready to exaggerate, people out to destroy one another, and malice and venom freely flowing, the Colorado political atmosphere became dangerously polluted. Fear, insecurity, and malevolence rarely generate temperate judgment.

The situation came to a head in August—Indian raids; political fights; public pressure, abetted by disappointment over the "gold bubble" failure; hopes dashed by the mining decline; and the frustration of losing population and headlines to Montana. The meager, scattered forces under Chivington's command could accomplish little, and Washington's only response, to allow a 100-day regiment to be raised, provided no immediate aid. But Evans kept trying: on August 11 he issued a proclamation authorizing all citizens to arm themselves and hunt hostile Indians. Then he declared martial law and began recruiting for the Third Colorado.

On August 13, Hal Sayre in Central City received his recruiting commission and promptly set about his task. Posters announced a war meeting at the Montana Theater, and a speech by Henry Teller netted about sixty men. Within a week, the number exceeded one hundred, including seventeen-year-old William Breakenridge, who said he joined to fight Indians and put a stop to their attacks. Miners, mill men, merchants, and workmen eagerly marched off to Denver. Andrew Hively joined another company, and his wife, Sara, to whom he had been married hardly a year, confessed to mixed emotions: "Oh to think of it, how can I let him go? I shall be so lonesome."

Off they all went to fight Indians, good men and ne'er-do-wells, permanent Coloradans and temporary, united by the goal of resolving a five-year-old territorial problem. The Plains Indians must be defeated once and for all.

During the next weeks Chivington and Evans endeavored to equip and train their 100-day warriors, but their best efforts did not produce professional, dependable, disciplined soldiers. Though they expended considerable effort to recruit experienced officers, only about half the men had any military experience. Their equipment, if it could be called that, would have been ridiculed by the battle-hardened veterans of the Army of the Potomac.

Coloradans, including the anti-state Journal, seemed nonetheless proud of their boys. That pride waned somewhat as the undisciplined youths caused a ruckus or two in Denver, following in the footsteps of those heroes of Glorieta Pass, the First Colorado.

Suddenly, in the midst of war preparations, Evans was astonished to receive a letter from Maj. Edward Wynkoop, now commander of Fort Lyon, saying he planned to bring several chiefs to Denver to discuss peace. This was the same man who, a month earlier, had stated, "In all events, it is my intention to kill all Indians I may come across until I receive orders to the contrary from headquarters." Orders to the contrary never arrived.

The opposing groups came together at Camp Weld on September 28. The Cheyenne delegation, headed by Black Kettle, met with the governor (seriously ill at the moment) and his commander, Chivington. About fifty-seven years old, Black Kettle had seen what was happening to his people and wisely understood what the future held.

He had sent a letter in late August to Fort Lyon, offering to exchange prisoners and desiring peace. Truly a man of outstanding ability and strong character, even he had been unable to control his braves and prevent war. No chief could speak for all Cheyenne Indians.

The conference closed with little progress on either side. When no new understanding emerged, Evans and Chivington advised the Indians to surrender unconditionally, something they could not and would not do. Centuries of misunderstanding and distrust tainted Wynkoop's sincere attempt at peace. His change of heart had come when he trusted Black Kettle's message that allowed him to lead a column of troops to rescue white captives peacefully.

Wynkoop's idea of bringing the leaders face to face could have been a brilliant success or a terrible failure. Burdened by the responsibility for the security of the people of Colorado, Evans and Chivington felt unable to take any additional risks for peace. Wynkoop's gamble failed.

The meeting ended, the Indians returned to the Fort Lyon area, and Coloradans returned to the business at hand. As winter neared, the raids slowed and stopped as expected; Indians traditionally rested during the cold months. Such tradition swayed no Coloradans. The Third Colorado had only a few weeks left before enlistments ran out. To utilize their troops to best advantage, Evans and Chivington had to act quickly. Having raised such a furor over the need for the regiment, they could ill afford to let it stand idle and then simply be mustered out. In mid-October the regiment rode out of Denver and headed south for Bijou Basin, where it set up camp.

Criticism of Wynkoop led to his removal and replacement by Maj. Scott Anthony. Although sympathetic to the Indians' plight, Anthony seemed much less willing to acquiesce in the peace program Wynkoop had inaugurated. Black Kettle, meanwhile, established his village a few hours' ride from the fort. Was he at peace, or not? Did he receive army protection in exchange for bringing his people in? No one really knew.

A refusal by the local Indian agent, Samuel Colley, to follow Evans's instructions in dealing with the Cheyennes and Arapahoes further complicated matters. Colley insisted on reporting directly to "Dean Cousin," Indian Commissioner William Dole. Gossip mongers insisted that Colley sold, rather than gave, annuity goods to the Indians and personally used supplies intended for them. The Fort Lyon situation angered territorial leaders and raised questions in their minds about activities there.

Facing this multitude of problems, the governor decided to go to Washington, as he had done in previous years, to advance Colorado's interests and defend himself (there had been demands for his removal) and the statehood movement. He and his family left on November 16. His close friend, Territorial Secretary Samuel Elbert, once more became acting governor.

Chivington, with his troops in the field and confronting mounting pressure for action, both from within and without the regiment, found himself cornered. Time raced against him, and controversy over his leadership seethed within the regiment. Sayre considered him a "good-natured, well intentioned man, crude though he was," while Boulderite David Nichols believed him justly unpopular with the soldiers because of his ambitions for promotion. Jealousy among officers extended back to the days of the First, and the statehood hassle only intensified divisions.

The colonel also faced a military in-house crisis when the hero of the victory over the Indians at Bear River, Gen. Patrick Connor, attempted to take some of Chivington's troops for his own planned Indian campaign to end overland trail problems. Connor traveled to Denver from Utah to discuss the matter with Chivington in mid-November and did not concur with the plans for a winter campaign. His rejection touched a raw nerve. Chivington, although cordial, realized Connor had the reputation and influence to confiscate troops from his district. The contrast between the victorious Connor and the yet-to-take-the-field Chivington stood out in bold relief. The military and personal prestige to be gained from a signal victory raised the stakes.

Chivington's desire to reenter the political arena and regain the military fame of his earlier campaign demanded that he act speedily. His overall commander, Gen. Samuel Curtis, had instructed him that there would be "no peace till the Indians suffer more." Curtis expressed a similar sentiment to Evans, suggesting that the Indians would have to be "fully subdued or exterminated." There could be no misunderstanding in either case—Curtis wanted the Indians punished.

In the end Chivington chose to gamble on the inexperienced farmers, miners, and merchants of the "bloodless third." They would stop the Indian threat to overland transportation. While Chivington was meeting with Connor, the marching orders for the Third reached Bijou Basin. Short of horses, supplies, and arms, the troopers rode through cold, late-fall days toward Fort Lyon. With them rode the expectations of Coloradans from the plains to the mountains. Something had to be done about the Indian menace, and they were not particularly choosy what that might be.

Chivington and some other officers arrived on the twenty-third. He took command, which, according to Sayre, caused "pretty general dissatisfaction." The bleak November days that followed would be forever etched on the soldiers' lives. At daybreak on the twenty-ninth, after an all-night ride, the Third and some companies of the First Colorado Cavalry attacked Black Kettle's village at desolate, dreary Sand Creek.

Tired, aching, cold, and dispirited by the night's march, the men of the Third looked over the creek bottom and bluffs toward the village. Breakenridge noted that they had discussed their intentions during the ride—take no prisoners and fight them their own way ("scalp every one of them"). Only those tactics, they believed, would put fear into the Indians throughout the region. At long last they found in their grasp the murderous "animals" who had caused Coloradans so much grief, frustration, and expense. The Cheyenne and Arapahoe Indians meant nothing to them. Bugles sounded, shots were fired; they charged. In Denver, Byers noted in his diary that it was a "very fine day."

Sand Creek, as a military event, was finished. Chivington marched on beyond the site toward other villages. Finding nothing and with his men and horses worn out, he terminated further campaigning.

Fear, intolerance, and hatred rode in with the soldiers; recrimination, lies, and controversy rode out, outliving them all. The real victims that day were the Indian women and children who suffered and died. They constituted only part of a long chronicle of mistreatment, raping, and killing. In the man's world of Indian and white conflict, women and children on both sides suffered horribly.

The facts of the incident will never be known—the population of the village, the number of warriors, the number killed, the sex and age of the victims, the amount of mutilation, and whether these people were peaceful or simply renewing their energy for another fighting season. After analyzing the statements given at subsequent hearings, one must conclude that an astonishing number of innate liars participated in this fight. Either that, or they must have been universally myopic. Seldom in American history has such conflicting testimony been offered by seemingly rational witnesses.

The controversy surrounding the events at Sand Creek matters little. Of greater importance is an understanding of why the massacre took place at all. The Third, and the Coloradans it represented, was determined to have its hour of vengeance. When troops attacked the village, the hatred and frustration of generations poured forth. It may be honestly doubted that anyone could have stopped the bloodletting.

Chivington may have had other motives for attacking Sand Creek. Possible reasons include a desire for an overwhelming victory, too small a force to risk a longer campaign, favorable weather conditions, the nearing end of the Third's service, political and military ambitions, the risk of losing the element of surprise by attacking a village farther away, and the public's cry for action.

Coloradans would not tolerate interference with their lives and destinies. By fall 1864 they had had their fill of Cheyenne and Arapahoe Indians. Peace seemed unattainable; Wynkoop and Black Kettle's hopes were crushed. Evans and Chivington responded to the majority's wish in a way that seemed logical to them. A "civil war" had been waged for too many generations between two heterogeneous peoples who did not, and would not, accommodate each other. This was, in truth, America's longest war: American vs. American, each desiring to live in his own way on the same land.

Black Kettle's dream died that day, and the discredited chief and other survivors fled. An equally good man, Left Hand, was fatally wounded and died believing in peace as the answer. This Southern Arapahoe leader had welcomed fifty-eighters in their own language and served as one of the few bridges between the two cultures.

George Bent, son of the famous trader William Bent and his Cheyenne wife, Owl Woman, had been in the Indian camp when the attack came; though wounded, he survived. He recalled, as survivors escaped to villages to the northeast, "the terrible march, most of us being on foot, without food, ill-clad and encumbered with wounded and the women and children." Bent and his compatriots thirsted for revenge.

In an unprecedented winter campaign, Plains Indians attacked with vicious abandon. Overland transportation stopped, tele-graph wires were downed, and isolated parties found themselves in great danger. Julesburg was attacked twice and finally burned before the Indians retreated northward for the rest of the winter.

Denver and other communities rejoiced at the first news of Sand Creek. These people had been waiting a long time to even the score, and Chivington's report seemed to confirm that that had been accomplished. Other reports concurred with his. Sayre praised officers and men for conducting themselves bravely. Joseph Kenyon's first reaction on hearing the news was that the victory improved his "chances of getting through safe." Sara Hively hoped Andrew had survived unhurt (actually, he had never gotten into the fight) and that he would soon come home: "I want Andrew to get at something or other to make money. I am tired and sick of such things." When they returned in December, the "bloody thirdsters" paraded through Denver, forming a most imposing procession, according to Byers. The troops were eventually mustered out, ending their 100-day careers.

Sand Creek as a cause célèbre, however, was just beginning. By New Year's Eve, George Kassler had written Maria that Sand Creek was turning into a political affair; Chivington was accused of killing friendly Indians:

Although I am personally and politically opposed to the Colonel, still I do not believe any thing of the kind. From what I learn of those who were there, the scalps of their white victims, government horses they had stolen and numerous other articles found in their possession, seem to me the most convincing proofs that they were not of the friendly kind.

This is a great country, where from the small Indian fight in the far west to the greatest battles of the Potomac, that "bug bear" politics must have something to do with them.

By January, people were choosing sides, and Sand Creek came

under a cloud from which it would never emerge. The legislature stood firmly in its conviction: the Council and House passed a joint resolution thanking the officers and soldiers for "bravery displayed." Acting Governor Elbert reiterated the same theme in his annual message.

Newspaper articles and editorials, personal statements, letters, rallies, and finally the calling of a military commission in February to investigate charges all kept the topic fresh. The three-member commission, headed by Lt. Col. Samuel Tappan (no friend of Chivington), convened from February 9 through May. The conflicting testimony called into question the credibility of evidence and the commission's procedures.

During the last weeks of winter, the *Journal* and the *News* tore into each other again, this time at odds over the responsibility for Sand Creek and the Indian war.

Militarily, the attack at Sand Creek accomplished little. Chivington soon "relinquished command," pursuant to orders. The House and Council praised him for "ably and skillfully discharging his duties." In his place came Col. Thomas Moonlight, who was bombarded by the same old problems.

Moonlight heard pitiful cries for help, found himself short of troops, declared martial law in February because of the "threatening attitude" of the Plains Indians (and also because of isolation and the failure of the legislature to raise troops), and listened to Coloradans who pushed for a scalp bounty. He attempted to increase his ranks and was told by Curtis to make the best of what he had and wait for spring. New commander, no new miracles.

Additional companies were recruited, including one led by former sheriff William Cozens. Captain Cozens and his men enlisted for ninety days. Moonlight sent patrols out to protect wagon trains and escort stages, generally suffering the same limitations as previous commanders.

Postmaster Byers disliked his job during these tense months. He wrote the assistant postmaster general in Washington on April 4 that, for more than half the past quarter, regular mail service had been interrupted, "materially reducing business." Now, he thankfully noted, mails were arriving regularly, the crisis had begun to ease. Sand Creek was finally being crowded out of the newspapers by events in the East as Richmond fell and the war drew to a close. On April 12 the *News* ran the headline, "All Quiet on the Plains."

Clerk Frank Young anticipated an uneventful journey when he left New York for Denver in late February, following "several months of pleasant castle-building." He dreamed of finding better things in Colorado than the crowded city and humdrum pursuits he had left behind. All along the road he saw remnants of the recent fighting: smoke-blackened walls, wrecked ranch homes, the ruins of Julesburg, graves, a nearly illegible "headboard" telling of a massacred family, and one dead, mutilated Indian. All were "ghastly testimony to the ferocious hatred engendered in the Plainsman against him and his kind by the barbarous warfare of the past year." Forty-two days on the trail brought Young to Denver and a new life.

"New life" was what Colorado was all about and, in a real sense, explained why Sand Creek had happened. Perhaps men had willingly sacrificed dignity and honor to impulses born of greed and fear. But most of them probably believed that their actions had been justified. Circumstances forced decisions and actions. The excesses of battle may be justly criticized; other events must be judged against what seemed at the time untenable circumstances.

13

"Water got the best of whiskey"

"NEXT TO A GOOD DIGESTIVE APPARATUS, the proper observance of all religious duties is the best preparation for the journey before me," wrote Nathaniel Hill to his uneasy wife back in Providence. Alice had every right to be nervous; crossing the plains in 1864 could be more dangerous than ever before.

Prior to reaching Atchison to board the stage, Hill had to traverse Missouri, where bushwhackers threatened every train. Because of Indian depredations along the overland trails, Hill and his fellow stage passengers had to dip more deeply into their pocketbooks for tickets, up from April's $100 to November's $150. Like Twain and others before him, Hill found the trip to Colorado a revelation: "As for hardship and discomfort, I had underestimated it." Hot days, dust ("we are all of one color & that nearly black"), cool nights, and poor food (consisting usually of "fried pork or ham, potatoes so far soaked that I cannot possibly eat them & shortcake as fat as the potatoes") further disillusioned him. After seven miserable days and nights of uninterrupted travel, Hill arrived in Denver.

Except for the increased danger, a temporary problem, travel conditions had changed little during the past four years. If one wished to travel in what comfort and speed were available, he had to pay the price. James Willson journeyed from Boston to Nevada City in October to inspect some mining property. His total expenses for tickets, luggage, meals, and miscellaneous expenditures exceeded $330, far beyond the reach of the ordinary American, who still lumbered along by wagon.

Once in Denver, travelers found territorial roads fair to miserable and made worse by every storm. Stages left the metropolis daily for Golden and Central—weekly for Boulder, Pueblo, Breckenridge and other communities—providing the best connections yet available if one could ignore dust, bumps, and general discomfort.

Visionary Coloradans continued to dream of railroad connec- tions, not simply to Denver but to the mountains beyond, where profit awaited the bold. In March 1865, an overland camel com- pany proposed to establish an Omaha-to-Sacramento freighting business. This novel idea was dismissed in favor of a quest for the railroad.

Up in the mountains, poor transportation created the same old headache. John Dyer resorted to trying a "packcow." He aban- doned the idea when she took off on a bawling warpath. To con- quer snow, stage companies commonly substituted runners for wheels, a tiresome innovation that at least kept passengers and mail moving until the worst of the weather passed.

As winter lingered on (locals regretted that Rocky Mountain weather ignored spring), Coloradans hoped immigration would increase. Acting Governor Elbert propounded this theme in the governor's annual message, encouraging legislators to devise a plan to promote the territory in Europe. If successful, such a plan might balance the outflow to Montana, which continued at an alarming rate. Colorado could ill afford to lose people such as Denver's pioneering townsman, John Ming, who went to Virgin- ia City and opened a book and stationery store. Newlyweds John and Nettie Kinna left Central for Bannack. Others made money from the outgo: ambitious Henry Porter turned a small fortune by bringing wagons and well-broken cattle to the territory the past April to sell to Montana-bound folks. The commodities sold like "hot cakes," a bonanza for Porter, a bust for Colorado.

Profit continued to be the name of the game—for Horace Tabor in Buckskin Joe and David Moffat in Denver. Tabor stayed with his small store and his practice of grubstaking miners, which was interrupted occasionally by a business trip to Denver. Entrepreneur Moffat, on the other hand, dreamed of railroads, and of Denver as the banking and business heart of the Rocky Mountains. Working overtime as Colorado's adjutant general, Moffat could do little more than dream.

Byers, who continued to earn extra income as Denver's postmaster, pursued a seemingly endless round of duties in the territory's busiest post office. During the four months before he became postmaster, 100,000 three-cent stamps had been ordered and over half of them sold. He attempted to educate Washington about the special problems of his office. A "characteristically transient" population frustrated Washington-mandated carriers; general delivery could do the job at less cost and provide better service. The post office department, however, had instituted carrier delivery the same day the battle at Gettysburg began and wanted Denver to modernize.

The government relentlessly pressured Byers to find a new location. Some people had alleged that the post office was being run in the interest of Woolworth and Moffat, which occupied the same building; Byers denied the allegation. The high cost of answering letters of inquiry, which "daily flooded" his office, (most without stamps to cover replies) irritated him.

After months of searching, the postmaster finally leased a wooden building in April 1865. It did not meet the fireproof specifications demanded by the post office department, but the proper buildings, Byers resignedly told his superiors, commanded enormous rents and were all occupied.

More typical of the territory's post offices was the one at Empire. In June it received thirty-five letters; the biggest purchase was twelve cents' worth of stamps. Most of the letters came from within the territory. Volume of mail was not the issue, as both postmaster Tabor and Moffat knew. A post office in your store increased business by bringing in customers who might not otherwise have stopped.

For most Coloradans the daily or weekly visit to the post office provided their only contact with the federal government. The postal department did its best but was hard pressed to keep up with the shifting population. As Byers found out, complaints outnumbered compliments.

An unusually high number of complaints bombarded businessmen in general during the fourth year of the war. Transportation difficulties and Indian problems caused most of the griping; as shortages emptied shelves, costs soared and customers' tempers rose with them. Prices increased across the board, from food (flour jumped from the $12–$16 range to $20–$23) to services. Central's male population booed a 100-percent increase for a shave, from twenty-five to fifty cents in November. Billy Smith saw so promising a future that he quit the restaurant business and opened a barber shop. Frank Hall grumbled, "Aren't barbers of this country crowding things hugely?" He did not consider a haircut for $1.00 or coloring of a moustache for $1.50 any bargain either. For whatever reason, within a fortnight the barbers reduced their prices to the previous twenty-five cents for a shave; the customer won this round.

Even newspapers felt the economic pinch. The paper shrank in size as the price, along with the cost of advertising, increased. Not until November did Hollister finally get his *Journal* back to regular size; the price stayed put. He justified the increase by noting that the cost of a ream of paper had risen from $5 to $20 in the past year and every other expense had escalated fifty to seventy-five percent. A single copy now cost ten cents, a year's subscription was $24. Citing similar woes, Byers raised the *News'* price to $24, too. The eastern press gave no relief to the harassed reader, either—the price of the *New York Times* increased to four cents.

Although they agreed on price, Hollister and Byers agreed on little else. Now that Gibson had finally ceased publishing in Denver, having been unable to compete successfully, Byers felt free to aim his editorial guns at Central and Black Hawk. Through all the tumult, the newspaper business continued to be as chancy as ever. The Gold Hill *Message* ceased to publish after five weeks. Hollister sympathized with the *Message's* plight and hoped the "boys" had retired in time to save themselves.

The Denver Typographical Union, initially organized in 1859, kept the publishers on edge by repeatedly demanding higher wages to match the rising cost of living. Not awed by Byers's threats to discharge union members, the members threatened a walkout. Local #49 supported the demands of its fellow printers in Central City and Black Hawk, which did not endear the union to the mountain editors, either.

Although the union did succeed in raising wages, 1864 was not a good year for the organization. In the face of Indian troubles, a struggling newspaper economy, and rising prices, members decamped or fell into arrears with their dues. By April 1865, only sixteen held good standing; eight had withdrawn, two were suspended, and one had been expelled over the past year.

Lawyers also discovered that the going could be rough at times. The general attitude of disdain toward them had softened somewhat, but it had not gone away. Hollister took a swipe at the bar in May:

Central is full of vultures. (Ah! excuse us gents, we intended to write lawyers.) The mistake is all the more pardonable, because terms convey to the minds of disinterested parties suggestions of synonyms, and things quite natural you know.

Recent arrival George Watson discovered how arduous establishing himself in the profession could be. "I like the west," he wrote to a friend in July, "but do not wish to practice here unless I strike a d——d good chance." He preferred the East, finding Denver too rough-and-tumble and expensive.

The legal profession proved lucrative for Henry Teller, whose reputation rose quickly. When he helped ex-Coloradan George Ingersoll, now living in Chicago and recovering from a severe illness, by collecting a debt and resolving a problem with a onetime partner, Henry received this note of gratitude:

. . . and could you have seen the silent tears flow from the eyes of my wife, one of the most patient and helpful women that ever lived, you would feel that you had done a deed that amply paid you.

For all its Victorian sentimentality, the comment showed that Colorado had become a place where justice and law would prevail.

Butcher Joseph Block in Black Hawk experienced justice both as accuser and accused. He took his neighbor, who owned a hotel, into court for discharging kitchen slop onto his property, then was similarly summoned to answer a misdemeanor charge when he obstructed the street by leaving a woodpile and delivery cart on it.

Murder still generated the most interest; it created a sensation when one of the participants was the old fur trapper and frontier legend, James Beckwourth. When "Nigger Bill," a "savage and dangerous character," tried to break into Beckwourth's ranch and saloon a few miles up the Platte from Denver, the proprietor responded with his double-barreled shotgun. A jury acquitted him. Savage characters were becoming unfashionable.

Counterfeiting of those unloved greenbacks also caused the law some trouble. In March, Byers warned that everything from $5 to $100 bills was being passed in Denver. The $50 and $100 bills were the most dangerous, being "better calculated to deceive."

As they had since the beginning, Colorado's merchants struggled to build the territory into something more than a temporary mining site. Times had not been easy since Fort Sumter; now, in the spring of 1865, some problems seemed to be passing. "I Scream, You Scream, *Everybody* screams over the frigidity of the Ice Cream now manufactured by our friend Simon Louis of the Ballon Restaurant," hailed Hollister, probably after receiving a free sample. Colorado had come a long way in six years—in 1859 ice cream was a luxury that had been left back east.

The communities where these merchants worked and lived had also changed. Newspaperman Albert Richardson visited Denver in 1860 and 1865. He brought joy to Denverites' hearts by describing the positive changes, including increased population, imposing buildings, improved bills of fare (not materially different from New York or Chicago), and the "habits, dress and surroundings" of older states. And these refinements had survived a trauma unequaled even by the previous year's fire—May's great flood.

Mollie Sanford, living at Camp Weld and just returned from a visit to her family in Nebraska, awakened to these events:

On the morning of the 19th about 3 o'clock the night watchman at the corral came pounding on our door with the startling cry, "Get up. There is a flood in Cherry Creek, and hundreds of people are drowning." . . . We could not believe but that he was fooling, until we heard the distant roar and the shouts of men like the coming of a mighty tempest. Great inky waves rolled up 10 or 15 feet carrying on their crests pieces and parts of houses, cattle, and for all we know human beings too.

Fortunately for Denver, the loss of life nowhere reached the watchman's prediction (eight people drowned).

The monetary loss proved less than the fire's. Byers's office, which had been strategically placed on piles across Cherry Creek so as not to offend the former rival towns of Auraria and Denver, was swept away, and water damaged his home. When the Platte again overflowed on the twenty-seventh, the Byerses found themselves marooned on their ranch. They had to "move out with a boat," as he wrote in his diary. Chivington and some of his soldiers converted themselves into temporary sailors and saved the day, thereby cementing a friendship between the editor and the military hero. Byers and his family lived with the Evanses for ten days before moving to the still unoccupied Colorado Seminary building. The Typographical Union lost its books, papers, charter, and $120 in funds on hand. Its president later admitted ruefully, "we almost lost our identity."

During the next two weeks, the rains played no favorites, hitting mountains and plains alike. As far south as Pueblo, drownings occurred, and farmers suffered damage to their crops when the Arkansas overflowed its banks. "Outrageous, outrageouser, outrageousest, superlatively ridiculous and inconsistent," complained Hollister. His partner, Hall, wrote to his mother in mid-June that Colorado had had a terrible time generally and all transportation, except by foot, had stopped. As the weather improved and things started to dry out, Hall found a humorous side to it all:

Well this Platte River is noted for its extreme sobriety, is now and then inclined to "spree it" in the most outrageously ridiculous manner. . . . Denver's pretty cottages move upon the bosom of waters down to New Orleans. The people of D. seldom go to New Orleans after their cottages, when once they take a notion to float thitherward.

As Denver rebuilt, so did the territory. Byers purchased the *Commonwealth*'s plant and resumed publication within a month; the City of Denver, not so lucky, never recovered its lost safe and records. As late as August, with aftereffects still being felt, Joe

Kenyon jokingly wrote Barlow that for the "first time in the history of Colorado, water got the best of whiskey."

From this recuperation, Denver moved right into the Indian scare and all its attendant troubles—bad luck did seem to run in threes. Eighteen sixty-four had not been a great year. That Denver survived and could be so highly esteemed by Richardson marked its destiny.

Farmers also suffered the flood's ravages. They also had to grapple with grasshoppers, sunflowers choking the crops (a "greater curse to Colorado than Canada thistles to the Eastern states"), and the persistent threat of Indians, as the farmers broke sod farther out on the plains. But they had proven they could survive and prosper; so had the ranchers. Agriculture had taken root permanently in Colorado, despite comments published in the *New York Times* (July 12) describing the country as "really, naturally poor" and not in any sense an agricultural region. Local boosters bristled at the insult, but the writer was correct in one respect: The territory still could not produce enough home-grown "eatables."

By November Empire was facing a potato shortage. An angered resident, who signed himself "Index," accused farmers of hoarding potatoes until the price climbed higher: "Your course is very hard on poor people in the mountains who support you all, for without the miners ranchmen could not live!" Empire eventually received its spuds.

The thrust of the *Times's* statement could not be completely denied, even in light of agriculture's great gains over the past years. Farmers depended on mining for their livelihood, but miners could not depend on farmers. Farming had nonetheless made progress, shown clearly by the organization of the Colorado Territorial Agricultural Society, which received its charter in 1864. At the April 1, 1865, meeting, members laid plans for an agricultural fair, and, thanks to an appropriation of five hundred dollars from the legislature to pay premiums, the organization's venture looked promising. Among the trustees elected that day were none other than William Byers and, unexpectedly, Central City's Henry Teller.

All indications pointed to a flourishing year for agriculture in

1865. Spring showers propelled plains farmers to a rousing start, while slowing travelers and angering stage drivers. Byers saw his vision being realized—the garden would bloom.

In contrast, the same euphoria did not permeate mining; 1864 subdued even the most optimistic. "Can some curse be inflicted on this country for some previous sin that everything seems to be attended by bad luck," complained Porter to Barlow in January. Weather, Indians, lack of skilled miners, escalating costs, and re-fractory ore all conspired against ore digging.

These drawbacks burdened absentee-owner Samuel Barlow even more. He sent a young man west to help with the mining, but Barlow was advised that "from association, education and other surroundings," the new man proved ill fitted to encounter all "the rough usage" that everyone was obliged to "submit to in this *very* rough country." Poor Barlow, for all his acclaimed business sense and judgment, could not control the destiny of his investments in Colorado. An endless stream of reports criticized or defended various actions, told of lodes doing well or not doing well, and informed Barlow of legal disputes.

Porter ran into trouble at Gregory Point with the neighboring Smith and Parmalee Company, which contested ownership of the vein. The quarrel reached threatening proportions when Smith and Parmalee men drifted under Porter's shaft, put a shot in the roof, and gave his men the alternative of climbing out or being blown out. Porter's employees chose to exit peacefully; the ex-general prudently told his miners not to incur any violence because he had hired them to work, not fight. Porter closed down the New York Gold Mining Company in mid-April. To Barlow, the situation was rather confusing; he could not seem to make a profit no matter what he did.

Ovando Hollister also bemoaned the current state of mining. Investment had dried up, companies had discharged hands, and the cost of living and wages remained too high (management's view). These conditions boded ill for opening the season. Action had to be taken, or a great deal would be "lost in the bye and bye." Hollister warned that real mining had to take the place of speculation, wages had to be scaled down, merchants had to lower prices, and a competent class of men had to be employed to superintend mining operations. If these goals could be accomplished, mining would "come out all right"; otherwise, work on the mines could cease and bring absolute ruin to Gilpin County.

This uncharacteristic gloom reflected the bitter remnants of a shattered gold bubble more than anything else. But every cloud supposedly has a silver lining, and that adage proved true when spring came. The warm days motivated prospectors, who swarmed over the mountains above Georgetown to stake claims on silver ore. Would this be the rush of 1859 all over again? No one knew for sure, but Hendrie and Butler, in the meantime, prepared to build and repair all kinds of mining machinery in their Eureka Foundry. They were still defying competitors to match their reasonable prices and excellence of work. Territorial mining was becoming more home-based all the time.

Gloomy thoughts never discouraged William Byers, who delightedly called attention to Canon City oil when another new well was struck in March. He gloated that Colorado's "sumptuous oil supply" could meet the needs of the Rocky Mountains with only a little effort. Byers always found something positive even in the worst of situations.

Another forward-looking group, those people favoring statehood, commenced to beat their drums again as the new year progressed. Their anticipation might have seemed unwarranted in light of the previous year's vote but, undeterred, they called on all loyal Americans to rally to the cause. A few Coloradans were calling for Evans to resign; he had become somewhat of a scapegoat for all the territory's troubles. From Washington, the governor fought the attacks on him and planned to return to the territory to resume his official duties.

Evans and Acting Governor Elbert faced a minor secession movement of their own. Conejos and Costilla counties, unhappy with Colorado's jurisdiction, preferred to secede and be annexed to New Mexico. In the opinion of the predominantly Anglo population, these southern counties had always been poor stepchildren—largely Democratic, Catholic, and Spanish-Mexican. Chaffee and Evans displayed their intolerance when they accused the Mexican population of being totally anti-statehood, whereas the "loyal" American population almost unanimously favored it. Even Hill, hardly in the territory two months, demonstrated cultural prejudice on his tour with Gilpin. He complained about the unappetizing cuisine, the predominance of Mexicans in the southern San Luis Valley, and the "easy indolent life." This hard-working New Englander was shocked that the men never worked, as long as they had a few cents in their pockets, and that virtue was "entirely wanting among the women." The two cultures could rarely be merged in the Victorian mind, and the bias showed in Coloradans' attitudes.

J. L. Gaspar, from San Luis, eloquently stated the case for his maligned brethren in a letter to the *News* on March 22. He stoutly defended the people of Costilla County as peaceful and law abiding. He explained that Colorado law and customs differed so much from Spanish-Mexican practices that they found them difficult to comprehend, which would not be the case in New Mexico. If the laws were printed in Spanish, Gaspar believed, many of their grievances would disappear. He also pointed out that local members elected to the Territorial House had not reported for the last session, not because of an avowed determination to secede, but because they could not pay the "exorbitant prices" up north. The quiet voice of the southern counties had spoken, but at the moment no one heeded it or the hurt of these people. The fourth year of the war was drawing to a victorious close and diverted attention to other things.

Coloradans appreciated that they now had a history, a place and time to call their own. (One ambitious historian already had plans to write that story.) Overlooking the storage problem, Byers urged people to preserve their newspapers: "It brings up the very age with all its bustle and every day affairs, and marks its genius and spirit more than the labored description of the historian." Byers understood the need to save Colorado's history; he and his contemporaries were a vital part of it.

Despite the recording of past events, Coloradans looked to the future. Conscientious Denverites already talked of the need for parks, the "lungs of a city." They wanted to start work now in a community still only a short walk from the open prairie. Their visions and expectations boded well for the territory.

14

"Jubilee tonight . . . of the second birth of the Republic"

THANKS TO PORTER PENNOCK, Ellen Coffin found romance at the end of her Colorado rainbow; her teaching also fell victim to love. Married on May 1, 1864, the young couple settled down to farm-ing on Left Hand Creek, named for the Arapahoe chief who had once lived there. Their five-room home was equipped with a few things considered "extras" in those days: a small cook stove, dishes, three chairs, a lounge, and bedsteads. Pennock had been to Omaha for supplies earlier. For those things that were not available, substitutes were improvised. Bleached and fringed flour sacks made good table cloths, and one of Ellen's calico dresses was converted into a very pretty lounge cover. The Pen-nocks joyously (and bravely) set forth to challenge married life.

No Victorian family considered itself complete without a baby. "Babies ought to be plump, ruddy . . . something is wrong with children not chubby," advised the *Christian Advocate* via the *Rocky Mountain News*. The threat of childhood illness and death stalked parents east or west. Central City newspaper editor, Dave Collier, described the pain death inflicted when his only child, Charles, died at age two.

Undesirables sometimes created friction in a household. Sara Hively rented rooms to a couple and later discovered, to her hor-ror, that they were not married. She suffered further embarrass-ment when the police appeared to make inquiries about the man and woman. Sara evicted them as soon as possible.

Domestic conflict occasionally enlivened the routine of married life. One story, circulating in Colorado on the Pennocks' wedding day, told of a rebellious husband who sold his wife for $250 when their two hearts no longer beat as one. "Rather a cool but happy transition, even for Colorado," mused bachelor Frank Hall.

Some couples suffered the strain of extended separation. Lonely Nathaniel Hill wrote his wife that he spent July Fourth at the Coberle ranch fifty-five miles south of Denver. When the two daughters came home from a dance, he "noticed the ladies in question dressed in the height of fashion. The days of low necks & short sleeves were revived in my memory."

Those pleasant occasions contrasted with Hill's encounters with armed men. "I do not enjoy living in a country where every man you meet, thinks it safe to carry a loaded pistol. The practice is universal in all parts of Colorado." Hill, traveling during the height of the Indian scare, probably acquired a distorted view of the prevalence of arms. The lawless days and consequent need to bear arms had almost disappeared by 1864-65. Carrying a pistol possibly reflected some men's attempts to live up to the frontier's image of masculinity. Drinking and carousing were also aspects of this stereotype. For all the women on the frontier, it remained a man's world. Ellen knew it and so did Augusta Tabor, who had lived there longer. If rowdiness were to be tamed, women would have to do it, and they went about their duty with ruthless efficiency.

For the Pennocks, Tabors, and Hill, maintaining good health was a priority. Before starting west, the knowledgeable college professor laid up a stock of medicine for the journey, including lemon juice, cayenne (a pinch in his drinking water), Persy Davis' Pain Killer, "senna in prunes," ginger, and five small bottles of brandy and whiskey, "none of which I expect to use," he told Alice. Most people still doctored themselves and sought a physician only as a last resort.

Byers continued to praise the climate and published health hints and remedies. He even went so far as to analyze fourteen ways people could get sick and advised how to avoid those pitfalls. He warned about eating too fast, drinking poisonous whiskey, keeping late hours, wearing tight clothes, and neglecting to wash the body. As an extra pointed reminder, he cautioned against starving the stomach to gratify the "vain and foolish passion of dress." "Trashy and exciting literature" was most emphatically to be avoided.

Contaminated water contributed to many stomach ailments, fevers, and "mountain sickness." Samuel Leach considered finding pure drinking water his most difficult chore. Mining residue polluted streams, and some of the nearby springs were highly mineralized and alkaline. He wrote brother George of his horror in seeing scum gather on drinking water.

Colorado provided an abundance of churches to save the souls of those who overindulged in stronger drink. For all his acidic comments, William Crawford dutifully organized Congregational churches, including one in Boulder that was launched in July with eleven members. The active Methodists had moved so far along that they now published the strangely named *Rocky Mountain Sunday School Casket*. The Baptist church in Central City was forced to adjourn its Sabbath school during the fall when needed books, Bibles, and papers failed to arrive from the East. They had been sent out in June but disappeared during the Indian raids on the overland trails.

Neither wars, floods, nor Indian raids stopped the Central City Methodists, who finally laid the cornerstone for their new church in September. The energetic Bethuel Vincent, founder and editor of the *Casket*, conducted appropriate ceremonies with the help of several other local ministers. The church would be a structure finer than its counterpart in Denver, the *Miners' Register* crowed. The walls were nicely started when winter brought work to an end.

To further improve the moral climate of their community, Central church members campaigned for a modified Sunday closing law, from 10 A.M. to 2 P.M. for business and amusement establishments. On the Sunday following the mayor's proclamation to that effect, the city attorney was discovered playing billiards during the hours in question! Colorado had not been domesticated enough to close down for even a few hours on Sunday.

The red-light districts conducted their activities undisturbed by moral outrage. The *Clipper* raised its price to ten cents a copy but still titillated readers with such offerings as "Susie Knight, the raciest poem ever published," new card photographs of "before and after" the bath and French dancing girls, and, for two bits, "Gems for Gentlemen," an illustrated book of amorous songs and poems. According to Byers's way of thinking, the *Clipper* must have been one of the great contributors to ill health among Coloradans!

Society, though improved since 1859, did not quite measure up to "good old settled towns in the East," someone named AB admitted in a letter to the *New York Times*. His confession was somewhat surprising, as Coloradans endeavored to keep up with current styles, support the theater (opera recitals, however, were not "thoroughly appreciated"), and increase the female popula-tion to bring balance to the male-dominated territory. One trait that especially upset AB was "the meanest characteristic of this country, the disposition of people to gossip." In some social circles, such chitchat probably provided the spice of life.

Public schools were now well established, and the Colorado Seminary had been founded in Denver. "Time may be necessary to make it equal to Harvard or Cambridge, but we must remem-ber that it will not flourish by neglect," advised Hollister. The territorial library contained over eight hundred volumes (mostly Congressional and state laws and documents), thanks to the work of Hiram Bennet and others. Parsimonious legislators decided, however, not to fund the position of librarian, which paid forty dollars per month, and abolished the appointment. The territorial treasurer assumed the librarian's duties.

For the musically inclined, Woolworth and Moffat promised the largest and choicest stock of sheet music "you ever saw out west." Coloradans shed tears over the sentimental "Just Before the Battle, Mother," danced to the catchy "Listen to the Mock-ing Bird," and worshiped with the hymns of the well-known Lowell Mason. The best-selling books related to the war and included a biography of General Grant and another of General Butler, who hardly seemed worth reading or writing about. Poets Longfellow and Whittier each published a volume, and Louisa Alcott produced a book of hospital sketches. Artemus Ward con-tinued to supply humor. The story of Theodore Parker's life and the speeches of Wendell Phillips enticed buyers of religious and abolitionist literature. *Everybody's Lawyer* promised a way to cir-cumvent the legal profession. Colorado seemed to be right in step with the rest of America, AB's comments notwithstanding.

Coloradans also fell in line with northerners when it came to blacks. To all appearances, blacks were making progress toward acceptance. Barney Ford's restaurant was hailed as the only first-class establishment of its kind in Denver. Kentucky-born William Hardin, a recent arrival, made a noticeable splash on the cultural scene. When this recognized orator and champion of blacks spoke in Central on the Haitian "Black Napoleon," Toussaint L'Ouver-ture, the *Daily Mining Journal* praised Denver's "Octoroon Orator" for his eloquence. Then, after noting he had attracted an "overflowing and attentive audience," the paper drove home an unspoken but prevalent sentiment: "Not withstanding the deep rooted prejudice which exists between the white and that to which he belongs."

The "deep rooted prejudice" did not evaporate after the slaves were freed; the issue of race replaced that of servitude. Evidence of segregation surfaced in many ways. Black church services and a black school in Denver were examples. Occasionally a protest was heard, as in a letter from a "colored man" in Central City. Since other Central Citians were usually identified by name or nom de plume, the identification of the letter writer reflected underlying prejudice. He observed that "colored children cannot enter a single school . . . thus we stand, debarred of light, but paying our hard earned money to educate those who, in turn, are willing to expel us from every avenue of learning, and who then stand ready to ridicule and debase us."

No more poignant letter was published in Colorado than this one; it spoke volumes about attitudes and atmosphere. Freeing the blacks was only a small step on a long road, even though over 600,000 men had died in a war that still dragged cruelly on into the spring of 1865.

War or no war, life went on. Con Orem, the "famous pugilist," wearing a belt proclaiming him "Champion of America," fought a few exhibitions in the spring before leaving for Salt Lake City. Before his departure, Denver had to defend its favorite against

"unmanly and unjust innuendoes" in eastern papers; one journalist, the "slandering scribbler," called him a "shocking bad
fighter." Colorado's "right, good gentleman" did not stay long in
Mormon country, moving on to Virginia City, Montana, where
he opened a saloon and fought again.

Con Orem's departure, declining mining districts, abandoned
camps, and collapsed buildings testified to an era's passing. In
other ways, life changed little or not at all. Boulder celebrated
the "glorious" fourth at Butte Grove, four miles below town,
with about six hundred ladies and gentlemen present, a far larger
number than would have gathered four years before. Speeches,
delicacies prepared by farm and town women, special music, and
impromptu toasts contributed to a pleasant holiday that concluded with a dance that lasted into the wee hours.

Thanksgiving, a recently declared holiday, was observed with
more solemnity and worship, along with the feasting. Turkeys
reached fifteen dollars apiece in Black Hawk (at Christmas, they
sold for three dollars per pound, feathers and all; farmers only
regretted they ran out of birds to sell). Governor Evans's proclamation reminded Coloradans that, despite floods, Indian wars,
and temporarily dampened prosperity, they had abundant reason
to unite in thanksgiving.

Sand Creek occurred a few days after the November holiday,
but Christmas quickly supplanted the tragedy in most people's
minds. George Kassler suffered a business setback when he failed
to receive his order of Christmas books until December 31. Making the best of a bad situation, he attempted to persuade his
customers that New Year's was as good a time as Christmas to
give presents. He justified his action in a letter to Maria: "But as
the Irishman thought, St. Patrick was as good a man as the
Fourth of July." Christmas fell on Sunday that year, so George
went to church and spent the afternoon at the Moffats discussing
"roast turkey, etc." For the moment, he forgot the lost books; a
violent wind storm later that night also kept his mind off his
troubles.

Hal Sayre and the boys of the Third spent Christmas in camp
waiting to be mustered out. Getting drunk helped some pass the
day.

On New Year's Eve Kassler escorted two married ladies, including Mrs. Moffat, to a party. "As usual [Dave] managed to
get up an excuse for not going." Kassler had fun, and it must be
hoped that Maria suffered no pangs of jealousy.

Parties, ice-skating, fishing, pool, and a host of other entertain-
ments were available to Coloradans in 1865. Jack Langrishe and
his company performed in Denver, although the ever-popular
Mike Dougherty had left the company to return east, breaking up
the partnership that had dominated the Colorado stage. The
gaiety, however, could never obscure somber news from the war
front. For the predominant Unionists, the news was getting better and better, though casualties increased.

Even out here, war's inherent tragedy touched individual lives.
William Byers learned that his brother, wounded and captured
during the Vicksburg campaign, had died in a Southern prison;
John Dyer's eldest son was killed and his youngest crippled for
life. Of the 4,903 Coloradans who served in the Union Army,
323 were dead by war's end. Totals for those who fought for the
Confederacy are unknown. Probably about one fifth of the territory's 1860 population fought on one side or the other.

Sherman and Grant, meanwhile, relentlessly attacked the battered Confederate forces blocking the way to Richmond and
Atlanta. Sherman reached his goal first. While Grant pinned Lee
down at the key railroad center of Petersburg and settled into
trench warfare, Sherman launched his drive to the sea. Eventually he turned northward toward Grant to trap Lee and his army
between them. He left behind him a smoldering trail of destruction; war had become hell. Coloradans were kept apprised of all
the action and knew the end was near.

The men of the Second Colorado continued to patrol and fight
in Missouri. They tendered little regard for their enemies, whose
"cowardly dispositions" entitled them to a term no higher than
"bushwhackers" (*Soldier's Letter*, September 17 and October 15,
1864). The troops wanted this dreary, deadly war to be over so
they could go home.

Other Colorado troops equally wished out of the army, but
they were stationed at Fort Garland, where the Utes were causing troubles. Capt. Charles Kerber gave an indication of attitudes

to come when he reported, "I am very sorry that these depredations happened, but if they go on in this way they will find me a
hard fellow to deal with."

By late spring, even the most die-hard pessimist had to admit
the tide had turned in favor of the Northern armies. Charleston
fell in late February, causing widespread rejoicing. Kassler
described Denver on that occasion as "brilliantly illuminated" by
torchlights and transparencies. The Elbert Guards' little gun
"barked so joyously" in Black Hawk over the same victory. Next,
Coloradans knew, would be news of Richmond's fall, an event
eagerly anticipated for nearly four years.

They would have to wait a while longer. Sherman drove
ruthlessly north, and Grant prepared to launch a flanking movement to force Lee's battered army out of Petersburg, Virginia,
the gateway to Richmond. What once had been a gentlemen's
war had evolved into total war; civilian and soldier alike were fair
game. The few remaining southern sympathizers in Colorado lay
low—they had no reason to celebrate. Their cause had died
months ago at Gettysburg, Vicksburg, and the hellfire of the
Wilderness.

Unionists could relax enough to enjoy a good chuckle over
some of the contemporary humor:

What is the difference between a good soldier and a fashionable
young lady? One faces the powder, and the other powders the face.

Why is Sheridan the Prince of Broom Scavengers? Because he wakes
up Early and sweeps a Longstreet.

As always, women bore more than their fair share of the kidding.
At eighteen, a woman prefers the best dancer in the room; at
twenty-five, the best talker; at thirty, the richest man; and forty
is a period no young lady ever reaches!

April had not been so full of fun since the warm, golden days of
1859. The light-hearted mood contributed to a spate of April
fools. Hats with rocks under them ambushed pedestrian hat
kickers, and asking for a drink in one's favorite saloon might produce a bottle of "pure Platte water or some of that colored stuff
from turbid Cherry Creek." Prankster and victim laughed
together and waited for someone else to fall into the trap. One

Central rogue carried on the celebration a couple of days longer by spreading red pepper on the post office stove, just as the crowd gathered to await the eastern mail. "Soon the promiscuous mass took up line of march wheezing away," all the while cursing the playful fellow who did the mischief.

The lightheartedness disguised but did not replace the grim reality that men, north and south, were still dying as the final of' fensive opened. When Richmond fell, Central City celebrated— "every way in which joy could be expressed was resorted to." Several windows were broken in the noisy celebration that in' cluded firing of guns and powder blasts. The cheering crowd tramped around in "mud half a leg deep," almost until morning. Out in the St. Vrain River Valley, north of Boulder, the farmers also rejoiced. Burlington unlimbered its artillery—two huge an' vils—and fired a thirteen-gun salute as a "goodly" number of citizens celebrated.

From Richmond, the road to Appomattox proved mercifully short for the war-wearied country. The end came on Sunday, April 9, springtime in Virginia. A "cloudy & chilly" day, noted Byers, where winter had been hanging on disagreeably for the past week. Denverites took the news pretty much in stride.

Untiring John Dyer heard the news while on a missionary trip to New Mexico; George Kassler, just before he started east to be married. Nathaniel Hill, back in Colorado less than a month, took time off from wrestling with the refractory ore problem to celebrate. William Byers could finally furl the flag that he had vowed to fly on the masthead of the *News* until victory, "We'll not furl THAT flag until over our Nation, ALL the stars blaze again in one grand constellation." Not until late November did he fulfill that promise. Veteran Romine Ostrander and his company made no noise about Lee's surrender, nor were "any great demonstrations of joy manifested. Everybody seems to think it a matter of course."

Civilians were not so blase. Central planned a big celebration— "Jubilee tonight . . . of the second birth of the Republic."—for April 13, the day four years earlier when "the noble Anderson" had lowered the flag after the attack on Fort Sumter.

The nation celebrated, and so did a tired president. For the

Lincolns, it would be a night at Ford's Theater to see the play that had been a Colorado favorite for years, *Our American Cousin.* Mollie Sanford spoke for her generation:

> There comes to us sad news, the assassination of President Lincoln. He died a martyr, died by the hand of a cowardly assassin, J. Wilkes Booth. He had been one of the noblest and best of our Presidents. How can our country spare him? O! what a cruel thing! The whole nation mourns. O could he have but lived to see Peace again in our land.

Peace again. Coloradans in their joy had temporarily forgotten the Sand Creek imbroglio, the threat to the overland trails, the mining problems, the failure to achieve statehood, western rivals, and the changes that had come since April of 1861.

The prospect of a better tomorrow came with the peace at hand. The Indian threat was lessening, the boys were coming home, a transcontinental railroad was under construction, and a new mining rush had begun. With these long-awaited tomorrows now becoming reality, the war could be quickly put behind them.

Colorado had crossed a divide and would never be the same again. America and the territory had changed. An era had died, a new one was aborning. What had been lost could not be forgotten. Whatever lay ahead, the ever-optimistic Coloradans seemed confident enough to handle. The star of empire again took course toward a better, if unknown, future.

Epilogue

PEACE HAD COME TO AMERICA. The battle's fury, the killing, had ended and, like Lincoln, belonged to the ages. Bright flags, cheers, and last good-byes accompanied the boys as they marched toward home, most of them much changed by their experiences. The war had changed America, too, leaving behind a legend, a haunting memory, and places where the present would always be the past. Now the quiet folk, who had merely wanted to live in peace, could pick up the pieces of a war-torn generation.

Perhaps meaning could be found in the wreckage of lost lives and a vanished way of life. Perhaps the overall message would somehow be greater than the sum of its tragic parts. Perhaps a country's dreams could now take on new substance, new focus, new reality. In the confusion and agony following Lincoln's death, Coloradans simply did not know.

They did know that in four war-weary years their territory had changed. Where once the fifty-niners had come only to prospect, pan, and go home, they now had created stability, built towns, and carved for themselves a place in the new America, forging a permanence that gave new significance to their lives.

People had continued to come west regardless of the war. Some wanted only to escape the long arm of the army draft; most were following, in their own ways, the centuries-old American quest for a new life on the frontier. Colorado did not keep all of them; more often than not they drifted on to the mining fields of Idaho and Montana.

243

In some ways, a millennium seemed to have passed since 1861. It had been 1,461 days since that April morning in Charleston. Colorado had been more romantic then, full of greater opportunity and gold, offering more adventure and abundant hope. With its present statehood squabbles, refractory ore mysteries, and Sand Creek troubles, the territory beckoned less alluringly. Curiously, the legend of 1859 had already softened the sharp edges of memory, dulled the disappointments, and sired a growing band of Coloradans who longed for the good old days. Their memories, in many cases, enhanced the reality of events.

Behind the men and women who called Colorado home stretched innumerable long, dusty roads that reached the main streets of the towns and villages whence they came. Warm, lingering thoughts of a sweetheart left behind or a Christmas with family, were, perchance, all that remained of those earlier days. Now at home in Colorado, their future rode on tomorrow's fortunes. This new life had transformed them all, as had the war; there would be no going back.

The name Colorado commanded attention, as important in its own way as Bull Run, Shiloh, Chancellorsville, and Petersburg. Those who had helped shape the territory could take pride in being pioneers. Five men had looked out on the promising spring of 1861, and now the promising spring of 1865 lay at hand.

Boulder farmer Sylvanus Wellman had so prospered that he went back east for a vacation and was in Chicago when Grant and Lee met at Appomattox. Four years ago he had been breaking ground for spring planting while enthusiastic Confederate gunners shelled Fort Sumter, now in ruins, along with Charleston and the nation it once symbolized. Wellman exemplified the real strength of America and was a Colorado success story.

Still a bachelor, Frank Hall might have given up mining, but he intended to make his fortune and also find just the right woman to marry. The idea of returning home after two years had been supplanted by a determination to stay in Colorado. Confident that "Time, Faith and Energy" would give him "all I want of this world's goods," he lived in Black Hawk, one of the editors and proprietors of the *Daily Mining Journal*. His knack for writing served him well, and he proved adept at giving as good as he got in the feisty world of Colorado journalism.

William Gilpin had been in Washington in 1861, looking forward to assuming the reins of power as Colorado's governor. Now he lived in Denver and hoped to be nominated governor by the reviving statehood advocates. His aspirations for an "empire" in the San Luis Valley could be put on hold if the old warhorse were to again enter the arena of public affairs.

Colorado had not proven so promising for Edward Seymour, who mined, went home for a while, then returned. Oro City failed to provide more than just a living for the Seymour family. Seymour never found the opportunity to make his fortune and died in Denver in August.

Quite to the contrary, William Byers had climbed almost to the pinnacle of his prestige and power. No one seriously challenged the *News* as the territory's leading newspaper, nor the spunky editor as its foremost spokesman and defender. Byers could see many of the ideas and projects he had advocated, from farming to railroads, coming to fruition. He could ask for little more at the moment, except perhaps a reversal on the statehood question and a quieting of the Sand Creek controversy.

"Hurrah for Colorado" and its march of empire. This former wilderness had been transformed, not by any carefully arranged plan, but by youthful enthusiasm, a dash of luck, little enough money, lots of sweat and tears, and a confidence born of optimism undimmed by a setback or two. Far from the American mainstream, unsung heroes, not to mention a few scamps, had brought Colorado into this new era. A peaceful April dawn broke bright and clear for them once more.

> *Out, out, brief candle!*
> *Life's but a walking shadow, a poor player,*
> *That struts and frets his hour upon the stage,*
> *And then is heard no more.*

These words, spoken more than once on the Colorado stage by the brooding, murderous Macbeth, now speak for those pioneers. Before they "cross over the range" into the realm of history, grant them one more moment on the stage to discover what happened to their dreams.

Susan Ashley enjoyed camping in the mountains, helped raise funds for the Colorado exhibit at the 1893 World's Fair, and in 1908 still lived in Denver, forty-seven years after arriving there as a bride.

James Beckwourth, the old frontiersman and trapper, scouted for the army after the war and died in 1866 or 1867, like his era, a relic of the past.

John Xavier Beidler became a famous vigilante in Virginia City, Montana. He later worked as a gold-shipment guard and collector of customs for Montana and Idaho.

Hiram Bennet's career in Colorado politics never soared. He returned to Denver, resumed his law practice, and later served as Denver's postmaster and state senator.

George Bent recovered from his Sand Creek wounds and resumed fighting in the summer of 1865. Two years later he tried to arrange a new treaty and, when the plains wars ended, he went to Oklahoma with the Cheyenne Indians.

Albert Bierstadt achieved enormous popularity in the 1860s and 1870s as America's foremost painter. He sketched and painted in the west and Colorado on several occasions.

Amos Billingsley, chaplain for a regiment of the Pennsylvania Volunteers, was captured and spent the rest of the war in Richmond's Libby Prison. He married in 1865 and lived in the East and the South.

Black Kettle continued to work for peace. He died on November 27, 1868, when his village was attacked by George Custer and the Seventh Cavalry.

Edward Bliss, remembered as a most "eminent Bohemian," worked for London and San Francisco newspapers before his health failed. He died in 1876 on his way back to Colorado.

Joe Block left Black Hawk and Central City, moving with the Colorado mining frontier to Irwin and, finally, Crested Butte, where he operated a butcher shop.

William Breakenridge led an adventurous life in the West, which he recounted in *Helldorado*, his autobiography.

Bela Buell operated mines near Central City, and then moved to Leadville in the 1880s, dabbling all the while in politics. He returned to New York in 1896.

Elizabeth Byers busied herself with club work, travel, and church activities and "enjoyed poor health." She stood loyally by William when his affair with a Golden milliner became public.

William Byers remained editor of the *News* until 1878. His reputation had soured after the affair but he rebounded from the setback and became president of the state historical society and Denver's Chamber of Commerce. When he died in 1903, it was said of Byers that he had touched almost every aspect of life in Denver since 1859.

Mlle Carolista, the charming young actress and tightrope walker, dropped out of sight after the war.

Pat Casey, in 1867, was reportedly acquiring "an education" denied him earlier and owned a wholesale tobacco house. He apparently lost all his money in New York, went to Deadwood, South Dakota, during the gold rush and died there.

Jerome Chaffee emerged as Colorado's premier politician, a tireless worker for statehood, and finally became one of its first senators. He continued to invest in mining, became embroiled in a scandal or two, and, with Moffat and others, organized Denver's 1st National Bank.

John Chivington never fully rebounded from the aftermath of Sand Creek. He left Colorado but returned in the 1880s, found Coloradans' attitude pro–Sand Creek, and lived out his life in Denver. Despite all bitter feelings, he helped the Wynkoop family get a pension after Ed's death.

David Collier remained Gilpin County superintendent of schools until 1867. In the 1880s he was president of the Gilpin County Opera House Association.

Daniel Conner successfully fled the territory and from 1862 to 1867 prospected and fought Indians in Arizona. He returned east, then disappeared from history until reappearing in California in 1909.

William Cozens, rated as "the greatest sheriff" in Colorado, moved to Grand County at the head of the Fraser River, where he operated a ranch and hotel.

William Crawford organized Congregational churches in Boulder, Central City, and Denver and brought ministers to the territory to serve them. He left in 1868.

E. S. Cummins operated the Idaho Springs mineral springs until he sold out in 1866. In 1873 Byers listed Cummins, address unknown, as owing the *News* twenty dollars.

Matthew Dale returned to Pennsylvania and married in 1863. He owned a wholesale produce business in Scranton, and also invested in some coal mines.

Mike Dougherty, "Inimitable Mike," returned to Central City in June. He died on July 5, 1865, probably of acute alcoholism.

William Dutt stayed in the army and was killed in a battle with Indians near Butte, Montana, on December 25, 1866.

John Dyer became a Colorado legend, the snow-shoe itinerant (also the title of his autobiography). He was active in the Methodist church almost up to his death in 1901. The man had matched his destiny.

Samuel Elbert married John Evans's daughter in 1865; she and their son died three years later. Elected to the territorial legislature in 1869, Elbert also served as governor in 1873–74, until removed by President Grant. He later served as Colorado's chief justice.

John Evans resigned as governor in August 1865. Not seriously hampered by Sand Creek's blemish on his career, he remained in Denver and became involved in railroading. Long active in the Methodist church and Denver University, he was revered as a Colorado pioneer.

Margaret Evans had a daughter in 1871 and remained prominent in Denver social circles. She enjoyed traveling and could proudly say she had mothered one of Denver's first families.

Barney Ford sold his restaurant in 1865 and led a wandering life thereafter. He lived in Chicago, Cheyenne (twice), San Francisco, Bodie, California, and Breckenridge before returning to Denver in 1890. Fortunate mining investments and keen business ability brought him success.

J. L. Gaspar was living in Waukesha, Wisconsin, in 1898. He had temporarily returned to Colorado in 1896 in a failed attempt to find a gold vein he remembered seeing in 1860 near Canon City.

Thomas Gibson, after selling the *Commonwealth* in 1864, left Colorado and returned to Omaha.

William Gilpin never achieved the success he hoped for and did not regain the governorship. The die-hard bachelor married in 1873, and a tumultuous relationship followed. Despite his troubles, he was honored as the "elder statesman of the Rockies."

Benjamin Hall, Gilpin's supporter, returned to New York in 1863.

Frank Hall sold the *Journal* and purchased the *Register* in 1865. Territorial secretary from 1866 to 1874, he married in 1871. He also wrote a four-volume Colorado history, which contains much of his firsthand knowledge.

William Hardin, the outspoken, abrasive advocate of black rights, remained active in Colorado and the Republican party until 1873. A charge of bigamy (he had two wives, one white) drove him to Cheyenne.

Rose Haydee, "Charming Rose," did not survive the war; she died back east during the late winter of 1864–65.

Charles Hendrie was joined by his sons in 1864, and their foundry eventually became the firm of Hendrie & Bolthoff, renowned in mining circles.

Alice Hill and her children moved to Colorado after the war. Alice became the "social arbiter" of Central City and later assumed a similar role in Denver. The Kindergarten Association also attracted her attention.

Nathaniel Hill solved the riddle of refractory ores and became Colorado's leading smelterman; he moved his smelter from Black Hawk to Denver in 1878. Active in Republican politics, he served one term as United States senator and eventually owned the *Denver Republican*.

Sara Hively, housewife and mother, raised four children, the last born in 1870. Andrew worked as a broom maker in 1880.

Ovando Hollister sold his interest in the *Journal* and in 1867 wrote what became a classic, *The Mines of Colorado*. This former bachelor also succumbed to marriage.

Irving Howbert was elected county clerk for El Paso County in 1869 and held that position when Colorado Springs got its start. A fortunate investment in Leadville's Robert E. Lee Mine turned his dream to reality, as did later investments at Cripple Creek.

George Kassler remained in the book and stationery business until 1873. The next year he joined the 1st National Bank. As
did many Coloradans of his day, he invested in mining and
railroad companies.

Maria Stebbins Kassler married George on May 31, 1865, ending
their courtship by mail. She moved to Colorado to become a
housewife and mother of two sons.

Nathaniel Keith left Colorado in 1869. His experiments finally
paid off, and he became famous for his work with electricity
and refining; he worked with Thomas Edison and founded
Electrical World.

Joseph Kenyon, the "wealthy and esteemed" fifty-niner, died on
July 4, 1882, in Colorado Springs.

Jack Langrishe took his acting company elsewhere in the West.
He returned to Colorado in 1876, then rushed off to the Black
Hills. In 1879, he came back to launch the Tabor Opera House
in Leadville, a well-deserved tribute for "Colorado's favorite
actor."

Jeannette Langrishe, much loved in Colorado, continued with her
husband's troupe. She and Jack eventually retired to Idaho,
where he lived out his days as a newspaperman and state
senator and she a housewife.

Samuel Leach headed east in 1865. He led a wandering life in
Virginia City and Helena, Montana, and Independence,
Missouri, before returning to Denver in 1874. He teamed up
with John Smith again in the mercantile business in Denver.

Emanuel Leutze's most famous painting, *Washington Crossing
the Delaware*, kept his name alive after his death in 1868.

Wolfe Londoner left Oro City and opened a store in Denver. Active in Republican politics, he was elected mayor. Before that,
however, he fell victim to one of Eugene Field's classic jokes
and scrambled to find watermelons to pacify Denver's black
voters.

William Loveland, Colorado's "Mr. Democrat," enthusiastically
promoted his beloved Golden, only to see it fall far behind rival
Denver. Newspaper owner and railroad developer, Loveland
maintained the role staked out by him during the war.

James Lyon was considered the territory's leading mill man until

Hill solved the refractory ore riddle. He left Colorado and several years later became involved in Utah's infamous Emma Mine scandal.

Isaac McBroom kept farming and became an expert on grain and forage crops. He died in 1914 at his home near Fort Logan.

David Moffat, ambitious and hard working like Byers, was Chaffee's partner in the 1st National Bank and various mining operations. He became fascinated by railroading, and his millions finally went into building the Moffat Tunnel.

Frances Moffat, "Fannie," adjusted to life in the West, and Dave built her one of the finest homes in Denver, as befit one of the state's pioneering families.

Con Orem fought several classic bouts in Virginia City and ultimately became a rancher near Dillon, Montana. His family included a wife and four children when he died in 1892.

Romine Ostrander stayed in Colorado, and the 1870 census listed him as a farmer and railroad contractor. He married Kate McMahon in September 1872.

Ouray became the most famous Indian of Colorado. This Ute leader tried valiantly to keep his people in their homeland. In the aftermath of the 1879 Meeker massacre, that proved impossible, but Ouray died before the final removal of all but the Southern Utes.

Ellen Pennock and her family returned to Illinois in 1865, but her ill health and her love for Colorado eventually brought them back in 1874. They settled near Longmont.

Fitz-John Porter returned to New York in 1865 and entered the mercantile business. Turning down an offer to command Egypt's army, he became police commissioner for New York City.

George Pullman did not play a significant role in Colorado after the war, except when his famous cars were introduced. Eighteen sixty-seven was a banner year for him—he got married and organized the Pullman Palace Car Company.

Mat Riddlebarger, a thirty-eight-year-old Virginian, lived in Greenhorn, Pueblo County, in 1870 and worked as a bookkeeper.

Mollie Sanford spent a long and useful life in Denver, remembered

as a "tower of strength." Her husband, By, worked at the U.S.
Mint for forty years.

Hal Sayre, following his discharge after Sand Creek, returned to
Central City to work at his surveying business. Involved in
mining and banking, he moved to Denver in 1885 and lived
there until his death in 1926, one of the last of the pioneers.

Bennett Seymour worked at various Gilpin County mines into
the 1870s. He then became a grocer and, during the next forty-
eight years, saw Central City prosper and decline.

Eben Smith married the year after the war ended. Before his
career was over, he became one of Colorado's foremost mining
men, working at various locales, including Caribou, Aspen,
and Cripple Creek. Among his partners were Chaffee and
Moffat.

Richard Sopris served as Denver's mayor and park commissioner,
was elected Arapahoe County sheriff, and became involved in
railroad building. A mountain was named after him.

Irving Stanton, mustered out of service as a first lieutenant, spent
two years in the East before returning to Colorado as registrar
of the land office at Central City. Transferred to Pueblo, he remained there for the rest of his life.

Learner Stateler stayed in Montana, hailed as one of that state's
pioneering ministers.

Augusta Tabor, ever-loyal wife and ultimate Colorado pioneer,
followed her husband back to Oro City and on to Leadville,
where they found the fortune they had sought in the 1860s.
For Augusta, wealth brought only heartache and the end of
her marriage.

Horace Tabor became the most famous Coloradan of his generation. Eventually elected lieutenant governor and a thirty-day
senator, Tabor wheeled and dealed throughout the state and
the West. He divorced Augusta, married Elizabeth Doe, and
bestowed a legend upon Colorado.

Samuel Tappan finished his term as chairman of the commission
to investigate Sand Creek and was not active in Colorado after
that.

Henry Teller grew in stature and leadership as the years went by.
Along with Chaffee, he was chosen one of the first senators

and served until appointed secretary of the interior in 1882, after which he was reelected to the senate. The state's most famous silver spokesman, Teller emerged as Colorado's beloved politician of his era.

Ten Bear used his influence for peace until he died in 1872.

Joseph Thatcher became one of Colorado's successful bankers, first at Central City, and then in Denver. Stock breeding also caught his fancy.

Alexander Toponce went to Montana, where he worked as a miner and freighter before settling in Utah. He led an adventurous life, which he recounted in an autobiography.

Mark Twain traveled on to Virginia City, Nevada, and fame as a writer.

Bethuel Vincent, the energetic minister devoted to Sunday-school work, labored in Colorado before going east in 1875. He returned west in 1889 and finally retired in 1908.

John Wanless served as Colorado's superintendent of public instruction in 1866-67.

Lewis Weld traveled east to enlist in 1863. He helped organize black regiments and died in January 1865 from exposure and cold during the Petersburg campaign.

Sylvanus Wellman married, fathered four children, and continued to farm in Boulder County. He eventually owned a coal mine and became a businessman.

Peter Winne settled near the future site of Greeley, where he served as superintendent of schools for Weld County before moving to Denver.

Clara Witter had five children. In 1868 she toured Colorado with her brother, vice presidential candidate Schuyler Colfax. A new house in Denver in 1871 brightened her life; she and Daniel celebrated their golden wedding anniversary in 1905.

Ed Wynkoop resigned from the army and became an agent for the Cheyenne and Arapahoe Indians in 1866. Unable to accomplish what he set out to do for these people, he left that position after two years and went back east. He later returned west and died in Santa Fe in 1891.

Frank Young settled in Central City and in 1865 worked with Hollister and Hall on the *Journal*. He then went into banking and moved to Denver in 1880. The man who came west because of ill health lived on to write about his experiences in a delightful book, *Echoes from Arcadia*.

In the words of the hauntingly beautiful ballad "Lorena," which was popular throughout the war years:

> *The years creep slowly by, Lorena,*
> *The snow is on the grass again;*
> *The sun's low down the sky, Lorena,*
> *The frost gleams where the flow'rs have been.*

Bibliographical Essay

THE PURPOSE OF THIS STUDY was to examine the era and the people through primary sources. This essay therefore contains very few secondary works; for these the reader must consult the bibliographies of recent general Colorado history texts and Civil War studies. This essay is divided into sections that reflect the major sources utilized.

Newspapers

Without question, the dominant paper and a major historical source is Denver's *Rocky Mountain News*, (weekly and daily editions). The city's rival papers, including the *Colorado Republican and Rocky Mountain Herald* (under various titles) and *Weekly Commonwealth*, provide a balance for some of Byers's views.

No other Colorado community could equal Denver's newspaper coverage during the Civil War. Central City's *Tri-Weekly Miners' Register* (later the *Miners' Register*) and *Colorado Mining Life*, and Black Hawk's *Daily Mining Journal*, provide a mountain perspective, beginning in 1862 (*Life*) and 1863 (*Register* and *Journal*). Only teasingly short runs of other newspapers remain. This lack of geographic diversity forces the historian to rely on a Denver-oriented press, which obviously slights important happenings elsewhere in the territory.

The *New York Times* (indexed), *New York Tribune*, and *New York Clipper* offer the eastern view of events, though Colorado during the war incited little interest from that part of the country, except for the "gold bubble." A sampling of the *Deseret News* (Salt Lake) and the *Aurora Beacon* (Aurora, Illinois) proved disappointing for Colorado material, as did *Harper's Weekly* and *Harper's New Monthly Magazine*.

Diaries, Letters, Journals

The Scott J. Anthony Papers (Colorado Historical Society, Denver) harbored only a few gems. Susan R. Ashley, "Reminiscences of Colorado in the Early Sixties" (*Colorado Magazine*, November 1936) is excellent, as are the Henry Douglas Bacon Papers (Huntington Library, San Marino, California) and the Samuel L. Barlow Collection (Huntington Library). The Bent-Hyde Papers (University of Colorado, Boulder) and the George Bent Letters (Colorado State Historical Society) provide the Indian view of Sand Creek.

Amos Billingsley's diary (University of Colorado) provides great insights, as do the Alonzo Boardman Letters (Denver Public Library) and, to a lesser degree, the William Byers Papers (University of Colorado) and Diaries (Denver Public Library). Daniel E. Conner's manuscript, *A Confederate in the Colorado Gold Fields* (Norman: University of Oklahoma Press, 1970), is unsurpassed for the Confederate view. The William Z. Cozens Collection (Colorado Historical Society) has a variety of material about this interesting man.

The Matthew Dale Letters (University of Colorado), Correspondence of the Superintendent of the Denver Mint (National Archives Branch, Denver Federal Center), the Denver Typographical Union #49 Collections (University of Colorado), the William Dutt Letters (Huntington Library), the Empire City Post Office Records (Colorado Historical Society), and the Edward H. Edwards Letters (Yale University, New Haven) furnish a variety of information. Samuel Elbert, "Public Men and Measures" (Bancroft Interview, University of Colorado), the John Evans Papers (Colorado Historical Society), and Letter Press Book 1863-64 (Colorado State Archives, Denver) present views of Sand Creek.

Paul H. Giddens, "Letters of S. Newton Pettis" (*Colorado Magazine*, January 1938), and the Gilpin County Court Records (Colorado State Archives) deal with some of the legal ramifications. Colin Goodykoontz, ed., "Colorado as Seen by a Home Missionary, 1863-68," (*Colorado Magazine*, March 1935); the Frank Hall Letters (Denver Public Library); the N. P. Hill Letters (Colorado Historical Society); the Sara Hively Journal (Denver Public Library); the George Kassler Collection (Colorado Historical Society); and Philip Alexander, "George W. Kassler: Colorado Pioneer" (*Colorado Magazine*, January and April 1962) are invaluable to the study of these years. Robert Horne, "James Fergus in the Colorado Gold Fields" (*Colorado Magazine*, Winter 1973); "Nathaniel S. Keith and Two of his Early Colorado Letters," (*Colorado Magazine*, March 1940); and Liston Leyendecker, "Young Man Gone West: George M. Pullman's Letters from the Colorado Goldfields" (*Chicago History*, Winter 1978-79) are less helpful.

Samuel Leach's "Reminiscences" (*The Trail*, 1911 and 1926) are an aid to understanding this period. The Samuel Mallory Collection, David Nichols Collection, and Harper Orahood Papers, all at the University of Colorado, contain a few nuggets. The Romine H. Ostrander Diaries (Colorado Historical Society); Ellen Pennock, "Incidents in My Life as a Pioneer" (*Colorado Magazine*, April 1953); and the Hal Sayre Papers (University of Colorado) are "musts" for examination.

The Learner Stateler Collection (Denver Public Library) provided only marginal help. The Samuel F. Tappan Collection (Colorado Historical Society) contains material on Chivington and his activities. Both of the above depositories contain Irving Stanton letters and papers. The Henry Teller Papers

(University of Colorado) illuminate this significant individual, and the Sylvanus Wellman Diaries and business records (Colorado Historical Society) proved invaluable. Mrs. Daniel Witter, "Pioneer Life" (*Colorado Magazine*, December 1927) and the Daniel Witter Letters (Colorado Historical Society) present homey topics, as do many of the other collections.

Published Material

A large number of mining company prospectuses from the 1860s, most located in the Huntington Library Special Collections, Colorado College Library, and the Denver Public Library, Western History Department, were utilized. All provided some information about mining and investors' expectations. Edward Bliss, *A Brief History of the New Gold Region of Colorado Territory* (New York: John W. Amerman, 1864); William M. Breakenridge, *Helldorado* (Glorieta: Rio Grande, 1970, reprint); S. W. Burt and E. L. Berthoud, *The Rocky Mountain Gold Regions* (Denver: Old West, 1962, reprint); and John L. Dyer, *The Snow-Shoe Itinerant* (Cincinnati: Cranston & Stowe, 1890) give first-hand accounts of a potpourri of subjects.

William Gilpin, *The Central Gold Region* (Philadelphia: Sower, Barnes, 1860) helps the researcher understand this man. Frank Hall has much original material in his multivolumed *History of the State of Colorado* (Chicago: Blakely, 1889–95). Ovando Hollister's two books, *Boldly They Rode* (Lakewood: Golden, 1949, reprint) and *The Mines of Colorado* (Springfield: Samuel Bowles, 1867), offer the same. Irving Howbert defends Sand Creek, among other things, in *Memories of a Lifetime in the Pike's Peak Region* (New York: Putnam's, 1925). Thomas Marshall deserves thanks for his *Early Records of Gilpin County, Colorado 1859–1861* (Boulder: University of Colorado, 1930). Maurice O'Connor Morris, *Rambles in the Rocky Mountains* (London: Smith, Elder, 1864); Nolie Mumey, *History and Proceedings of Buckskin Joe* (Boulder: Johnson, 1961); and Albert D. Richardson, *Beyond the Mississippi* (Hartford: American, 1867) address numerous topics.

William Rockwell, *Colorado: Its Mineral and Agricultural Resources* (New York, 1864) promoted the territory, and Helen Sanders, ed., *X. Beidler: Vigilante* (Norman: University of Oklahoma Press, 1957) traces the career of the book's subject. Required reading would include Mollie Sanford, *Mollie* (Lincoln: University of Nebraska Press, 1959). Only slightly less imperative is an examination of Irving Stanton, *Sixty Years in Colorado* (Denver, 1929). Alexander Toponce includes a few comments on his Colorado experiences in *Reminiscences of Alexander Toponce* (Norman: University of Oklahoma Press, 1971, reprint). Metta Victoria Victor's *Maum Guinea* (New York: Beadle, 1861) illustrates the popular novels of the day.

Eugene F. Ware, *The Indian War of 1864* (New York: St. Martin's, 1960, reprint); John Wetherbee, *A Brief Sketch of Colorado Territory and the Gold Mines of that Region* (Boston: Weight & Potter, 1863); J. E. Wharton, *History of the City of Denver* (Denver: Byers & Dailey, 1866); and Ellen Williams, *Three Years and a Half in the Army* (New York: Fowler & Wells, 1885) are somewhat disappointing but worth researching. Frank Young's sequel to the well-known

Echoes from Arcadia, Across the Plains in '65 (Denver: Privately printed, 1905), is narrower in scope, and Frank arrives in Colorado as the war ends.

Government Publications

Territorial and federal publications and records are rich sources of information for the Civil War years in Colorado. For Colorado, the Interior Department Territorial Papers, State Department Territorial Papers (Colorado Series), Colorado Territory Supreme Court Records (Colorado Historical Society), *Council Journal of the Legislative Assembly* (Denver, 1862–65), and *House Journal of the Legislative Assembly* (Denver, 1861, 1864, and 1865) provide fine places to start. *General Laws and Joint Resolutions . . . Colorado* (Denver: Byers & Daily, 1865) shows the development of Colorado's laws. Annual messages of Evans, *Governor Evans Message* (Denver: News Office, 1862), and Elbert, *Annual Message* (Central City: Collier & Wells, 1865), which praise the present and promote the future, have been published.

There are a few county records for these years, Gilpin County being the best represented with court records and miners' court records, along with mining district laws (Colorado State Archives and Colorado Historical Society). Some other counties are represented only by mining district records.

Federal documents run the gamut of research possibilities. The *Report of the Commissioner of Indian Affairs* (Washington: G.P.O., 1861–65) touches repeatedly on the territory. The *Report of the Joint Special Committee, Appointed Under the Joint Resolution of March 2, 1865* (Washington: G.P.O., 1867) includes the Sand Creek testimony, as does the *Report of the Secretary of War . . . Ex. Doc. No. 26* (Washington: G.P.O., 1867). The multivolume *The War of the Rebellion: A Compilation of the Official Records of the Union and Confederate Armies* (Washington: G.P.O., 1881–89) is invaluable for military and, to a lesser degree, political affairs. The United States District Court Records (National Archives Branch, Denver Federal Center) are a gold mine of information.

In the final analysis, the researcher is limited only by time and imagination in the search for records of all types. Half the fun of researching Colorado is the challenge of finding new material in order to throw new light on the mystery of the past.

Index